FLINGS
AND FAUX PAS OF
AN AMERICAN GIRL
IN LONDON

# SLEEPING
# AROUND

# CATHERINE TOWNSEND

SOURCEBOOKS, INC.®
NAPERVILLE, ILLINOIS

Published by Sourcebooks, Inc.
P.O. Box 4410, Naperville, Illinois 60567-4410
(630) 961-3900
Fax: (630) 961-2168
www.sourcebooks.com

Originally published in England in 2007 by John Murray Publishers.

Library of Congress Cataloging-in-Publication Data

Townsend, Catherine.
    Sleeping around : flings and faux pas of an American girl in London /
Catherine Townsend.
        p. cm.
    1. Girls—Sexual behavior—Great Britain—London—Case studies. 2. Sex—
Great Britain—London—Case studies.  I. Title.
    HQ27.5.T69 2009
    306.7092'2421—dc22
                                2009010285

Printed and bound in the United States of America.
        VP  10  9  8  7  6  5  4  3  2  1

*For Mum*

This is a true story.
Some names, identifying characteristics, and time sequences have
been changed simply to protect anonymity.

# DOUBLE STANDARDS: WHY I SHAG ON THE FIRST DATE

Well, that was four hours of my life that I'll never get back.

My date tonight was a very cute thirty-six-year-old English screenwriter, and I was dressed to kill in a tight black dress and the kind of four-inch heels that were meant to be worn horizontally rather than vertically.

After discussing the mechanics of everything from *South Park* to string theory over two bottles of wine at Les Trois Garcons in east London, he dropped the "So, how many people have you slept with?" bomb. I tried to be vague, but he insisted that honesty was very important to him.

"No, really, tell me," he pleaded, putting his hand on my knee. "I'll bet I can guess, six?" In a moment of temporary insanity, I forgot that for men, the only "honest" answer about sexual history involves the phrase, "Yes, you're the biggest and best I've ever had!"

"Add a zero to that number, honey, and you'll be in the ballpark." I smiled sweetly, involuntarily raising my left eyebrow.

"Are you serious?" He paled visibly. After too much red wine, the looming taxidermy on the wall was beginning to look rather sinister. Even the dead moose appeared to be judgmental.

"I don't know why you sound so surprised. I mean you are talking to a girl who just spent the afternoon fellating an aubergine." I explained that I'd had an oral sex masterclass as part of my research for an upcoming column, and threw in what I thought were a few amusing anecdotes.

But he didn't even try to laugh; instead, he paid the bill and fled into the night.

Back at home, I pulled on my writing uniform—the torn, drawstring-waist tracksuit pants that I've had for the past decade with "Rock Star" printed in tiny rhinestones on the back, fuzzy leopard-print house slippers whose soles are starting to peel off, and a Hanes paper-thin men's cotton tank top.

Judging by my emails, most readers like to imagine that a sex columnist would lounge around in a red silk negligee and furry, high-heeled, slip-on mules. But I save my risqué outfits for dates. Not that any of my underwear got a workout tonight. Some readers even refer to me as a "posh tart," which I find hilarious since, as an American living in London, I'm actually an outsider. I'm from the Deep South, so I spent my childhood playing near trailer parks, not polo fields.

I headed to the refrigerator in search of a Diet Coke. As usual, we've got slim pickings in our kitchenette—two unopened bottles of champagne from a recent film after-party, a half-eaten jar of Nutella, and a loaf of wheat-free bread that looks as if it's growing a winter coat.

Our kitchen is a culinary wasteland. Last week, in a moment of optimism, I decided to heat ready-made soup. The stove wouldn't fire up, so I had to call the gas-man. He got a good laugh out of the fact that I had lived here for six months without realizing that the gas wasn't connected.

"Hey, baby. How did the date go?" My flatmate Victoria, who's also my best friend, was curled up on the couch watching *Dangerous*

*Liaisons*. In the buttery light from our living room lamp, I could see why people mistake Victoria for my sister: She's five years older, and has the same full lips, hazel eyes, and dark hair except that she's five foot two and curvy, and I'm five foot ten and still stuffing my bra.

Sitting down next to her, I told her about my date's disappearing act, because I knew that she would tell me if I'd been at fault. Victoria is the "fat trousers" friend who I'll ask for an opinion before I buy because, with both clothes and men, she's brutally honest. I love her for the fact that she isn't afraid to tell me the truth.

"God, that's so stupid," she said, shaking her head. "I can't believe that there are guys out there who are still so scared of a woman with a bit of experience." She paused. "Then again, maybe women are to blame as well. I've known girls who would go home with a guy they'd slept with before just to avoid upping their numbers. What kind of warped moral logic is that?"

"I know! I read in the *New Scientist* that the national average was nine partners. But the interesting thing is, once the women knew they were attached to a lie detector, they doubled their numbers."

"Well, Cat, there is an old saying: 'Women halve their number, and men double it.' And you have to admit, there is a definite double standard. A woman who has loads of sexual partners is still seen as a slapper, while guys who hook up constantly are considered studs."

"I think that's crazy. We've had the sexual revolution—women should feel free to date and have sex like men. Men have always been permitted to sleep around until they find 'The One' so why do women still have to feel sensitive about 'The List'?"

"You're right," Victoria said. But then a cheeky smile spread across her face: "Though to be honest, I'm occasionally tempted to edit some things out. Like I don't really add anything that lasted under thirty seconds to my list."

I laughed as we started to debate what else "doesn't really count." Mutual masturbation in the back of a cab? Unreciprocated oral sex? Women?

Then there's the fact that my memory gets fuzzier with time. These days I tend only to remember the really good, the really bad, and the really bizarre.

Victoria echoed my thoughts: "It's getting harder to keep track as I get older. Have you ever tried to make a list of everyone you've ever shagged, as research or something?"

I giggled. "That's what I do instead of counting sheep."

"You still can't sleep? Cat, let me give you some pills. I'm sure I've got some knocking around in my handbag somewhere." Victoria is a walking pharmacy, but she knows that I don't even take paracetamol. Caffeine is my drug of choice.

"No thanks," I told her. "I've got to push through this. When my body needs sleep, it will get it. Then again, that's what I said about sex."

"Whatever, darling. See you in the morning, then?"

I blew her a kiss and went into my closet-sized bedroom, allowing my mind to wander. I was disappointed about tonight. But it wasn't the first time that my sexual frankness had got me into trouble.

I still remember my first sexual fantasy, which happened when I was five years old while my teacher was reading the Cinderella fairy tale in class.

Always a precocious child, I waited until she got to the "and they lived happily ever after" part to raise my hand and ask, "So does that mean they are going to take their shirts off and get into bed to kiss?" She made me sit in the corner and called me a bad girl, which I also quite enjoyed.

A few days after that, my best friend Whitney and I found ourselves in a standoff over Barbie dolls. "I want the dream house," she said, "because my Barbie is married and has three children."

"Fine," I shot back. "My Barbie is rich and famous and has two Kens, so I only want the Corvette." I'm afraid that, like my miniature plastic counterpart, not much has changed for me since then. Whitney's Barbies baked cookies and sang songs. My Barbie dolls spent most nights in a pornographic tableau despite the absence of discernible genitalia. As for Rock Star Ken, I always suspected that his tight shiny pink shirts and studded earrings conveyed homoerotic undertones.

I fished out a mauled Marlboro Light from the bottom of my handbag, and was about to start on this week's column, but first I cracked open the window and attempted to check out my hot neighbor with amazing pecs. Fortunately for me, he tends to walk around shirtless. Unfortunately, he's had the bad manners to put up curtains. Spoilsport. I curled up under the duvet with my laptop and began to type.

*I read somewhere that men think about sex every seven seconds. This sounds about right to me, because I'm so often horny that I end up having sex on the first date. So do several of my girlfriends.*

Some people are horrified by women admitting to the hedonistic pursuit of pleasure for its own sake. Yet most of my male friends seem to think that they will sleep around and have adventures until the right girl comes along. So why should women be any different?

Which is why I was so surprised to see the results of a recent University of Sheffield study that said nine out of ten women believe that casual sex is immoral. Apparently, single women rarely have sex for physical pleasure, but rather as a result of their quest to meet a long-term partner.

But why do the two have to be mutually exclusive? With a few exceptions, most of my serious relationships have started out as one-night stands where the chemistry between us was too great to ignore.

I've never understood those people who say, "It all comes down to compatibility and good conversation" when it comes to finding a soulmate. Of course I want those things, but I also need passion, love, and gut-wrenching, mind-blowing orgasms. On the occasions when I click with someone mentally, I would rather find out on date two than date twenty that we're not sexually compatible. If I just want a sympathetic ear, I'll ring my mum.

Still unable to sleep, I called my friend Michael, a fellow night owl, to get some insight. Michael and I hooked up several times early in our friendship, which I think made us much better friends, because we got the sexual tension out of the way early. I trust his judgment about men completely because as a political journalist he has to constantly determine the meaning behind politicians' words. He's a serial monogamist who lately seems to have been leaving a long time between girlfriends because his standards are so exacting.

"It's premature intimacy that's the problem, not premature nakedness," he said. "If I'm into a girl, I'm going to call her again, period. I don't like people who set up artificial barriers; I think the whole 'Ooh, I can't do it on the second date but on the third is fine' is bullshit. It shows that she doesn't have enough self-confidence, which is the real turn-off. But, Cat, it's almost 2:00 a.m.; are you sure this is just about an article?"

I had to laugh, because even though I'd only mentioned the piece, he knew me well enough to guess that something was up.

I exhaled slowly and dropped my cigarette butt into the remnants of my soda can. "Okay, well, I had another bad date tonight."

"What happened this time?"

"He asked me how many people I slept with, and I was honest. Do you think it's a deal-breaker?"

"Frankly, Cat, I don't see how it's any of his business."

"That's what I thought! But I guess I'm just wondering when I'm going to find a man who can handle me. I mean, I'm smart, funny, and reasonably attractive, so why is the fact that I can deep-throat an aubergine a hindrance?"

"Well, I can tell you that the thought of you sexually molesting a vegetable is a serious turn-on for most of the male population. I think it's probably more about him than you; you know, the idea that some guy somewhere along the line is better than him."

"You have a point," I admitted, thinking back to an ex-boyfriend who found out that I once dated a semi-famous Manhattan photographer known as The Horse, and not for his equestrian abilities. I never heard the end of it.

"Then again, sleeping with a sex columnist is a bit intimidating, kind of like performing open-heart surgery on a cardiologist," he continued. "Maybe men *are* afraid of your experience. Or the fact that you're this feisty, outspoken American who also happens to be very tall in heels. The combination *is* pretty terrifying."

"It cuts both ways, you know. I sometimes worry that they are going to expect me to morph into some kind of sexual superwoman."

He laughed. "Well, sweetheart, I think you kind of are. You're definitely, shall we say, very imaginative."

I stifled a giggle as I looked down at my faded gray tank top and baggy tracksuit.

"Yeah, right, I'm looking seriously hot now," I laughed as I made a face at myself in the mirror. My hair was messily piled on top of my head in a faux-denim scrunchie that hadn't seen the light of day since the mid-eighties.

"Anyway, if I am considered hot, I deserve to be after the crap I took in primary school. The cheerleaders were all so cute, and I looked like some kind of freak."

That was putting it mildly: In a school where the kids' idea of fashion was wearing a shirt that had buttons, I wore mesh tops and silver ballet flats. I was teased mercilessly, and nicknamed Alien Girl because of my height and wide-spaced eyes.

"You're lucky babe, you bypassed the 'cute' stage completely and went straight from being an ugly duckling to sex kitten," he said. "I'll bet those cheerleaders all weigh twenty stone, have five kids, and live in trailer parks right now."

I laughed. "Thanks, Michael. I'll talk to you tomorrow, okay?"

"Sure thing. Sweet dreams."

Fat chance. On the rare occasions when I actually do sleep I have incredibly vivid dreams. Which wouldn't be so bad, except that lately they are erotic dreams about Gordon Brown. I shudder to think what fucked-up things must be happening in my subconscious to bring that on.

So I pulled out a yellow legal pad and tried to make a list of all my previous shags. The earliest entries were highly detailed, while later ones were full of holes ("Number 24: Jon or Joe?? Photographer With Nice Teeth"). My eyes soon blurred, and I debated whether to download some Internet porn, but I'm paranoid about giving my credit card number out online and inviting tons of spam.

Besides, the media players giving free previews aren't that compatible with my Mac, and I feared I would end up with a bunch of jerky footage of thirty-five-year-old "teenagers" having "first-time" lesbian experiences. At that time of night, I usually preferred online erotic stories, which I have put neatly into labeled folders on my laptop: straight, gay, group, etc. But not tonight—I was too tired for any elaborate fantasies.

So I licked my fingers and slid my hand between my legs to massage my clitoris in quick, deliberate pulses. The thought of my neighbor, peeping through his curtains to watch me, getting hard and moving his hands down his rippled stomach to stroke his cock, watching me watching him, did the trick. It only took about ninety seconds.

Lying in bed afterwards, recovering, I thought about how much I've learned since I came to the UK and began the sex column, and how each date—the good, the bad, and the ugly—has taught me more about what I want in a partner.

It's been an emotional and physical rollercoaster, but what doesn't kill me will ultimately make me stronger. And it's going to take a lot more than an idiot like the one tonight to break me.

It would be fantastic if any of my casual partners turned out to be the love of my life. But if not, I'll still respect them all in the morning.

As I drifted off to sleep, I spurned Gordon's invasion of my REM sleep and started thinking about how my career as a sex columnist began.

# ONE

Like many things in life, my sex column in the *Independent* began with an ending. However much most people claim to hate clichéd breakup lines, there has to be a reason why "It's not you, it's me" has become as ubiquitous a relationship catchphrase as "I love you." I found this out the hard way the day my ex-boyfriend Patrick kicked me to the curb.

I've never been a great believer in the quintessentially female idea of "closure." But the trick to surviving what I call the "relationship exit interview" is to focus not on what your partner is saying, but on whatever it is they are trying to hide.

Unfortunately, for most of us, the phrase "I need some space" generally ends with "to sleep with other people." Likewise, "We need to slow down" is missing the ending, "so I can keep my options open, in case somebody more interesting/hotter/richer comes along." This isn't always a bad thing; in fact, telling a white lie to help initiate a break up can often save the dumpee a lot of time and heartache.

But Patrick was different, or so I thought. We based our relationship on "absolute honesty," which was why I agreed to move in with him after a whirlwind five-month courtship—even though I was still living in Manhattan at the time, and he worked in London as a banker.

I'd recently given up my job as a New York gossip columnist, and for ages I'd been flirting with the idea of relocating to London permanently. I figured that with my years of journalistic experience, landing a job, or at least a work experience placement, couldn't be that difficult. In the past few months I'd started flying back and forth looking for openings.

In retrospect, my career judgment at that time was almost as poor as my judgment in men. My efforts in London hadn't exactly been going swimmingly: The *Independent* had shown an interest in the stories I'd sent them but I'd only sold them one piece so far, and my last work experience placement (which I soon discovered was codespeak for "slave labor") at *The Times* came to a screeching halt after I screwed up an arts guide by listing a Kevin Spacey play one year too late. "It was only sixteen words, and I still managed to fuck it up," I had said when they dismissed me.

So I had continued to supplement my income by taking freelance assignments back in New York, the latest of which was writing entries for a fashion guide. Every day, I would trek through Manhattan, then run up huge phone bills on late-night calls to Patrick to talk about our future together.

Finally, I felt ready to take him up on his offer. I packed my stuff and got ready for the adventure of a lifetime.

But two days before I was due to fly to London for good, he sent me an email to say that he "didn't feel that we were on the same path" and never wanted to see me again. Clearly lacking a sense of irony, Patrick insisted that we meet one last time at the Bleeding Heart pub in Farringdon, where he would explain why he wanted to split.

I was in a state of shock, but nonetheless I cringe when I remember my pathetic selection of clothing that day. For women, there is only one relationship ensemble more monumental than the first date: the breakup outfit.

Legs shaved, bikini line waxed, and eyebrows plucked into perfection, I squeezed my size-8 frame into a black pencil skirt that I knew he loved, with a white off-the-shoulder silkscreen print Blondie T-shirt, my distressed leather biker jacket, and four-inch Christian Louboutin stilettos. Underneath I was wearing my lace La Perla corset in anticipation of a best-case scenario.

"I don't feel the same way about our relationship as I did and I think it's best if we call it a day," he'd written. This was in no way ambiguous, but I guess somehow I hoped that he would rush in, claim temporary insanity for the email, sweep me into his arms, and declare, "What was I thinking?"

However, one look at the bright lighting and strained faces of the couples around me told me that there would be no reconciliation: The Bleeding Heart was a place where relationships came to die. The room was cozy enough to ensure that I wouldn't raise my voice and "make a scene," yet the tables were sufficiently wide to prevent me from scratching his eyes out, or whatever men imagine women do in the face of a breakup.

I arrived fifteen minutes early, hoping to have downed half a dirty martini and smoked a stealthy cigarette to steady my nerves before he came in. But Patrick was already sitting at a corner table, tie loosened, looking slightly disheveled but gorgeous. He appeared to be sending a text.

He attempted to stand up when our eyes met, but his knee slammed the bottom of the table and he sucked in his breath, sharply, then gave me a perfunctory kiss on the cheek. "Hi, Cat, um, can I get you a drink?" he said, sliding his mobile into his pocket.

"What are you having?" I asked, trying to keep my tone light even though my voice was shaking. Despite my rock-star façade, I was a nervous wreck.

"A tomato juice," he said flatly. For a half-Irish bloke who drinks Guinness like water, this was not a good sign.

"I'll have a vodka tonic, please. Better make it a double." I sat down and took off my wraparound sunglasses, trying to steady my trembling hands. Unlike most of my friends, I prefer comfort drinking to comfort eating in the face of adversity. I tend to overthink everything, so in trying times I use booze to deaden my brain against the pain.

The trick to keeping the buzz going is to stay at exactly the right level of inebriation to stay merry, not morose, which for me is usually about three drinks. Any more than that and I'm crying in the toilets or sitting on top of someone random. It's a delicate balance.

Once he returned with my cocktail, sat down, and fixed his gaze on me, I wasted no time. "Is there someone else?" I asked, fighting back tears. I was not going to cry. I wasn't going to give him that satisfaction. "I can understand if there is. In fact, I think it might help me accept why this happened."

He sighed and loosened his tie further. "God, I only wish it was that simple," he said, cagily casting his eyes downward, his hand wrapping around the viscous red liquid. I had always loved Patrick's hands. My friends swear by the size of a man's feet, but I could never look at his long, thick fingers without imagining them sliding inside me, stretching me out. "I don't think you have any idea how hard this is for me."

"Hard for you? You begged me to move in with you for months, then after I quit my job in New York, left my apartment, and was two days away from flying here, you tell me that I have nowhere to live? What were you thinking? Do you even care?"

My heart was racing, and despite the seriousness of the situation I could feel myself tingling down below. *Even if we don't patch things up for good*, I was thinking, *the make-up sex would be amazing.* It must have been my blood pumping and the booze, lulling me into thoughts of a temporary reprieve. I kept rattling on about work, manically, because I knew that the minute there was a pause in conversation the end would come and the pain would be too much to bear. Besides, Victoria didn't get off until seven-thirty, and had no spare set of keys. Even though we'd only met for the first time three weeks ago, at the hairdresser, she had kindly looked after me in my moment of need and was letting me stay at her flat.

It was either this, or crying in a Starbucks wedged between tourists with rolling suitcases. It sucked to be homeless.

I was also thinking that I might never get to fuck him again, and I wasn't sure when I'd have chemistry that good with anyone else. Part of the bitch of breaking up is the laziness that comes with being a couple, when you know each other's sexual preferences and are completely in sync. The thought of investing that kind of energy and time in someone else after getting kicked to the curb was daunting. I felt nauseous.

He sighed. "I did that because, frankly, I thought you might stay in New York after I sent that email."

This made me angrier than anything he'd said so far. He knew that I'd wanted to move to London since I came here at age fourteen with my school choir, and managed to ditch the adults and go to my first pub. I fell in love for the first time in the UK; not with a man, but with the drinking culture. And while writing about the Oscars had been fun, I was starting to get seriously bored with doing stories about celebrities and their rather frivolous concerns. I had frivolous concerns of my own.

I realized that if I stayed where I was, one day I would be forty-five, still regurgitating pop culture crap and trying to analyze the decline of D-list pop stars' marriages. I knew that I had to leave New York to get away from it all. I didn't know a soul in London, but that had never stopped me before. I love a challenge.

"Patrick, I've been talking about moving to London for a year now. Since before I met you. Why would you think I would change my plans?"

"Because, well… what is it that you want to do here?"

I saw him sneak a glance at his phone. Was he meeting someone else? Was it that petite blonde who sat next to him at work, the one he'd always insisted was "just a friend"? I was probably being paranoid. Then again, what difference did it make? "I kind of thought you were moving for me. I mean, it's not like your unpaid work experience is going that well."

I felt like I'd been slapped. At twenty-seven I had found it difficult to be demoted from mingling with celebrities as co-writer of a trendy New York gossip column to brewing cups of tea for a grumpy *Times* editor who told me constantly he wasn't sure if I had the "feel" for features, before dismissing me over the Kevin Spacey debacle.

I took a deep breath. "Well, I really want to write a sex column for a national newspaper. The *Independent* has been very receptive to all the ideas I've sent them, and I've had one piece published. I'm hoping that a staff position will open up. I just have to be tenacious and make sure that I'm in the right place at the right time. Whenever that is."

"See, that's what I'm talking about, Cat," he said, exasperated. "I can't go out with someone who has her head in the clouds the entire time. A national newspaper column? Some of us have to have realistic dreams."

*Fuck this*, I thought.

He was allowed to dump me, but not to doubt me professionally. How dare he? "I have to go to the loo," I blurted out, because I knew that I wasn't going to be able to hold back the tears much longer. I flung open the door, walked up to the sink, and started my primary school trick of giving myself a mirror pep talk. "You are a rock star," I kept repeating, steadying myself against the crumbling brick wall while dabbing at my mascara and trying to regulate my breathing. "You are a rock star, and he is an idiot."

"You okay, love?"

I spun around and saw a tall, lean, shaggy-haired rocker boy leaning against a urinal. In my haste to flee the scene, I must have stumbled into the men's bathroom. Great. This night just kept getting better and better.

"Yeah, I'm fine. I've just been outside getting dumped, and I'm trying to psych myself up. Nothing to worry about."

"Someone binned you?" he said kindly, a smile crossing his friendly, open face. "He must be crazy." He was wearing a Sex Pistols T-shirt with some artfully torn jeans. Despite myself, I forced a smile. I appreciated his, apparently sincere, incredulity that someone could end it with me.

"Are you sure it's over?" he said, handing me some tissue from one of the stalls. "I mean, can't you two work things out?"

I blew my nose really hard and flung the disintegrated tissue into a bin. "No, I think the fat lady has sung on this one. Thanks anyway, um, what's your name? I'm Cat."

"Nick," he said, shaking my hand before we headed towards the door. But he hesitated slightly.

"Look, this may seem a bit weird, but should I give you my number, in case you need anything?"

My mind reeled off a variety of reasons why this was a bad idea. *It's too soon. I don't know you. You have unsightly facial hair.*

But I found myself fishing through my handbag; the time lapse in finding a writing utensil told me I was well on my way to being three sheets to the wind. "Um, I have a pen, but no paper," I said, sticking my hand out. "Write it on the back in case I have to wash them." I attempted a feeble smile. He scrawled down a mobile number, and held my hand a bit longer than absolutely necessary. "Listen, my mates and I are going out to a rock club tonight, so feel free to give me a ring any time. And good luck, Cat."

I followed him out of the loos, and felt my heart drop to my stomach as I went back to our table. This scene was so surreal; the last time I'd seen Patrick he had made me breakfast and kissed me goodbye before I left for the airport to go and do one last freelance assignment in New York. And he was wearing my favorite suit, maintaining the illusion of manly control that had snared me in the beginning.

Patrick and I met when I was on a trip to London, while I was still debating whether or not to take the plunge and move permanently. Since I knew almost no one in town, I had come to Amy's, a friend of a friend's, party alone and spent the better part of the evening talking to the birthday boy's Italian father, while he spoke to my cleavage. My Italian is pretty much limited to Frank Sinatra tunes, so I was miming enthusiastically as I nursed a glass of wine. Normally I have no problem chatting to strangers, but the cliques at this party were difficult to infiltrate.

In New York, people tended to open with the "What do you do?" line, but the girls here seemed to be bonding over where people went to school. They probably also wore elaborate hats to summer sporting events. I didn't really fit in.

"This party is boring," a baritone voice behind me whispered. "What do you say we go out on the terrace and share a bottle of wine?"

I whirled around to see a tall, solidly built, dark-haired guy with piercing green eyes and a very posh accent hovering over me brandishing a bottle and two glasses. I wasn't overwhelmed with passion, but I'd already found out the hard way that most British men's idea of an approach involves furtively staring across the pub until after their twelfth pint of liquid courage, at which point they blurt out something charming like "Nice tits!" and stumble outside. So I had to give him points for trying.

I touched the top of the bottle. "Just want to make sure it's corked and you're not some kind of date-rape serial killer who has severed heads in his fridge. I don't mind dismemberment per se, but I prefer that my dates keep them in the basement. Otherwise it's, like, totally unsanitary." I used my faux-Valley Girl accent and rolled my eyes.

He laughed. "You must be American. Well, I have to admit that I never leave the house without my Rohypnol. What would happen to my success rate? But I haven't graduated to homicide yet."

Hmm, cute and a sardonic sense of humor. This was starting to get interesting. Over the next hour I found out that his name was Patrick, he worked in high-risk finance, and he was in his early thirties.

Amy warned me that he had a reputation as a "bit of a womanizer," which of course only made me want him more.

Back in New York, the craziness of my job meant that I was always attracted to bad-boy tattooed biker types who would never invade the neatly regimented reality of my day-to-day life. But this was a real man, with a grown-up job. I love men in suits, because I imagine stripping them off and unearthing their kinky side.

Our first date took place two nights later, where we split two bottles of champagne over a four-course dinner at Hakkasan. "Cat," he said, stroking my face in the cab, "why can't I stop thinking about you?"

This is the typical ploy of average-looking men. They will spout phrases like "Don't break my heart," complete with the wounded, puppy-dog face, right until the moment you get comfortable in the relationship. The about-face is like having a finger severed by a benign-looking chihuahua.

But I fell for it. We went to an underground hip-hop club near King's Cross where the ratio of metal detectors to patrons was frighteningly close. We wove through the sweaty throngs to the bar, where I waited until we were on the last third of our second beer before I pulled my signature move. "This is nice," I said, taking his hand and linking it through mine. "It's a comfortable silence."

"It's fantastic," he said. "I can't remember when I've been more entertained. Really. I feel like I could talk to you all night."

"Well, now that you mention it…" I moved my hand from the bar to his knee and leaned in conspiratorially. "If you were planning on asking me to come home with you, this is the perfect opportunity."

He looked shocked and delighted. "Um, of course, if you want to come back I would absolutely love that," he said, signaling for the bill with the international "miming pen writing on pad" flourish.

We hadn't even kissed at that point. But I'm one of those people who hates awkward transitions: I'll always pay an entire restaurant bill rather than argue about who only had the mineral water and salad vs. the foie gras. If I left it to him, I was worried about facing the awkward "cheek or lip" kissing dilemma while hailing a cab. Out of politeness, he probably would have walked away at the end of the evening for fear of offending me. But I was way too horny to let that happen.

Ten minutes later we were in a cab headed east, and his hands were headed south. I slid my legs across his lap and rested my head on his shoulder. Then we kissed, and I took his hand from my cheek and started sucking on his fingers. He moaned and I could feel his hardness beneath me. I was instantly, totally soaked: I've always been self-conscious of my wetness, which was already threatening to drench his lap and the seat. I didn't let him touch me because I felt so horny I might come right there. And I wasn't ready for that yet. I moved my hand up his thigh, tantalizingly close, but kept teasing him.

The cab pulled up outside his east London high-rise, and his tongue became more insistent. Then I guided his hand outside my panties. "Can you feel how wet you're making me?" I whispered in his ear.

"I can't wait to feel you properly," he said, moving his fingers in gentle circles outside my underwear, driving me wild.

By the time we made it inside the door, clothes were already flying. Once our shirts were off, I asked him to get me a glass of water. While he was in the kitchen I marveled at the neatness of his life: The Zegna and Armani suits, hanging in rows on a rail outside his walk-in closet, probably pressed by his cleaner. I wondered, even then, if my chaotic life could ever meld with his "if-it's-Tuesday-it-must-be-the-pink-shirt" existence. I envied him.

I remember wrapping my legs around him and feeling surprised at how solid and safe he felt; after grinding together for a couple of minutes, he reached into the bedside drawer and pulled out a condom.

This highlights another dilemma: I had long ago mastered the art of putting on a condom without using my fingers. The prophylactic moment is critical, and some men freeze like deer caught in headlights and can wilt at the slightest interruption. I wanted to see this guy again, so I didn't want to intimidate him with my experience. We didn't need to break out the whips and chains for our first night together.

I decided to let him handle it, reaching my hand between his legs to fondle his balls while he slid it on. "You're so hard," I murmured.

I've never really had a problem with talking dirty. It's often just a matter of stating the obvious to add a little narrative color, the way that boys sometimes say "Wow! You're tall!" or "It's raining really hard, isn't it?"

He pushed me back onto the bed with my knees bent over the side, parted my thighs, and slid his tongue inside me, and even in my drunken state I could feel that what he lacked in technique he made up for in enthusiasm. But three drinks is normally my maximum for coming through oral sex, and even then it can take twenty minutes.

Most men don't realize that the time to give women oral sex is after fucking them for a few minutes, after a bit of G-spot stimulation, to tip them over the edge. They treat sex like a storyboard with beginning, middle, and end. But this was no time to talk about literary analogies.

So I sat up. "I want you inside me," I murmured, and he needed no further encouragement. However much I love contorting like a pretzel, the missionary position remains one of my favorites. I think it's because I don't have to worry about imitating the *Kama Sutra*; I can just lie back and let myself go.

I wrapped my legs all the way around his back and locked my ankles together (another advantage of being five foot ten) and he pushed back so that he was sitting up, watching himself plunge inside me. I've always been so jealous of men's ability to see everything, since a girl could be a yoga master inside a hall of mirrors and still not get the full picture.

"God, this is so amazing," he said, looking down at me. "You are so fucking gorgeous."

No matter how many times I hear this line, it just never gets old. The only one that gives me the same kind of thrill is the concerned "You look so thin! Are you eating enough?"

Then I squeezed my legs together and threw my ankles over his shoulders, clenching the sheets between my fists as he pushed even further inside me, up to the hilt, and said that he was close to coming. "Do you mind if I touch myself?" I asked him, fingering my clitoris before waiting for an answer. I guess he figured that it was a rhetorical question.

"That is such a turn-on," he said, grunting and increasing the pace of his thrusts.

It mystifies me why women have such hang-ups about masturbating in front of men—they seem to love it. But I also love to watch men touch themselves... I massaged my clit in rhythm to his thrusts, and felt myself tighten around his cock and clench tighter until the spasms started as I came around him.

Just as my orgasm subsided, he came inside me, then we both lay back, breathing heavily, in the dark. "You know how you were saying earlier that, in Manhattan, you have to have a 'talk' before you decide whether you're boyfriend and girlfriend?" he said.

"Uh-huh," I said, rolling over on my stomach and involuntarily grinding my hips against the bed. I was already getting ready for the second round.

"Well, just so there's no confusion, I want you to be my girlfriend," he said. His tone of voice was gentle, but insistent. "I want us to be a couple."

Even then, I could tell that this was a guy not used to taking no for an answer.

Back at the Bleeding Heart, the tirade continued. By the time Patrick got to the phrase "It's not you, it's me," I felt nostalgic for my childhood boyfriend, who dumped me in the playground by yelling, "You're dumped! You smell!" At least he was direct.

"Look, let me stop you right there. There's no way to make a breakup 'not personal.' If you don't want to be with me any more, well, I'm a big girl and I can handle that. But I'd really appreciate it if you wouldn't patronize me."

I picked up a cocktail napkin and dabbed at the corners of my eyes, where black Kohl was pooling like ink.

"Well, I guess there's not much more to say here—Wait, what the hell is that?" He had spotted the felt-tip pen scrawls on the back of my hand.

"Oh, I ran into some guy in the bathroom who wanted to hang out with me tonight and said he was worried about me." Despite holding my breath, I felt a traitorous tear slide down my cheek. "At least someone is."

"Well, it certainly didn't take you long to move on," he spat. "Do you really think that was appropriate?" His eyes narrowed, and I saw a flash of something unpleasant lurking underneath. I had seen this look once before, and it wasn't pretty.

Our first fight had happened after five weeks of complete bliss. We went to a party with a few of Patrick's friends, and I began chatting to his cousin Celia. Early on, she had told me that she fancied a really hot guy with dreadlocks standing over by the bar. Holding Patrick's hand, I told her that she should go talk to him. "He's really cute," I said, "and it's a birthday party, so he probably knows someone here. Go on, you're gorgeous! He'll totally consider himself lucky."

"I'm too scared," she whispered. "You're good at this kind of thing, Cat. I think Americans are just more blunt. Would you mind approaching him for me?"

"Sure thing," I said, giggling as I walked up to the guy and introduced myself as someone with a friend he should get to know better. Ten minutes later I pulled him over, triumphant, and introduced him to Celia. They started chatting, and I was truly chuffed at how well things had gone when Patrick grabbed my forearm and dragged me into a corner.

"What the fuck were you thinking, ignoring me like that?" he said.

I was genuinely shocked, and my mind was reeling as to what could have set him off. "I was just trying to hook her up," I began feebly. He gritted his teeth and started his lecture. "You are my girlfriend," he hissed, "and you were talking to that bloke who was trying to chat you up in front of all my friends—"

"Hang on," I said, "this is insane. I came here with you, all of your friends know that. And I was just talking to him."

Patrick's Jekyll and Hyde act was so complete that I actually began to second-guess myself. I was pretty drunk, had I maybe been a bit flirtatious? Looking back, it's easier for me to understand how women get sucked into emotional abuse. It starts out so innocently.

Though I was still madly in love with him, in hindsight I should have known that our relationship was doomed a couple of months after the party incident. We were in Rome on a romantic weekend, holding hands. "It's so nice to be able to be with my boyfriend, holding hands on a gorgeous afternoon." I nuzzled next to him. "Somehow, I never thought that it could happen to me."

He looked down at me and gripped a bit tighter. "What do you mean—didn't you hold hands with any of your exes?"

I paused, slowing down. "Well, not really. I've never been a super tactile person in public. But it's nice holding hands with you."

"What about your ex-boyfriend, the bartender? Didn't you ever hold hands with him?"

I could feel something shifting, and his lilting voice seemed to have an ominous undertone. But I spoke falteringly, still not comprehending how our gorgeous outing could have gone so wrong. I realize now that I was searching for the right response. Not a good sign.

"Well, no, because he wasn't really my boyfriend," I said, feeling my cheeks blush. I told myself that I had nothing to be ashamed of. This was part of my past, and had all happened way before I met Patrick.

"What do you mean, not your boyfriend? You were sleeping with him, weren't you?" Still, he kept his tone casual; his verbal attacks were subtle sometimes. I felt the hairs on the back of my neck stand up.

"Well, what I meant was... Yes, I was sleeping with him, and he was the only person I slept with for several months, but it was more a 'friends with benefits' arrangement. I wasn't in love with him. Which is why I wouldn't call him my boyfriend."

"Well, if he wasn't your boyfriend, Catherine, why the hell did you expect him to show up at the clinic? Or give you any money? I'm not surprised that he bailed. He probably had no idea who the father was. I mean, you were behaving like such a slut back then."

According to the laws of physics, nothing had changed. We were still in Rome, chatting in front of the Colosseum, and the sun was moving westward across the sky. Anyone looking from the outside would have seen a slightly tipsy couple in love. And yet, the tectonic plates of our relationship had shifted irrevocably. In that instant, I had the first glimmerings of doubt that he wasn't the person I thought. I started to cry, got a bit upset, and he apologized.

When we had very perfunctory sex that night, I dug my nails into his back, not out of pleasure but because I wanted to wound him. He wasn't my soulmate; he had been devalued to the role of human dildo. I began to withdraw into myself, so that he couldn't hurt me anymore.

I had taken a risk, and told him my deepest, darkest secret, and he had waited until the perfect moment to strike. The suspicion grew in that moment that, contrary to what he'd claimed in the past, he didn't celebrate my experience—he hated it. I think, in some twisted way, that he was jealous.

Men always say that they want an equal partner. But in most of my relationships, there's been a crucial moment when I feel like the Jack Nicholson character from *A Few Good Men* on the witness stand screaming, "The truth? You can't *handle* the truth, son!"

I realize now that I was so vulnerable to Patrick because he seized on my weakness—the one event in my life when I felt completely out of control and blamed myself. I suppressed my doubts because I thought I was in love, and I didn't want to face the enormity of my mistake.

In the pub, I snapped back to the present. "What business is it of yours? You've made it very clear that you don't give a shit what happens to me."

"Okay, okay. How are you getting home? Can I walk you to the Tube? Or are you getting a cab?"

I could hear in his tone that he wanted to be somewhere else, probably with the girl he was texting, and that his asking me was strictly an obligation, rather like shepherding home the unwanted, slightly tipsy aunt who overstays her welcome at Christmas. Which is what made my next request even more pathetic. "I want to go home with my boyfriend," I said, my voice finally breaking. "I'm still in love with you, and I have no idea what has happened to us."

He sighed. "Cat, that's not going to happen," he said. "The bottom line is I don't see any future in this relationship, with someone who has no real job and no future plans."

I took a deep breath. I'd like to say that I maintained my dignity at this point, but the truth is that I cried like a little girl. "Well, I'm sorry you feel that way about us, Patrick, because I was—I am really in love with you and didn't realize that our future together was dependent on me having the perfect résumé. But I'm going to make it in this town, with or without you."

"I'm sure you will," he simpered. The insincerity of his tone irritated me. But underneath the pain I could feel something stronger that I was too afraid to tap into fully. It was rage. Or maybe righteous indignation. Logically, I knew that the breakup was for the best, but I was also devastated that I could have gotten things so wrong. I suppose I'd thought of Patrick as a safe landing, since I was moving to a foreign country where I barely knew anyone. In the back of my mind I couldn't help thinking: *What if he's right about my career prospects? What if I am a fantasist loser doomed to making tea runs for the rest of my life?* His dumping me seemed like an omen of worse to come.

I hated him for being so blunt, and myself for being so pathetic. We walked outside, where sheets of seemingly permanent dirty rain slammed into the side of my crappy New York deli umbrella. "Well," I said, "goodbye, then." The man who had told me three weeks ago that he couldn't live without me couldn't muster more than a lame, half-hearted top-half-of-body hug—the kind you give to your slightly lecherous uncle to avoid any below-the-belt contact. Tears blinding my eyes, I watched him walk down the side street and disappear in the direction of the Tube.

I felt too fragile for public transportation, so paced to the edge of the sidewalk in search of a cab. Two cars passed by, splashing freezing cold gutter water onto my shins, but I didn't care. I just stood there, shivering, until I saw a yellow light come on and slide past me to the curb. As I started towards it, the flimsy metal exoskeleton of my umbrella gave way and snapped. Flinging it on to the sidewalk (I changed this mentally to "pavement" since I was a Londoner now), I opened the door and stepped inside, thinking that, whatever happened, my night couldn't possibly get any worse.

Lonely, crying, and devastated, I decided to call Bathroom Boy. But when I looked down at my soaked hand, the ink had run and spilled all over my white T-shirt. Yep, I was definitely cursed. I pulled out my mobile to find three texts from Victoria, asking what was going on. I punched in her number and started sobbing uncontrollably when she picked up the phone. "Sweetie, I'm so sorry," she said. "I'm on my way home, so I'll meet you in twenty minutes." I told the cab driver to head towards Hoxton.

"Maybe he's right. Maybe I should go home," I slurred, throwing back another shot of Absolut Mandarin. We'd unearthed the mummified bottle from the freezer the minute I walked through the door. It burned going down, and I hoped that the slowly unfurling coil of heat in my stomach would dull the pain.

"What, so you're going to let your breakup with this guy run you out of town? You're stronger than that! And the *Independent* likes the ideas you pitched. The editor said that he wants to take you out for drinks, right?" Victoria was spooning Strawberry Cheesecake Haagen-Dazs—my favorite—into a Sex Bomb mug and handing it to me. Hoovering down ice cream and crying into my drink? God, I was such a walking cliché.

"Yeah, but there's still no contract in sight; it'd be strictly pay-as-you-go freelance stuff," I said. "I'd still have no job security, no friends, no place to live, and no money," I told her, swirling the ice cream around in my cup and watching it liquefy. "Besides, what makes me think that they'll give me a job writing weekly about relationships when my own love life is such a fucking train wreck?"

"You've got me, so that's friends covered," she said, pouring me another shot and handing me a tissue. "You're a talented writer, I've read your stuff. Besides, you're not a relationship expert, you're a sexpert, right? You just need to be out getting more material!"

"That's the last thing I feel like doing." I blew my nose, shredding my tissue. "I'll never meet anyone like Patrick. He was so charming and chivalrous."

"He held doors open, Cat, but frankly, on the few occasions when I met him, he struck me as immature and sulky. Plus, he obviously had the emotional depth of a puddle." She paused and sat on the arm of her tattered living room chair to put her arms around me. "Sweetheart, he dumped you by email. How chivalrous was that?"

"Well, I still don't have anywhere to live, and I can't keep camping out on your sofa. You've been way too kind already. I'll miss this place, believe it or not." Victoria has the world's tiniest living room, but it's very charming and homely. The walls are lined with bookshelves that contain mostly travel guides, covering every region of the globe from Cuba to the Maldives and Vietnam.

The only view she has from her front room is of her neighbor's much larger and more palatial flat. At that point he had yet to put up curtains so we had coffee with him every morning, through two panes of glass. The effect was quite surreal. Still, she has a great deal, because it's basically an illegal sublet. The fact that the landlord left two fire extinguishers on her bedroom wall tells me that the place probably isn't up to code.

"Look, you know that Jennifer is moving out in five days to her boyfriend's place. Why don't you move in here? It's really cheap, even if Jen's room is the size of a closet."

Returning to Manhattan and begging for my old job back wasn't my style. I wasn't leaving London until I had conquered this town, on my terms. "God, that would be great. Are you sure?"

"Totally. I was going to advertise on Craigslist and asmallworld, but maybe this is destiny, or kismet, or whatever. But I should warn you about a few things: We have no water pressure, and limited hot water."

"Yeah, I kind of already figured out that the only thing more unreliable than the men in this town is your boiler." When I showered, the nozzle on the wall only distributed water in two temperatures: freezing or boiling hot.

Victoria started ticking off her fingers. "You can't wash dishes and do laundry at the same time, because the sink backs up with murky water.

The windows don't shut fully. You can't really turn the radiator in your room off. Oh, and we have a wee bit of a rodent problem."

"Stop!" I said, laughing as I raised my hand. "I don't want to know any more. I'll take it." I stood up. "And I'm having drinks with the editor in two days. If I'm going to wow him with the first installment of my sex column idea, I'd better figure out a topic."

She looked up at me. "How about something timely, like, I don't know, male vs. female approaches to breakups?"

# TWO

Lying on my bed, listening to the Nine Inch Nails' *Pretty Hate Machine* album to stop myself from crying, I thought about how my female friends try to support me after a split. They dissect every aspect of the guy's personality while encouraging me to talk about my feelings, and reassure me that I was too good for him. We usually try to find some life lesson from the experience, which can only be gleaned after obsessing over every detail of the end of the affair. I inevitably listen to bleak, sad love songs by Joy Division and the Smiths in the early stages of a breakup, but the nihilistic lyrics of the Nine Inch Nails' albums are perfect when I'm ready to move on to the rage phase.

My male friends, on the other hand, don't care about dissecting emotions. They just encourage me to get laid.

"Got dumped?" Michael said the next day when I called him. "You need to stop wallowing and get back on the horse ASAP. Meet me at the Westbourne at nine-thirty."

But Michael got held up at work, so he texted Rick, one of his banker mates, to look after me. We chatted to a group of his friends, boys from New Zealand who were celebrating their very cute female friend's birthday with a massive crowd of people. So far, the pub was certainly living up to its reputation as a meat market. Crossing the room to the loo, I felt as if I were walking a rickety plank over snapping crocodiles with a raw chicken dangling from my waist.

They suggested that I went along with them to a West End club, just for "one drink." But somehow one drink became ten, and I found myself in the middle of the Kiwi horde, bumping and grinding to Kanye West with the birthday girl. Petite and tanned, she had dirty blonde hair and an attitude to match. She was wearing a teal dress with a neckline that plunged almost to her stomach, and she caught me looking more than once when we went to the bathroom together. It was only a bit of innocent flirting, or so I thought.

"Do you want to come back with us to party?" she asked me, lacquering on several coats of sheer red lip gloss.

I figured, why the hell not?

There were four of us in the cab: Me, Rick, Birthday Girl, and a guy whose name I can't recall. I'll call him Mr. X.

En route, Birthday Girl stroked my legs as we headed somewhere south of the river. We settled into the living room, opened another bottle of tequila, and started playing strip truth-or-dare, heavy on the dare. When Rick's turn came, he said, predictably, "Okay, so we want you guys to kiss. For twenty seconds."

Shyly, Birthday Girl put her hand on my cheek and pulled me to her, kissing me softly. Her tongue parted my lips and I could feel a jolt running through my nether regions. She wasn't the first girl I had ever kissed: That honor belonged to my university friend Irina. One night she and I had gotten a bit experimental in the female toilets of a nightclub, but the sound of knocking outside stopped our exploration. I had regretted the interruption ever since. Because even though I could never become a lesbian—I simply love cock too much—I have always wondered what it would feel like to go all the way with a girl.

"Fine, but you guys have to kiss too," I said. I've never had that much experience with gay male porn, except when turning up the volume on a pilfered DVD called *Ass Masters VI* really loud to annoy Patrick, who would frantically try to grab the remote from me to drown out the moans. But I have to admit that watching two bare-chested, muscular lumberjack types who were clearly not taking this seriously turned me on. They kissed, awkwardly, laughing the entire time.

"Okay, now," Mr. X said, taking a belt of tequila. "Cat, why don't you suck on her nipples?"

"Do you mind?" I asked her, leaning in to take one of her round, brownish-pink areolae in my mouth. I flicked my tongue lightly over one, then the other and sucked gently. I don't know if it was part of her act, but I felt them stiffen and she seemed to enjoy my attentions.

While Rick put another log on the crackling fire, Mr. X was cutting lines of cocaine. "Do you girls want some?" he said.

"Should we? I've heard that if you put it on your clit it feels really intense," she whispered in my ear, sliding my hands between her legs.

"Um, no, I'm fine, thanks," I said. "You have to be careful how much you put on," I warned her. "It's a mucous membrane, just like your nose, and you don't want to overdose." My mum was a biology teacher, and I've read way too many science textbooks. Besides, I treat illegal drugs like anal sex: Okay for very occasional use like birthdays and Christmas, but do it every day and you'll start to feel seriously worn out.

We kissed again, but this time she lightly bit my bottom lip. I was aware that we had an audience, but alcohol had dulled my inhibitions.

"Ready to up the stakes, girls?" Mr. X asked.

"I don't think I'm going to need anything to feel stimulated right now after all," she giggled.

I felt really nervous, like the time I gave my first blow job on a beach during spring break when I was thirteen. At the same time, I was seriously turned on. I slid one finger inside her and made a come-hither motion to stimulate her G-spot, while circling my thumb around her clit, trying to keep a steady rhythm.

She turned to Rick, who had been wanking while he watched us, and motioned for him to come join in. Mr. X just kept cutting lines; that's the shame of Class A drugs, they tend to make the boys randy but flaccid. I kissed down her tanned, flat stomach, then found myself face to face with her perfectly smooth shaved pussy. Even in my hyper-aroused state I found myself wondering if it was Atkins or just loads of sit-ups that made her tummy so flat that it was practically concave. I guess I can't stop being a girl, even when I'm going down on one!

She smelled of baby powder and jasmine perfume, and tasted strange but vaguely familiar, almost metallic. I licked around her nub, then probed my tongue between the folds while continuing rhythmic pressure, pumping my first two fingers in and out. I felt her gasp and tighten so hard that I worried the circulation would be cut off in my fingers, then the minute but unmistakable contractions. I made her come! I felt a flush of pride.

While Rick switched places to slip his cock inside her, she leaned down to return the favor and we slipped into a half-hearted 69 position. But whatever they say about a woman knowing what a woman wants must not be true in all cases, because when she put her tongue on me I couldn't feel a thing. Maybe it was because the booze had deadened me, or because I got distracted by trying to give and receive at the same time, but I did something I would normally never advocate: I faked it. It was probably the addition of the third party that caused me to freak out a bit.

Though the sight of Rick pushing into her was way more erotic than any porno I'd ever seen, coordination has never been my strong point. When I was a kid, my ballet teacher compared me to "a bull in a china shop." So it's no surprise that when performance anxiety sets in during a multiple-partner encounter, part of me feels like the cruise-ship director walking around with a clipboard, saying, "Is everyone all right for cock over here? Anyone need more oral?" Mr. X finished himself off, watching us, before the three of us collapsed in a heap.

Afterwards, we all retired to the kitchen for toasted cheese sandwiches, which I tore through gratefully as I was suddenly ravenous. With no pajamas, I re-dressed and passed out on an overstuffed blue sofa. At some point in the night I caught a whiff of jasmine as Birthday Girl covered me with a blanket.

I woke up in the morning with a hangover from hell, sore thighs, an inexplicable sprained wrist, and no idea of my location. Through one half-closed eye, I could see the outline of a guy wrapped in a Spider-Man duvet, several overflowing ashtrays, and random articles of clothing scattered around the room. I tiptoed gingerly through the overturned wine bottles, and without saying goodbye I stumbled outside into the indiscriminate street next door to a park, underneath a gray sky, and hailed a cab.

I texted Victoria on my way home to let her know that I was alive, and added, "I had a threesome. Details later. Are you shocked? Should I feel guilty?"

"Menages-a-trois are to the noughties what anal sex was to the nineties," she texted back. "Don't feel bad. Hell, in your case it was probably therapeutic."

Of course, I still missed Patrick. But for some reason I couldn't stop laughing, and my body was tingling all over. In a weird way, I had never felt more alive.

In my head I was already composing my next column:

> *I followed my first rule of three-ways: I'm always the guest star, never the main attraction. Because, despite my liberal attitudes towards everyone else's sex lives, paradoxically, I'm far too jealous to ever share a serious boyfriend.*
>
> *But sometimes, a night low on drama and high on nakedness is just what the doctor ordered . . .*

# THREE

Spent the afternoon in therapy, a.k.a. Selfridges, with Amy in tow. I had met her on the same fateful night I met Patrick and we had become firm friends. She works nearby in St Christopher's Place, so we nipped in after a late lunch.

"How are you, babe?" she asked, concern in her voice. "Victoria told me about your little 'group sex therapy' adventure last week. Do you think that perhaps you should see a therapist for real?" she asked, pulling out a Matthew Williamson sequined sundress with white leather cutouts. She's probably the only person I know who could pull off white leather—she's lithe, toned, and healthy with natural blonde hair and no makeup.

While Victoria is concerned about appearances, Amy is completely into mental health. When I have a crisis or lover's spat, Amy offers me one of her self-help books, or suggests that I take up yoga or channel my inner peace. Victoria focuses on helping me get revenge.

"I think I overanalyze myself enough as it is," I told her.

"Makes sense," she said as we walked to the women's designer shoes.

"But I still think that a therapist is a good neutral third party to help you vent all your frustrations. In any case, it would be a nice escape from sex and dating."

"See, that's the thing," I said, pulling out a pair of black Stella McCartney over-the-knee boots. "Sex has always been my escapism. Do you think these are too slutty?"

"Of course not, if you're planning on charging by the hour." She laughed. "I'm only teasing, they're foxy. Try them on."

We sat down and I told Amy about my weird sex dreams, and my hero Carl Jung, who believed in the power of the unconscious. "I don't buy into all this Freudian nonsense about harping on endlessly about what happened as a child. Jung is cool because he's all about balance. He says we should develop a healthy relationship with our unconscious self. If we obsess too much about it, we become psychotic. And shutting ourselves off apparently causes empty consumerism and a life devoid of meaning."

She smirked. "So a Jungian is buying £375 boots?"

"Yeah, right! I have exactly £8.20 in my bank account," I said. "I just bought a latte on my credit card. Anyway, I'm going off Jung a bit. I read the other day that he thought monogamy was totally unnatural. His actual quote was something like 'the prerequisite for a good marriage is the license to be unfaithful.'"

"You look fabulous in those," Amy said, glancing up and down my legs. "So, basically, he thought that we want a fairy-tale ending that is scientifically impossible. And he believed that was the cause of our cultural malaise?"

I unzipped the boots and struggled to get them off. "Pretty much."

She absentmindedly stroked a suede Sigerson Morrison boot. "But you still believe in the fairy-tale, right?"

I smiled. "Yeah, well, I've known that I was living largely in a fantasy world of my own creation for some time now. Luckily, I'm comfortable with that."

I got the "How about a night in?" text late in the afternoon, while I was heading home in a cab after my "therapy" with Amy. My reply was short and to the point: "Only if we can camp out at your flat with nothing but a box of porn, a bottle of water, and a few choice accessories."

I had the ideal arrangement with Mark, a hunky half-Australian ex-boyfriend. He's tall, dark, handsome, and muscular, but incredibly gentle except when I expressly command him to be rough. We got along famously, but soon realized that we were so similar our personalities clashed, rather than complemented each other, so we agreed to split up a couple of years ago. Fortunately, we stayed great friends.

He moved to Hong Kong but works between three continents. So we had an understanding: We saw each other when we were both in the same location and were both between relationships, but not often enough to get bored, or too attached. He's a fantastic shag.

Oddly enough, that's one of the reasons we couldn't stay together long-term: Every night in bed with Mark was a three-ring circus, and sometimes all I needed was a cuddle.

Part of me did wonder if, so soon after Patrick, I was setting myself up for disappointment. Ultimately I do want a committed relationship, but until then I'm looking for the sexual equivalent of Switzerland: Someone who is safe, fun, and not too emotionally draining. For the most part, I've ruled out sleeping with exes because the risk of a one-sided relationship or overdosing on nostalgia is too great. Mark is the exception to the rule.

He called me five minutes later. "What did you have in mind?" he asked, his voice sounding jet-lagged but still very sexy. "I've missed you, sweetheart."

I'd missed him, too. I've always believed that having a steady diet of sexual activity can actually take the pressure off dating, and makes me less likely to leap into bed with the wrong guy; or as Victoria says, "It's like a job that you know isn't permanent—it's a place to get a steady salary until you find something better." And I trust Mark implicitly: He's the sort of friend I can be completely myself around, and our on-off scenario has outlasted most of my romantic relationships.

Since my breakup, my more promiscuous male friends had encouraged me to try the Internet, where a hook up can be delivered faster than a pizza on sites like Craigslist "Casual Encounters." But scrolling through I found descriptions like "trusty motor needs a good run-out" and "fat hairy smelly misogynist seeks sexy intelligent waif," and realized that I'm looking to get laid, not end up in a seedy motel with a guy who looks like the villain from *The Texas Chainsaw Massacre*. Erica Jong's "zipless fuck" may be the anonymous ideal, but I need to have chemistry (or at least a decent digital photo); otherwise, I'd rather stay in with my vibrator. Besides, in my opinion spontaneity is the key to passion. Exchanging countless emails about what we are going to do to each other is like seeing the same trailer for a film over and over: The main event almost never lives up to the hype.

So I rushed home to change from my strictly functional "day" underwear into an Agent Provocateur pink and white lace demi-cup bra and tie-side knickers. I pulled up to Mark's Kensington flat just after six, with my professional-looking black laptop bag packed with "accessories" for our late-night tryst.

He let me in, wrapped in a pilfered Hilton Hotel white terrycloth bathrobe, and gave me a huge hug. At six foot two with an incredibly defined and muscular chest, Mark is one of the few men who has ever managed to make me feel petite.

"Do you need to write tonight?" he said, taking my bag.

"Sort of. I just got assigned to do a piece on environmentally friendly sex toys," I told him, helping myself to a Grey Goose on the rocks from his living room wet bar and unbuttoning my blouse as I walked to the bedroom. "So I have to, um, road test them."

While he headed to the loo, I wriggled out of my trousers (skinny jeans were definitely not made for sexy stripteases!) then put my heels back on.

When he reappeared, I peeked back over one shoulder and let the silk blouse slide to the floor, arching my back, accentuating my long legs and keeping my chest hidden, for now.

"Environmentally friendly? What the hell does that mean?" His black hair was still wet from the shower, and he smelled faintly of cinnamon and Hugo Boss cologne. I'm not sure if it was my pheromones that reacted when his scent wafted across the room, but I felt wet already.

"Well, I've got a battery-powered vibrator, but it wasn't really a sunny enough day to get it charged. So we can take our pick: We've got some gold-tipped glass dildos, organic lube, and phthalate-free silicone vibrator—or any combination thereof."

"Well, that depends on what you want to do," he said, scooping me up so that I could feel how aroused he was beneath his bathrobe. "What's a 'phthalate,' anyway?" he asked.

He pushed me against the wall while I wrapped my legs around him, then started sliding his hands between my legs and up inside my panties.

"And judging by what I'm feeling, I don't think we're going to need any lubricant tonight, do you?"

"Not for that, honey," I said, biting his earlobe as I whispered in his ear. "I do have a fantasy that I've never fulfilled, but it might be a bit too much for you." I was putting on my sweet little Southern girl accent to the max, and adding an extra syllable to draw out every word.

"Since when has anything ever been too much? Tell me, sweetheart," he said, as he carried me over to the bed and dropped me onto the duvet.

I've always dreamed of trying double penetration, but found the idea of two men at the same time a bit intimidating. So, in a tone more suited to asking for more milk for my afternoon tea, I whispered, "I want you to fuck me in the arse, and slide a vibrator inside of me at the same time."

"Whatever you say," he said as I untied the robe and wrapped my right hand around his cock. Obviously he was excited by the idea. "That is so dirty!"

Finding the right one was a bit tricky: The glass dildos were enormous. "Jesus Christ, this is a bit scary," he said, laughing. "These things are huge."

"You pick one, and try not to kill me," I said, sliding up to the headboard and spreading my legs so that he could take in the sight of me in my tie-side knickers, still wearing the stilettos. "But please, make me beg."

I pushed my hand down my soaking knickers so that I could stroke my throbbing clit.

"No, you're not doing that yet," he said, playfully pulling my hand away and attaching my wrists to the bedposts with silk scarves that he, knowing my tastes, had already pre-attached. I have tiny arm bones and he didn't really bind me tight enough, but I wasn't going to let on and ruin the fantasy.

Mark loved me to play the helpless damsel in distress, but we'd never done anything this elaborate. Since I have to be so dominant in every other realm of my life, from managing my career to hailing a cab, is it any wonder that I long to be submissive in bed? He gently licked me through the thin satin fabric of my knickers, which he knows drives me wild.

"Please," I said, my eyes glazing over.

"Please what?" he asked me, staring intently at me with his intense hazel eyes while stroking my cheek. "Do you want me to fuck you? Say it."

"Please fuck me, baby," I said, arching my back to grind myself against his tongue.

"Not yet," he said, loosening my ties and flipping me over, before climbing up to straddle my chest as he stroked his cock. The sight of his hairy, muscular chest looming above me was amazing: I've always preferred manly men to shaved and buffed metrosexuals. After all, I want to be the pretty one in the relationship.

"First, I'm going to put my cock all the way in your mouth, right to the back of your throat, then I want to taste you. Then, if you're a very good girl, I'll fuck you so hard that you come all over me." He kissed me lightly, biting my bottom lip. "So, are you going to be a good girl?"

I nodded, and he pushed himself up on his knees and plunged the entire shaft into my mouth. I was fine with relinquishing control because he knows my limits. I felt him pushing down into the back of my throat and could hear his grunts of pleasure as I deep-throated him, while concentrating on breathing control. Back in high school I used to be able to hold my breath for two and a half minutes, a skill that has served me well in bed. I felt him get even harder and knew he was getting close; then he stopped, and began feather-kissing his way down my stomach before taking my knickers off with his teeth.

Which was a pleasure, because Mark has some serious oral skills. He has never fallen into the relatively common trap of relying on the lizard tongue-flicking in pornos to learn how to go down on a girl. He alternated small circles with his tongue to sucking on my clit. When he slid his fingers inside to press against my G-spot while lavishing his tongue on me in rhythm, I told him I was close to coming.

"Not yet," he said teasingly. "Are you ready to have me inside you?"

"I'm soaking the sheets," I said. "What do you think?"

He plunged all the way into me with one stroke and started thrusting slowly at first, before building up the tempo. At the same time he spread some lubricant (I didn't have time to find out if it was organic or not) on his fingers and gently massaged my bum, before sliding his finger inside. "Are you okay?" he said as I tensed up. "Is it too much?"

"No," I gasped. "Oh my God, it feels amazing. Don't stop."

I've never been much of a believer in organized religions. My parents are lapsed Presbyterians and I couldn't link the boring sermons in church to the animal pleasures I experienced at home, by myself, under the duvet.

Ironically, orgasms are the closest I've ever felt to God, and my mind often wanders when I'm on the brink. It's like an out-of-body experience, and during my moment of detachment I began to wonder if anal sex serves any purpose in Darwinian evolution. Then I thought, "Why am I thinking about Charles Darwin when I'm about to be sodomized?"

When I snapped back to reality, I saw that Mark had fished one of the smaller, pink silicone vibes from under the bed, the G-monster if I'm not mistaken, and turned it on low. It's one of the best to use in the heat of passion, since the glass ones can be a bit chilly in cold weather.

He took his fingers out and slid his cock into my bum, gently, waiting for me to relax against him before pushing further inside. "Are you okay?" he asked again.

"Fuck, this feels amazing," I said, not articulating everything else that it encapsulated: It felt dirty, taboo, and as if he had utter control of me. He kept still inside me while he positioned the vibrator against my clit, first buzzing it in small circles then sliding it inside me while he gently rocked against me. Once I pushed past the barrier of pain, it was sheer bliss. He was stimulating what textbooks call my "A spot," and my pussy was the event horizon. The sensation of being filled to the hilt from both sides was almost more than my body could bear. I was being stretched, turned inside out. I was on fire.

"Oh God, oh fuck, I'm coming!" I screamed, and could tell by the look on his face that he was not far behind me. I felt my muscles tense and spasm, and the vibrator pulsing inside me made my orgasm prolong itself.

"Jesus Christ," he said, breathing heavily as we linked hands and collapsed onto the pillows afterwards. "That was incredible."

Afterwards, we took a bath together and he soaped my back with almond shea butter body wash while we discussed the relative merits of cheesy eighties horror movies, and our emergency escape plans in case of zombie invasion.

"I would totally steal someone's boat and head for the water," I said, taking the sponge out of his hands and rubbing the back of my neck.

"This flat would be pretty secure, I reckon," he said. "I guess it depends on whether they are the slow-moving, George Romero *Dawn of the Dead* type ones or the ones that run really fast like in the 2004 remake."

And then I just lost it and actually started to cry.

"Sweetie, what's wrong? It's Patrick, isn't it?" he said as he jumped out and grabbed me an oversized bath towel.

"Yeah, I'm sorry, it's not you, it's just that talking about horror movies reminds me of our weekends together in New York and—" My voice broke. "Mark, do you think I'll ever find someone… someone permanent?"

"Absolutely," he said, wrapping a towel around me and ruffling my hair. "And next time, it will be someone man enough to realize what an amazing person you are. Passionate, smart, and sweet. And a complete nightmare neurotic, but hopefully he won't figure that out before it's too late!" I chucked a half-melted bar of soap at him and we both burst out laughing.

That night I drifted off into a dreamless sleep. The next morning, Mark made me a cup of coffee, which I downed in two gulps, then I opened his refrigerator in search of food. Like most bachelors, he had nothing of note inside except for some basmati rice from a leftover Indian takeaway, which I microwaved for breakfast.

"Hey, sweetie, what about these?" he said, gathering up the remaining toys from last night. "Do you want to take them for your next hapless victim?"

"No, keep them here," I purred, casting him a quick sideways glance and blowing him a kiss. "Because next time, I'm going to turn the tables and use them on you."

# FOUR

It was Valentine's Day, some five weeks after my split from Patrick, and Victoria and I were discussing the need for space in relationships—in her case, specifically, a shelf. She'd been spending loads of time at her new crush Mike's house, but he lived south of the river and the commute back to Hoxton had been a bit hellish.

"I'm sick of using his shampoo—no conditioner, of course—smelling like Old Spice and everyone at work asking me if I'm okay because I look tired," she said. "But I've been burned before."

"I know what you mean," I agreed. "The one time I left a hairdryer at a man's house he gave it back to me in a plastic bag the next time I saw him." It was mortifying, so I'm completely with Victoria on this one: I never leave anything inside a man's domain. Somehow, knowing which brand of eye makeup remover I use destroys the illusion I'm trying to project. Leaving tampons behind feels more intimate than sharing sperm, because it implies a future connection. Besides, he may think I left it on purpose to see him again.

"Why don't you start smaller than an electrical appliance?" I asked. "Leave an umbrella or something, and see how he reacts to that." I also told her never, under any circumstances, to leave anything that she couldn't live without. One friend of mine had to wait a month to get her very expensive Chanel cuff bracelet back after she "accidentally" left it at some German guy's house. "I don't think you have anything to worry about, though, he seems really keen for you to stay over. Then again, you never know. Patrick sent my shit back in a box—he couldn't even bring himself to hand it over in person." I felt a painful twinge in my stomach.

"Do you want to be my date tonight, sweetie?" she asked, squeezing my shoulder.

"What about your *boyfriend*?" I asked, gently teasing her. Victoria normally hates the "B-word" but she seemed really smitten with Mike.

"He's still in Stockholm, and not getting back until late tonight. So we're going out tomorrow instead; he's got some kind of 'surprise' planned and as usual I have no idea what's going on. So why don't we hit a few bars? It'll be super romantic!"

I agreed to meet her at the Bricklayer's Arms down the road later, and tried to work on my next column until then. My drink with the *Independent* editor had gone well. He'd liked my idea of a sex column and when he read my pieces he agreed then and there to give it a whirl. The reaction to my first few had been very encouraging.

That week I was under pressure to come up with something romantic, but, honestly, I find blood orgies much less offensive than an artificial day that encourages grown men to brandish teddy bears and gaze into their lovers' eyes over bottles of cheap pink champagne. As a single girl, I hate Valentine's Day. I loathe it so completely that I decided to immortalize my despair in the column.

*Passing yet another window filled with cheap cuddly toys last week, I found myself yearning for St. Valentine's Day of old. You know, back when saints were beheaded and, during the pagan fertility festival of Lupercalia, men ran through the streets whipping women with animal skins.*

*Public humiliation, revenge, and a sound whipping: It reminds me a bit of my last relationship.*

Nor do couples escape the wrath of Cupid's arrow. Experts recently estimated that half of all relationships end around Valentine's Day, since the pressure and expectations of the "most romantic day of the year" can compel people to re-evaluate the state of their relationships. I can understand that, because the soundtrack to my love life has always been more Depeche Mode than Céline Dion.

Ever since my awkward days at secondary school I've dreaded the cut-throat competition of Valentine's Day and the crushing disappointment when I realized that my letterbox was empty, except for a card that featured little green men and said, "Take Me to Your Leader" (in reference to the "Alien Girl" nickname).

As an adult, things haven't been much better; I've seen successful, gorgeous girlfriends reduced to sending themselves flowers. Some of us are fighting back, though, and anti-Valentine's Day parties seem to be on the rise. New York has the Black Hearts Party, an annual event at which hundreds of black-clad skeptics gather to eat black wedding cake, play raunchy games, and write their vitriolic rants on a giant blackboard.

Still, V-Day has a bright side for singles. Michael has a theory that an un-coupled person's chances of a random hook up rise exponentially on the fateful February eve. "Think about it: All these unattached people are freaking out, feeling lonely, and getting pissed. It can be one of the most fun nights of the year!"

I stubbed out a cigarette, saved my work, and called Victoria.

"What do you think, Valentine?" I asked. "Should we stay in and watch *Thelma and Louise*, or perhaps head to an overpriced restaurant to chuck bread rolls at loved-up couples?"

She laughed. "I think we should stick to pub karaoke. And we're definitely switching phones, so that neither of us is tempted to do any drunk dialing."

"By 'neither of us,' you obviously mean me. Don't worry, darling, I already have two hot dates tonight—with Jack Daniel's and Johnnie Walker."

Victoria was already at the pub when I arrived, looking fabulous, her ample chest squeezed into a red corset top under a black blazer. Her job in fashion PR has honed her sense of style and attention to detail—she never looks less than immaculate, which she says helps her feel in control of her life. Control is a big issue for Victoria. Her mum, a glamorous French former model, reared Victoria from a young age to be ruthless when it came to men. Her motto was "always find someone who adores you more than you adore them, darling." No wonder she takes dating tips from *Dangerous Liaisons*.

She enveloped me in a huge hug, and when she laughed the wall of Scotch in her breath hit me. "So he finally spilled. He's taking me out tomorrow night on one of those sunset riverboat trips," she said, giggling. "I love him to death, but I live in fear of feeling under pressure to be spontaneously romantic. And you know how allergic I am to seafood!"

"Oh, come on," I admonished her. "I think it sounds really sweet; anyway, at least you have a Valentine." I stuck my lower lip out in an exaggerated pout. "Nobody loves me."

"Cheer up, baby. I love you, and judging by the look of those guys"— she was gesturing to two lanky, curly haired collegiate types at the end of the bar who couldn't have been more than eighteen—"you've got a few other admirers."

From what she'd told me, Victoria had tended to go for completely inappropriate men in the past, which was why I was genuinely thrilled for her this time around.

"You know, it makes me anxious that Mike's so normal," she said after our first shot. "In fact, I find it a bit terrifying."

"It's good to have someone normal and solid," I reassured her. "We have enough drama going on inside our heads. You don't need to add another crazy person to the mix."

She laughed. "Think you should take some of your own advice?"

"In good time, my darling. Right now, let's sing. But we have to pick something really abysmally cheesy."

Two hours, three Jack and Cokes, and a tequila shot later, my tone-deaf arse was at the karaoke machine, wailing along to Journey's "Don't Stop Believin'." It was fantastic.

Back at home, Victoria and I stumbled inside and I immediately knocked over a pile of old *Vogue* magazines. She lit the Diptyque vanilla candle, and I swayed back and forth in front of it, almost singeing my eyebrows as I tried to light my cigarette.

"So do you think Mike likes me?" she slurred. "My mum's always saying, 'More mystery, less history,' and telling me that I'm supposed to be doing *The Rules*."

"Fuck *The Rules*!" I said, grabbing the offending book from her shelf and tearing off the cover. "I'm so fucking sick of these women chasing a quick buck by making women believe it's all their fault. It's so self-constructive…"

"Um, I think you mean self-destructive, Cat."

"Whatever… oops," I said, giggling as I accidentally dropped ash on my black leather ankle boots. "I'll tell you what we are going to do—we're going to ceremoniously burn this book right now."

I grabbed her lighter and headed out to the tiny terrace, Ellen

Fein's countenance beckoning me to melt that smug smile off her face.

"That bitch is divorced now, so you would think I'd get my money back," Victoria said, laughing. "But I'm not sure ritualistic fire is a good idea—this is Valentine's Day, not Halloween."

"Whatever, it's a pagan holiday, and it's time for some sacrifice." I set the book alight, and dropped it into a concrete flowerpot to watch it flame up. "Burn, baby, burn!"

We both giggled, then poured a bottle of tap water over the entire thing and watched the bestseller dissolve into a dank, pulpy gray mess. It felt cleansing somehow.

"The rule is, there are no rules," she said, weaving back to her bedroom, makeup smeared, and pointing her finger in my face. "Whoa, dude, that's really deep. Write that down for next week!"

# FIVE

I was astonished by how well my column was going. People, it seemed, loved to live vicariously through my misery. After only a few installments I'd become the literary equivalent of the Jerry Springer show—my misadventures seemed to make people feel better about their own love lives.

I had plenty to write about. It had been a crazy couple of months since my split, and I was starting to find that my voracious erotic expectations were back at their unrealistic peak.

Post-Patrick, I still didn't feel like entering into a full-fledged relationship. But if I was distancing myself emotionally, I was feeling the need to couple physically. I'd been rampantly horny. Besides, I was a sexpert now, a role that I was really beginning to settle into. I had to fill my "research" quota!

When I went on my first date with Tom, a six-foot four-inch blond surfer-boy look-alike, the conversation was standard boring first-date fare, all easy-to-digest, noncontroversial small talk that was the verbal equivalent of baby food.

The only surprise came at the end of the evening.

Tom wrapped his arms around me and kissed me for a full five minutes, and as our kisses became more urgent I couldn't help wondering why I felt no signs of life below the belt. Normally I'm a big fan of what I like to call "copping the obligatory feel," which means that I try to get some kind of sneak preview of the package via "accidental" frottage before any clothes come off.

Funnily enough, we had been talking about penis size earlier. We saw Mötley Crüe rocker Tommy Lee in the Electric, and when he swaggered in, the discussion inevitably turned to the infamous sex video with Pamela Anderson, then his wife, starring Lee and his massive member.

"But size doesn't matter anyway," Tom blurted out. "If it's too big it's a turn-off for women and hurts, right, Cat?"

I demurely sipped my vodka tonic and smiled. As the vagina is an elastic organ that can stretch—or shrink—to accommodate, unless a man is literally hung like a horse this is probably not an issue any man need worry about. Yet when a guy asks if he's big enough, we have to say yes, even though most of us have found ourselves at some point begging, "Put it in," in the heat of passion, only to be told that it's already there.

Back at his flat, he led me through a cluttered room that lacked any discernible decor. It was obviously a bachelor pad: There was a lone loafer thrown on the floor and camera equipment and piles of DVDs lined the walls. His bedroom was equally basic, and he sat down on the peeled-back comforter, with me grinding on top of him. We used to call this "dry humping" in high school, and it was refreshingly retro.

He started inching my asymmetrical skirt up, and I started to unbutton his shirt, laughing nervously as I kissed him. "I want you," I said, sliding my hand up his thigh and fumbling with his button-fly jeans.

"Let me help you with that," he whispered—and unearthed a member the size of a pickled gherkin.

At first I kissed down his chest, convinced that it had to be some type of optical illusion. I mean, the guy was six foot four. After teasing him with my tongue, I half-heartedly gave him a blow job, which didn't even activate my gag reflex.

The anticipation of having him fill me up gave way to crushing disappointment. I know it's shallow (no pun intended), but I feigned a giant yawn and told him that I was really tired.

"It's because I'm small, isn't it?" he asked, sitting up.

Feeling terribly guilty, I said, "No, of course not, it looks fine!" in the chirpy tone I'd use about a girlfriend's ghastly new haircut. God, I felt horrible. So I did the only thing I could think of: I faked stomach cramps, mumbled something vague about "female troubles," and ran to the loo to text Mark. I used our standard SOS text: "Au secours!"

He rang back immediately and I shouted through to Tom in the bedroom that I had to take this call. After giving Mark the low-down in hushed tones, I asked if the reverse had ever happened to him. "Once," he said. "I was dating this girl who was gorgeous, but we just weren't a good fit in bed."

"What happened?" I asked. But I could hear Tom getting out of bed next door. "I'd better go," I said. "It would be terrible if he overheard us."

"Let's put it this way," I heard Mark say as I hung up. "Sweet girl, very fit, but her nether regions felt like the Mersey tunnel."

Pulling a sad face, I came back into the bedroom and informed Tom that my flatmate had just been dumped and was having an emotional crisis. It's the perfect white lie because even if he didn't believe me he would have to be polite.

In the taxi home I wondered whether to feel guilty.

I'm not saying that porn-star proportions are a guarantee of being great in bed. I'll never forget one photographer who was huge, but just unzipped his trousers and smiled smugly, leading to the most anticlimactic night of my life. I also believe that emotional connection, oral skills, and imagination can go a long way towards compensating for any lack.

However, most women discreetly admit that, all things being equal, bigger is definitely better. So if Tom wanted another date, I was planning on letting him down gently. A massive member may not be essential for me, but a tiny one is, alas, a deal-breaker. Since men have no qualms about stating their preferences for purely aesthetic characteristics such as big breasts or a slim figure, I don't think that women should feel guilty about admitting to their own needs. Some of my girlfriends won't date anybody under six feet tall, so why should I feel bad about hoping for more than six inches?

Back at the flat, I did a Google search. Sixty-five years ago, Alfred Kinsey decreed that phallic lengths between five and seven inches were within the continuum of "average." The measurements have defined men's lives since.

But, while men today can pump up their pecs, sculpt their abs, get hair transplants, and pop Viagra, there's very little they can do about the size of their genitals. Obviously, it's still a male obsession— or the guys wouldn't be sending "Erectus Maximus 001" to my Hotmail account.

I heard the key in the door ten minutes later, and was about to launch into a tirade about the evening's events when I realized that Victoria had been crying. "What's wrong, baby?" I asked her, shoveling aside several unwashed socks and a lone black ankle boot from the sofa. (Victoria is one of those people who just does not seem to see dirt. Her hygiene habits freak me out a bit, which is why I tend to eat out of single-serving, self-service containers. But I still love her.)

"It's Mike. He told me that he's got some kind of weird discharge. Then he met me at this out-of-the-way pub, and said, 'I have a sexually transmitted disease, and I can only have got it from you.' I asked if he had been tested, and he just freaked out more. He basically accused me of being the whore of Babylon!" Her voice broke, and I gave her a hug.

I can't say that I was totally surprised. After our first encounter, Patrick and I never used—or mentioned—condoms. Having lived for eight years in Manhattan—where the testing conversation is as much a relationship milestone as leaving a toothbrush at a new beau's apartment—the subject was still burning in my mind two weeks later when I blurted out, "Have you ever been tested for STDs?" one Sunday morning over coffee.

He looked at me as if I had just suggested inviting the entire Arsenal team into our bed. "Why would I do that? I've never had anything wrong with me in my life," he said, fumbling for a cigarette.

I gently pointed out that many diseases, such as chlamydia, the most common and easily spread, can be asymptomatic for months or years.

Not only was he completely unaware of the symptoms of chlamydia and gonorrhea, but I also got the feeling that he thought they were some type of tropical storm. "Well, I don't know what kind of people you've been hanging around with, Catherine," he declared, "but, believe me, I know the type of girls I've gone out with and that's never been a problem."

I have discovered that, unlike in the U.S., where for the most part the safe sex message has become completely absorbed into the cultural Zeitgeist, London mating rituals are as steeped in 1950s nostalgia as the retro fashions dominating the high street.

As a student at New York University, I carried condoms in a chic and discreet vintage Gucci purse, and felt looked after rather than shamed if a man provided one. But British men tend never to mention safe sex or use condoms, at least not without my insistence.

Which poses the question: In a town where unbridled hedonism is becoming the norm and group sex makes front-page news, what has happened to the AIDS conversation?

Michael once told me that, in lieu of latex, he relied on a system of "social vetting" to weed out potential dangers. "I go to members' clubs like Soho House, where you know two things about the people you meet: That the membership committee has approved them, so they most likely work in a field like arts or the media; and they can afford to spend £600 a year to belong. Otherwise, I tend to meet people at friends' parties, so it's not as if I'm picking up women in a random bar."

British men also seem to associate condoms with illicit affairs, more suitable to a one-night stand than a proper girlfriend. By that warped logic, not having the STD discussion implies a sense of trust—and therefore greater intimacy.

Unfortunately, as Victoria discovered the hard way, the illusion of romance ends when the painful urination begins. "Don't worry, honey," I said. "We'll go and get tested together. It may not even be an STD, and if it is, he could have had it before meeting you. You've got nothing to feel guilty about. He should be the one apologizing to you."

"Thanks, Cat," she said. "So you'll really come with me?"

I promised that I would, and fished out my Mac; we spent the next half-hour poring over websites to figure out the symptoms, while guzzling red wine.

"So," she said a while later, dabbing at her eyes, "how was your date with the hunk? I need to be distracted right now."

I filled her in.

"You did the right thing," she said, pouring me a cup of tea. "There's nothing worse than when they keep grinding away. The last guy who did that to me almost broke my pelvic bone. Then he was like, 'Yeah, that's right, take it!' and I had to refrain from saying, 'Take what?'" She laughed.

I shivered. "Jesus, Vic, it's freezing in here."

"Yeah, I meant to tell you, the boiler guy is coming over on Thursday. Would you mind letting him in? I have to warn you though, he's a bit weird. He's a Zen Buddhist recovering alcoholic, and he'll probably want to tell you all about his spiritual conversion."

I laughed. "I can handle it. In fact, after this week I'm starting to think that I can handle anything."

"Oh, and Cat?" she said, as she headed towards the kitchenette.

"Yes?"

"There's a dildo in the dishwasher. Can I assume it's one of yours?"

# SIX

Judging by the amount of email I was getting, the column really seemed to be touching the spot with readers. I was thrilled that people seemed comfortable enough to share their problems with me, even if some of them verged on the seriously bizarre. I'd been corresponding with a guy who said that he could only get turned on "by watching women brush and floss their teeth for at least half an hour, preferably before bedtime."

At first I thought his note might be a windup, but he seemed distressed, so I tried to reassure him that all wasn't lost: At least he was concerned with oral hygiene, and with any luck he would find a toothbrush-wielding wench some time soon. I try not to make judgments and to keep an open mind.

I was always surprised when people referred to certain sexual practices as anti-feminist, because what's most erotic is not necessarily the most politically correct. Otherwise, the Spank Me Santa S&M bondage and paddle kit wouldn't be a Christmas bestseller.

Still, I had been getting loads of emails asking me where my penchant for sexual deviancy began.

If I'm honest, I suppose my infatuation with seduction began shortly after my parents' divorce, when I wanted to regain control of my life. I was turning fourteen in that magical summer when my breasts grew two cup sizes and my mum and I moved to a sleepy little town in the American Deep South whose greatest claim to fame is the annual Peanut Festival (it's actually classified as a county-wide holiday!).

I wanted to leave the shy, gawky girl of my primary school years behind as well—by reinventing myself, and becoming popular.

First I tried the Goth phase, where I dressed in head-to-toe black and listened to the Cure at lunch while everyone else was cruising the Piggly Wiggly supermarket parking lot with hip-hop blaring. The boys would bounce quarters off the top of their pickup trucks to see whose sound system could make the coins bounce the highest.

That lasted about a week. Although I still preferred alternative music, I had to admit that the Doc Martens and caked-on eyeliner just weren't cutting it on days when the heat index hit 110°F. I was tired of being the loser outcast.

So I scraped off the black nail polish and decided to pretend that I was a method actress who was fully immersing herself in her role. I dreamed up a character loosely based on Madonna in *Desperately Seeking Susan*, a rock star who was secure in her sexuality. And wore really cool black lace fingerless gloves. And eventually, if you fake something long enough it becomes part of you, until you can't tell the real person from the character she's playing. So after a while, my alter ego became me.

I also contrived a reputation for being outrageous. I would channel my wild side when I had my friends over—I was the one who always had my own hip flask of Southern Comfort and went skinny-dipping at 2 a.m. with girls and boys. Then something happened: My alter ego went from someone who existed solely on the other side of the mirror to one of the most popular girls in school. Boys wanted to date her, girls wanted to hang out with her.

My new girlfriends were already familiar with the pleasures of Jack Daniel's and the Marlboro man, so I found another way of becoming a rebel: In a Bible Belt town where (largely hypocritical) virginity pledges were as ubiquitous as large flying insects, I decided to indulge my budding obsession with sex.

In my mind, I had carved out a very definite separation between sex and love. This helped me stay sane, since I already knew that I was way too horny to wait. Besides, I knew that the boys in my school saw nothing wrong with "hooking up" with different girls every weekend. I did the same, and was classified a "wild girl"—basically, a slut with good grades.

My first time was born more out of curiosity and anticipation than burning desire. I was fifteen and my then boyfriend was a twenty-year-old college student with a lean, muscular build and his own car. I planned my deflowering with military precision, and after nine months of fumbling, my libido got the better of me one late summer night at his parents' hunting lodge.

I remember that my underwear came off when "Stairway to Heaven" came on—and the whole thing was over before the guitar solo ended. It was anticlimactic in more ways than one. While he was on top of me, pumping away, I threw my legs over his shoulders to examine the color of my pedicure, wondering whether I could get away with orange varnish. Nah, my skin was definitely too pale. Better stick to neutrals.

Afterwards, I was cool as a cucumber. My boyfriend was gentle, and receptive when I pulled a bottle of baby oil and a bag of strawberries and whipped cream out of my bag. "So," I said, "are we going to make things a bit more interesting? That can't be all there is to it." He taught me the importance of giving a great blow job, starting with the age-old advice: "More lips, less teeth."

Anyway, after I split up with the three-second wonder, I spent the bulk of my time hanging out at the Waffle House diner with my girlfriends Sheila and Nikki. We drank cup after cup of burned coffee laced with smuggled-in Southern Comfort and listened to Candlebox and the Smashing Pumpkins while detailing our sexual exploits. I wasn't looking for love—well, maybe eventually, but not back then—I was just hungry for adventure. Each of my sexual conquests, at that stage, was simply another notch on my belt.

Teachers always told me that it was easier to ask for permission than forgiveness, but where's the adventure in that? I justified my antics by telling myself that I would rather regret something I did than something I hadn't done, which is why I was always taking chances in the name of love—or at least rampant lust. As long as I wasn't hurting myself (well, beyond the obvious minor abrasions!) or anyone else, I think that life should be about charting my own path, not following the crowd. Even if the path occasionally led me astray.

I admit that I'd always had a fantasy about hooking up with an older man. The closest I had come at that point was a heated make-out session with a thirty-five-year-old musician from Panama City, Florida. He played bad covers of Dire Straits and Soul Asylum songs, which back then seemed really cool—despite the fact that his playing a buffalo wing joint should have given me a clue that a record deal was probably not imminent.

But like a lot of pubescent girls, I fell into the classic trap of believing that I was a mature sex goddess because I was dating older guys. I only figured out much later that if girls their own age wanted nothing to do with them, there was a very good reason.

Which is why Mr. Murphy was so different: Because not only did he not target me, he did everything in his power to avoid getting involved with me. But from the beginning, he was fighting a losing battle.

I think I fell in lust with him the first time he walked into the classroom. I was sixteen. He was in his mid-twenties but looked much younger, despite his horn-rimmed glasses and propensity for that news anchor staple: sweater vests.

Perhaps because he seemed so youthful, he made the fatal error of trying to be everyone's friend. He wasn't creepy or desperate, just a bit lonely, since most of his peer group in our town had moved away after high school.

During the first week of class, I was sitting in the front row, hanging on his every word. By Thursday I was ready to make my move. When the lunch bell rang, I hung back. I pretended to study intently my handout from health class, which explained the merits of calcium. Not that I trusted anything that the morbidly obese teacher had to say on the subject, since she brought doughnuts and muffins the size of baseball mitts to class on a daily basis. I guess it's sort of like having a fat personal trainer—it just doesn't work.

"Do you mind if I hang out here to do some reading?" I asked him.

He looked up expectantly. "Not at all. I'm glad someone is interested in French. I'm not having much luck getting through to most of the class."

"*Ne t'inquiètes pas.*" I leaned in conspiratorially and fluttered my eyelashes. "See, I was totally paying attention!"

He laughed, and I felt that I had broken the ice.

We chatted for a few minutes about my "favorite subjects" and "favorite hobbies" (if he only knew).

"Can I ask you something, Catherine?" he said, rubbing his creased forehead. "Do you find the course material too difficult?"

"Well, it's challenging, but I'm learning a lot, and you don't patronize us, which I like," I said. "Why do you ask?" I noticed nervously that he had a three-day-beard stubble and wondered if he was having an early midlife crisis, or just suffering from lack of coffee.

"Well, I've just been having a chat with the principal, and basically he thinks that I need to stop giving so much homework. But I don't want to dumb things down."

"Oh, I wouldn't worry about him," I said. "You know why he came to school today with a black eye, right?"

He shook his head.

I dropped my voice to a muted whisper. "Well, rumor has it that he got obsessed with his female neighbor, and decided that if he sent her a tape of him and his wife having sex, somehow she would want to sleep with him, too. So he made a tape of them screwing and left it out on her barbecue. But her husband found it instead. He's a bodybuilder."

His eyes widened, and he covered his mouth. He had huge hands, which even then I took as a good sign. "You are kidding," he murmured, laughing nervously. "I actually teased him about getting into a fight. So much for impressing the boss."

We both laughed, and were aware that we had taken the first tentative step towards friendship by discussing something mildly inappropriate.

After that, my trips to the French department became more frequent. He told me about his terrible childhood and his hobby of learning dead languages. I shared my dreams of moving to a big city and reinventing myself—just like Audrey Hepburn in *Breakfast at Tiffany's*.

So my campaign of seduction began. I sat in the front row, and swapped my sandals and cut-off denim shorts for a raunchy reform school look featuring black miniskirts and black thigh-high socks. I smiled at him and teased him, heavy on the irony. He put little notes and smiley faces on my papers.

He was the authority figure, but I was the one gaining control.

Our banter continued, but I couldn't get him alone outside school—until one weekend, when fate intervened. I was filling up my car with gas when I saw him walking down the street, covered in grease. "Hey," I said, waving at him, "what happened to you?"

"I was on my way to town, and my truck stalled," he said, fishing out his mobile. "I just called AAA, but it's going to take them an hour to give me a jump. I'm trying to get to the antiques fair. I've got to buy some stuff for my apartment."

I smiled. "I'd be happy to give you a ride," I said. *In more ways than one.*

After we'd perused the fair, he bought me lunch to say thanks. I ordered penne with sun-dried tomatoes and a glass of white wine. He didn't say a word about my underage drinking, which I took as a good sign.

When we got back to his truck, he shook my hand—but then gave me a dog-eared copy of Ovid's *Amores.* "I saw it at the fair, and you said you wanted to learn Latin, so I thought you'd like this," he mumbled, avoiding my gaze. "By the way, I'm moving tomorrow and having a few friends over to help; you're welcome to swing by if you get bored. See you later." I fished around in my backpack for a scrap of notebook paper so he could write down the address. I recognized the apartment complex; one of my best friends lived a few doors down.

Later, in the bathtub with an Oxford English–Latin dictionary in hand, I translated.

"Keep on with your present life, just don't admit to it. A modest/ Persona, in public, shouldn't prove too bad/ An embarrassment. Impropriety has its special off limits/ Enclave, where every kind of fun is the rule/ And restraints are unheard of." After setting the book aside, I picked up the shower head and locked the door, pretending that his hands were doing the work.

When I got to his apartment the next afternoon, he opened the door wearing a white shirt rolled up at the sleeves and ripped jeans—with bare feet. He looked gorgeous.

The moment of truth came at the end of the day, when I was three beers braver. I waited until everyone else cleared out and we were sitting by opposite walls of his empty bedroom, surrounded by boxes. The sun was settling, and the pink light played off the dust in the room, creating a kaleidoscopic image. The light was receding. I had to make my move.

"So, before I leave, what are we going to do about this, Richard?" I blurted out.

"What do you mean?" he said.

"About the fact that I'm incredibly attracted to you, and I think that you feel the same about me. Are we going to do anything about it, or pretend that it's not happening?"

He began to panic. His mouth kept opening and closing, as if he were gulping for air. "I—I, shit, I was never going to say anything about this. I can't deal with this, it's not right because you're a student and it can't happen." He ran his hands through his hair and stood up decisively, moving over to where I was. "Cat," he said, "this is not going to happen."

I kissed him. He kissed me back, tasting of spearmint gum. Then I pulled away, remembering the old adage about always leaving them wanting more. "I have to be home for dinner," I said, then, inexplicably, "I have to graph a parabola." I ran outside and started the car, my hands shaking. I looked up to see him standing at the window, head in hands.

So much for playing hard to get. The next night, after getting plastered on malt liquor at a party with my girlfriends, I realized that I was too drunk to drive home. The cops showed up to bust the party while we were splashing around in the swimming pool half naked so, naturally, I vaulted over two hedges and found myself at his apartment complex.

He didn't want to let me in, but I explained that I told my mum I was spending the night at a girlfriend's house.

"This isn't a good idea," he said, raking his hands through his sandy blond hair.

"It's two in the morning, please have a heart," I pleaded, pushing past him and dripping water on his kitchen floor, fully aware that he could see almost everything through my wet lacy bra and panties. "Plus, I'm freezing and I need to borrow a towel."

"God, you're drenched, and you're tracking it everywhere. What the hell have you been up to?"

I was a bit bummed that he prioritized mopping up wet leaves above satisfying the naked girl in his kitchen, but I soldiered on. "Well, a bunch of us went skinny-dipping in Sheila's pool while her parents were away, and the police showed up and I couldn't get my clothes in time." I put on my little-girl-lost voice. "Look, I'm really sorry. This was a stupid idea."

"No, it's okay—I'll just make up the couch. But you have to leave first thing in the morning, before anyone sees you walking out. My neighbors would freak out."

While I toweled off in the bathroom, he pulled out the folding couch and I checked his medicine cabinet. He had anti-depressants, like everyone else in the late nineties, but no lithium, which was reassuring. He also had an old-fashioned straight razor and brush, next to—very promisingly—a box of Trojan Extra Large Condoms. This was it: It was now or never.

"Cat?" he said, tapping on the bathroom door. "Look, I'm going to take the couch, okay? The bed's all made up for you. I'm hitting the sack."

"Fine," I blurted out, squinting at my reflection in the mirror, then used his toothbrush and Listerine to freshen up. For some reason, I felt like Alice in Wonderland about to fall through the rabbit hole and realized that this would be a defining moment in my adolescence. Which was pretty rare, really, since those usually come with hindsight.

I stripped completely, hung my clothes on the towel rack and wrapped myself in one of his terrycloth robes. Then I headed to the living room, where I could see him lying on his back, staring into the darkness.

"Richard?"

"Yes?"

I bit my lip and forced myself to do my meditation breathing: Inhale; count to five; exhale.

"I'm just going to strip naked and climb into bed now, because I'm really wet. I would love it if you would join me. But if not, I understand. 'Night."

I quickly shuffled into the bedroom, my heart pounding in my ears. I watched the analog clock on the bedside table count the seconds. Five minutes, I told myself, and then I'm giving up for good. I gave it my best shot.

Exactly two minutes and thirty seconds later he threw back the covers.

"Oh, Richard," I moaned, doing the over-the-top kissing thing that I'd picked up from too much daytime television.

"Don't swallow my tongue," he said, as he looked down at me and laughed. "Now, were you serious about learning a few things from me?"

I smiled up at him, spreading my legs. "Totally."

"Well, then, you can start by calling me Mr. Murphy in bed."

Over the next few weeks, he put me through the paces of light submission and domination—or at least his version, which included being tied up with magician's rope, blindfolded, with his cock in my mouth.

I reveled in our tutorials because in bed I considered myself his equal. I learned that being submissive ultimately gave me great power. And although I was too wrapped up in his fantasies to focus on my own climax—that would come later—I was learning an incredible amount, and couldn't get enough.

We experimented with hot wax—unfortunately, we used scented candles and I smelled like Windflower Medley, which activated my hay fever and had me sneezing through class all day. Though, really, I didn't need any props to get him hard: Young women have no idea of their power. Just showing up with a sixteen-year-old body was enough.

That's how I learned that paraffin candles burn at the lowest temperature, and hurt the least on skin. After that comes microcrystalline wax, then beeswax. Beeswax burns about 40 to 60°F hotter than paraffin, and if you don't keep blowing the candle out the pain is intense. I tried using baby oil, soap, and water to get rid of the hot wax glued to my forearms, but residue always remained. But I liked it, and the burnt smell afterwards was a reminder of our sex sessions.

Camouflaging the constant carpet burns when it was still pushing 90°F in an American South-style Indian summer was no easy task, so I relied on knee socks and discovered the wonders of Nivea yellow-toned concealer. The bruises were harder to mask. I tried everything—makeup, ice, and homoeopathic remedies such as arnica—all to no avail. My pale skin has always responded to pressure instantly, and I was starting to resemble an overripe banana.

In Politics 101, we discussed how the balance of power shifts between sovereign territorial states engaged in Machiavellian negotiations with each other, when both want world domination. Similarly, a few weeks into our fling, I suddenly found myself getting bored. He was Luxembourg to my United States.

"I love you," he told me for the first time during a two-hour sex session. He was trying to tie me up, but I needed to do my calculus homework.

Not wanting to start a fight, I looked up at him adoringly and smothered the sentiment with a kiss. I liked him and I was sexually attracted to him, so I figured that whatever we had was a close enough approximation.

Soon I couldn't ignore my increasing restlessness. We were entirely confined to his apartment, which could only be reached through extreme subterfuge. I had to park my car five blocks away in a cul-de-sac, and we still freaked out every time an unfamiliar vehicle drove by. A few weeks later, a friend asked me to the prom, and Richard sulked for days. Suddenly my mature lover seemed like a stroppy adolescent.

"I know I have no right to get jealous, but I just don't like the idea of you with someone else," he said.

I hated the thought of hurting him, but I explained that it was my senior prom, and I was going. "Besides," I said, "Chris is just a friend. We're going to be with a big group."

But he probably realized that I was slipping away.

In the end, I never made it to the prom, because our affair imploded a few weeks after Richard's psychotic ex-girlfriend showed up at his place. He hadn't been returning her phone calls, telling her that she couldn't come down because it was an "inconvenient time."

So she showed up on a Tuesday afternoon that was particularly inconvenient, since I was naked on his sofa, straddling him, my hands bound together with a sash when we heard the doorbell ring.

Richard ran out. I heard him tell her to wait outside, then she pushed him aside and threatened to smash his house up if he didn't let her in. Shit.

I panicked, struggled to untie my wrists, grabbed my clothes, and headed towards the bedroom, but decided against the closet because a) it was too obvious and b) had a squeaky door.

I could hear her screaming, demanding to know who he was sleeping with, punctuated by the sounds of her smashing the contents of his kitchen. "I want to know WHO [crash, probably a wine glass] YOU [judging by the clinking sound, silverware] ARE FUCKING [not sure, I think she slapped him across the face]."

Even though instinct told me that in horror movies the killer was always hiding under the bed, the first place anyone looks, in my panic I couldn't think of anywhere better.

He started pleading in a pretty wimpy fashion for such a dominant guy. "Look, you know that we broke up because it wasn't working. It had nothing to do with anyone else. Please calm down."

She began to cry. "But that's not what you said last week. You said that if you had some space things might work out and that we would keep talking and see how it went."

This was news to me. Poor girl. Even in my position, my heart went out to her. She was so naïve. Although I was only sixteen, I knew what a guy meant when he told me that he needed "space."

I heard her enter the bedroom.

"Please, just make love to me," she said through her tears, and I saw her sweater drop to the floor. "Just one more time. I love you so much."

Adrenaline shot through my body and I tried to get a glimpse of what was going on, but all I could see was her feet. He had told me that she was a hippy chick, so I wasn't surprised to see that they were tiny, with short gold hairs on the toes and really raggedy cuticles. She could, I noted in my terror, really use a pedicure.

"Look, this isn't going to happen—please stop taking your clothes off," he begged.

Suddenly, my eyes filled with tears, and I wondered if I was feeling overwhelmed by the emotion of the moment. But in fact, it was dust under the bed. Like most men, Richard had never braved the crawlspace beneath his mattress, and there were dust clumps the size of tumbleweed down there. I buried my nose in the carpet and tried to ignore the ticking, but it was no use—I was going to sneeze.

When pleading with him didn't work, she went back to the old female staple—anger. "If you're not fucking anyone else, asshole," she said, her voice rising an octave as she brandished a brush she'd nicked from his bathroom, "then why is there BROWN HAIR on this brush?"

My hair. I had let it down earlier, and suddenly I realized what I was missing. My rubber band, complete with its rhinestone skull adornment, was right by her feet. She was practically stepping on it. I tried my meditation breathing, wondering if Buddhist monks ever needed to scratch their noses.

They moved into the other room, and just as they shut the outside door I let out a huge sneeze. He finally came back twenty minutes later to release me, but the spell had been broken.

Despite his protestations of love, I knew that I had to get the hell out of town.

# SEVEN

Potential boyfriends are often shocked when I tell them that I've slept with most of my male friends. Some are former boyfriends, others fell victim to a mutual *When Harry Met Sally* moment after a bout of serious soul searching (and binge drinking). In school, I even kissed my gay best friend because he "just wanted to be sure" that his crush on Ricky Martin wasn't a one-off.

But all my male friendships fall into one of two categories: Those whom I've slept with, usually after a night of heavy drinking, and those whose naked bodies are still a mystery to me. It's not because I'm some sex goddess; I think it's natural for people who have personal chemistry to wonder what it would be like to take things to their natural, often orgasmic, conclusion.

Things are easier with the former type of friend, because there is no danger that years of simmering sexual tension will suddenly come to the surface. We have already been there, done that, and got the T-shirt.

Like my ex-boyfriend, David Parkside, who I was meeting for dinner that night at a morbidly overpriced sushi restaurant in Knightsbridge. As usual, jaws dropped when he put his hand on the small of my back and ushered me inside. He's handsome and beautifully dressed, but they were staring for other reasons: He's pushing sixty, and I'm in my late twenties.

David and I first met when I was twenty-three and working for the same fashion company in the States: I was on the editorial side, he was head of business development. He's British, and work often brings him to London. This was the first time I'd seen him here, in his natural environment, since I'd moved to the UK permanently. While fine restaurants could be David's habitat, I'll never forget when he took me for French fries and champagne on our first date at a gorgeous French bistro, which he termed the "anti-Atkins" date. Any occasion marked by carbohydrates was a big deal to David.

I had a huge crush on him back then, but was afraid to make a move, so I settled for flirting shamelessly. He was old enough to be my father; in fact, he was older than my dad. But he was kind, charming, sexy, and hilariously funny—the sort of person who lights up a room when he walks in.

When I finally summoned the courage to hit on him he was stunned, telling me that he was very flattered, but thought I was too young for him and didn't want to take the risk at work.

But I was extremely persistent. I looked up his number and called him. We talked all night, and one week later we were staring into each other's eyes over a candlelit dinner, then making out in a cab on the way back to his flat. The sex was fantastic, not least because this was a man who had had a lot of time to practice his oral technique. Although the background music was a bit off-putting: Men in their thirties often have standard-issue Maxwell or Massive Attack playing in the background, but for the over-fifty crowd it's all about Bryan Ferry.

There were other perks. Having dated a guy who thought that moving a pizza from box to paper plate was fine dining, the idea of munching lobster risotto while admiring the views from David's penthouse flat had a certain appeal. None of my friends thought it would last. They teased me about giving him a heart attack in bed, and changed my surname to Zeta-Jones.

Strangers were worse. Most people assumed that by dating him I was filling some void in my life by looking for Daddy. "I'll bet your parents are divorced, right?" was a common line. Of course, waiters who asked if he wanted a table for himself and his daughter didn't help.

However, David wasn't some guy with low self-esteem who wanted a younger woman to idolize him. He was just one cool character. He still is.

"God, darling, you look stunning as usual," he said, leading me to our regular table near the back. "How do I look?"

I told him, honestly, that his silvery hair was a bit more salt than pepper, but otherwise he hadn't aged a day.

"So, how's the column? And your love life?" he asked, while I tucked into the edamame beans. Our drinks appeared, shaken dirty martini for me and Grey Goose on the rocks for him. "I'm still on the Atkins Diet," he said. A rabid gourmand, David had a loose interpretation of "low carbohydrate." I'm not sure prawn tempura counts, but I wasn't about to spoil his fun.

"The column is great, and my love life still sucks," I said, filling him in on my latest disaster. "But things could be looking up—I'm going sugar daddy speed dating in a few weeks." All this writing was forcing me to think about what I was looking for in a man, rather than just randomly falling into bed with them. Though I'd been doing plenty of that recently. "At least the column gives me a sense of purpose. Every failed encounter isn't yet another disaster, it's a learning experience—or at least a funny anecdote, if I'm lucky." I laughed, but tears filled my eyes, which I quickly wiped away. "Though I still kind of miss Patrick."

"Patrick was way too narrow-minded to ever properly appreciate what he had," David said gently. "But sugar daddy dating? Now, that sounds like your area of expertise. See, maybe he was just too young for you!"

In a way, David had been the best boyfriend I'd ever had, and the only one who seemed to get my need for solitude. For a while, the age difference really hadn't seemed to matter. Until suddenly, one day, it did. I'd noticed that he occasionally popped pills, but nothing prepared me for the day I opened his medicine cabinet and found an alphabetized row of medicine for everything from angina to zinc deficiency. We tried to avoid the subject of his advancing age.

We used to get into huge arguments about his diet, because he always said he'd rather undergo a quadruple bypass than cut out Parma ham. I worried myself sick about his lack of health insurance, and secretly took out an extra policy for him. Then I started to have nightmares about changing nappies—and not for my children. And, though my crowd warmed to him, I couldn't exactly drag him to a punk concert. I started to miss my friends.

So, as quickly as it started, our relationship began to fade out. One night, I took him to a club where the bartender had safety-pin earrings and a "Jesus Is My Homeboy" T-shirt. "Look, I was in Studio 54 when Bianca Jagger rode in on a white horse, and I don't want to do this any more," he said. "This is your scene, not mine." Soon afterwards, we parted ways.

But the chemistry never went away. These days, we are like any two friends who meet to dissect the open wounds in our respective love lives—and the waiters still stare at us.

"So," I said, dropping my voice, "did you manage to get what I needed?"

"Yes, Cat, but if anyone asks where you got it—it was not from me," he said, sliding the little blue pills under the table. "People might start talking, and I have a reputation to protect. I don't want anyone thinking that I need help in that department." This was a one-off favor. David's erections were rock-hard, drug-free, and regular. In fact, I had dated twenty-five-year-olds with less rampant sex drives. But I'm a girl so couldn't get my hands on Viagra any other way.

"Don't worry, sweetie, it will just be between us," I said, smiling and stuffing them into my bag. "I'm only going to take it once; my friends swear that it's amazing. Something about increased blood flow to the clitoris, and readers keep emailing to ask me if I've tried it. I have a responsibility to the public." I grinned. "And I haven't had a truly decent shag in weeks."

He laughed. "If you get into a real emergency, you have my number," David said, putting his hand on mine. "Are you okay financially? I know you're too proud to admit you need help, but if you ever need to borrow any money…"

Tears filled my eyes. "I sometimes think that I was insane to make this move," I blurted out. "I mean, I wasn't satisfied with the work I was doing, but who is? At least I had a stable job, a paycheck, and could afford regular meals that weren't pilfered from someone else's fridge. What the hell am I doing here?"

He grabbed my hand. "Do you know what the majority of the most powerful CEOs in the world have in common?" he demanded.

I looked at him blankly. "Good dry cleaners?"

"No. They all take risks. Look at Steve Jobs, he got fired from his own company at Apple. He says, 'You can't connect the dots looking forward; you can only connect them looking backwards. So you have to trust that the dots will somehow connect in your future.' And they will, Cat."

"Well, they may connect in the future, but right now everything looks like a big random blob," I said, taking another gulp of warm sake, then spearing a spicy tuna roll. This was my only meal of the day, and I was determined to make it count.

I changed the subject. "Did you know that I majored in politics along with journalism? I actually used to think that I was going to be a war correspondent."

"In a way, that's what you are," he said. "Just be careful with this stuff. My friend gave me two kinds, 50 milligram and 100 milligram pills, so either take one or two, but he says never more than 100 milligrams at a time. And make sure you're with someone worth it, because once you're 'up,' so to speak, you're up for hours.

"At least, that's what I hear," he added hastily.

Victoria's health scare had got me thinking. Normally, I have a reputation for being really anal (no pun intended) about protection. I'm the girl who never leaves home without an array of condoms and spare knickers, in case of a best-case scenario, as well as cash and the number of a reputable cab firm in case of the worst. But her experience made me realize I needed a new way to incorporate condoms into foreplay—which is how later that evening I found myself browsing an online array of prophylactics that went way beyond ribbed or regular. I was taken with the fruit-flavored and glow-in-the-dark varieties. There was even a musical condom that changes tunes as the sex gets more vigorous, although I think a soundtrack emitting from my nether regions would definitely throw me off my rhythm.

The next afternoon Victoria and I headed to the Chelsea Westminster GUM clinic. She confessed that, although he apologized for his freak-out, Mike had been a bit incommunicado for the past few days. Apparently, he found declaring undying love less daunting than discussing abnormal discharge.

At least she'd kept her sense of humor: We were headed to an Angels and Demons theme party immediately afterwards, so had to go to the clinic in costumes that Victoria had hired earlier.

I had laughed when Victoria had brought them home. "I couldn't get much at short notice, so it looks like it's devil for me, sexy nun for you!" she said. I therefore went into the clinic wearing a habit with a lace corset underneath, feeling ridiculous and praying I didn't see anyone I knew, while Victoria was clad in a red PVC miniskirt with a long red satin forked tail protruding underneath. "This looks like a giant hemorrhoid," she laughed. "Not exactly sexy."

I needn't have worried: The posh-looking, besuited crowd could have been waiting in line at Boujis on a Saturday night. The exam itself was relatively painless, and the doctor was very reassuring. Plus I think the nurses got a good laugh—it's not every day you see a nun scooping up free condoms.

*In Alcoholics Anonymous, Step 9 involves making amends to everyone you've ever harmed. I wonder if the same approach should apply to sexaholics making up for crap one-night stands?*

It had been a slow week, and I hadn't had a chance to test my Viagra pills, so I started corresponding with one of my regular readers. I followed my own "rules," making sure that he emailed me from his work address, a firm in the city that I checked out, and sent photos of himself. He looked nice and easygoing, leaning against a tree, wearing a blue shirt that matched his eyes.

We met at the Pelican in Notting Hill, and I was dressed in one of my PWOS (potential walk of shame) outfits, including skinny jeans, a snug top, and Alexander McQueen shoes. It's a shame that women spend eons obsessing about dressing to impress other women. I spend an inordinate amount of time before each date trying to perfect my "look" with whimsical accessories, when British boys for the most part just want to see cleavage and a smile.

And there's nothing worse than stumbling out of a stranger's house in the morning wearing a vintage prom dress and carrying a gold evening bag. A kid in Clapham once actually gave me money—he thought I was some sort of homeless Miss Havisham.

My date's name was Nigel, and I was relieved to see that he was cuter in person than online. He had expressive blue eyes, a kind, open face, and full lips, thus avoiding the dreaded "turtle lip" syndrome.

We talked about our mutual love of sci-fi films, and argued over whether the *Back to the Future* or *Terminator* models of time travel were more practical. I must have gotten drunk quite quickly, because I vividly recall drawing my argument for circular causation on a cocktail napkin. He also listened sympathetically when I turned the conversation to the faulty heating unit in my flat. No matter how many times it gets fixed, we're constantly freezing.

"Well, you could always stay at my place. I've got lots more red wine, and a nice big fireplace."

I agreed, fervently hoping that this was a euphemism. His "place" turned out to be a multi-level house on a dead-end street in Chelsea, with ivy climbing the walls.

"Red or white?" he asked, walking into the kitchen as he turned the fire on with the flick of a remote control.

His living room was a Philippe Starck minimalist paradise, so I chose white lest I spilled anything on his pristine sofa. We sipped the sauvignon blanc and started kissing, then I excused myself to go to the loo where I took two Viagra pills. I wanted to see what the effect would be like in a blind trial, so I decided not to let on that I was taking them.

He might think I was some kind of crazed nymphomaniac and—well, best not to let that particular cat out of the bag yet.

I'm not sure if it was psychosomatic, but my pussy began to tingle and my breath got noticeably shorter over the next ten minutes. On our next round of kissing, I climbed into his lap.

"Do you want to show me your bedroom?" I asked breathily.

"Hang on, I've got something else you'll want to see first," Nigel said. "See, I always wanted to be a photographer, so I thought I could show you some of my travels around Africa." He opened a giant dusty album and proudly pointed out grainy, blurry shots of impoverished orphans.

"Um, why is this one a bit out of focus? Is it some kind of artistic thing?" I could actually hear my heart pounding in my ears—and everywhere else. When I closed my eyes briefly, I could see color, a pulsing, aortal red. Shit. This stuff was hitting me hard. Had I taken too much? I thought David said two 50 milligram pills for a total of 100, or were they 100 milligrams each?

He frowned. "Well, I thought that the composition of the photos was less important than their content. See, I fund a project that follows starving children around and gives them disposable cameras, then we show their work in London."

"But if they are starving, wouldn't it make more sense just to give them, like, a bag of rice?" That's when I started to suspect that Nigel might have a personal tic, even worse than men who say "guesstimate" and "face-time": He was showing signs of being a trustafarian.

"Well, some people think that art is a form of nourishment," he said, looking into my eyes while I searched desperately for a glimpse of irony. There was none. "It definitely touches the soul."

His hands were sliding somewhere well away from my soul, so I figured there was no point in disrupting that to press my point home.

I just nodded and agreed with whatever he was saying. Maybe I was being a bit harsh anyway—Amy was always telling me that I needed to be less cynical.

I took a deep breath, wondering when he was going to get down to business and fuck me. I was ravenous.

Finally—after moving the album carefully aside—we moved to the bedroom. Clothes started flying, and somehow a condom materialized. But ten energetic minutes later it was all over for him—twice—before I'd even really begun.

"Wow," he said, crossing his arms behind his head and lighting a cigarette he'd evidently pre-rolled, "that was amazing."

Smiling sweetly and totally pumped up from the Viagra, I moved alongside him and kissed his neck. "Baby, I'm not quite finished yet," I said. "I hope you don't mind if I touch myself." My whole body was throbbing, my head felt like it was going to explode, and I badly needed release. I swore, at that moment, that I would never ever take this drug again. Not even for research purposes. I can't imagine what possessed me. In fact, that's how I was feeling—possessed.

He actually recoiled in horror. "Nice girls don't do those things. My attitude with orgasms is if they happen, they happen. Maybe it's just not meant to be."

Easy for you to say, I thought, feeling as if I'd been slapped in the face. "But, um, don't you want me to have one too?" Now I knew what it was like to be a sixteen-year-old boy with blue balls. My crotch was on fire.

He took a drag and blew out. "Well, of course, as long as it's not too much work," he said with a laugh.

Failing to see the humor, I started to explain the potential pitfalls of the missionary position but he cut me off and told me that none of his other girlfriends ever had a problem with it (not that he'd ever actually asked them), so I "might be a bit abnormal."

"So, do what you have to do, sweetheart," he said, patting me on the forearm, "but you're not doing—that—in my bed. Anyway, what about whoever it was who said that it's better to give than to receive?"

I picked up my shirt. "That was Jesus, and somehow I don't think he had this situation in mind." I was stunned. This was the smooth operator who flaunted his private-school education and took pains to open every door for me—so why were his sexual manners so appalling?

I headed to his steel and glass kitchen, propped myself on the counter, and poured myself a glass of water. I may not be the *Debrett's* of dating, but I don't think it's unreasonable to expect a little mutual pleasure and respect, even from a casual fling. To my mind, selfish in bed equals selfish in life—which is a definite date-breaker. Aristotle would be seriously pissed.

Decision made, I headed back to the bedroom. "Look," I said as I threw off the covers and unlaced the corset that I had laced up so optimistically only a few hours earlier, "I'm going to have a bath. I'm frustrated, and I can't sleep."

"You need to calm down," he said, looking a bit like the cat that got the cream. "How about if we just hold each other?"

I declined. If I had wanted to cuddle, I would have stayed home with my teddy. I wanted to be hanging from the ceiling.

"I just need a few minutes alone," I told him, in my best impression of a good-little-girl voice. I'd always wondered how men's instincts could be so base as to lure them out into the night to get back-alley blow jobs from hookers who looked like five miles of bad road. But in Nigel's bed, I realized that after my pill-popping, he could be anyone. I needed release so badly I could literally feel my clit throbbing through my panties. I had a hard-on. Jacked up on Viagra, the unthinkable happened: I was becoming a Freud fan.

I ran the bathwater to cover my moans, pointed the shower head at my pussy, and felt the water racing against my skin as I clawed the side of the tub and bit my lip so hard that I drew blood. As one subsided, another began, and wave after wave of heat spasmed from my drug-riddled body. Finally, sated, I toweled off and went back to the bedroom.

"See, all better, right? Did you take a cold shower?"

"All better," I said, too tired to argue with him. "You were right. That was exactly what I needed."

"Look, Cat, I know I'm a bit of a dour Presbyterian in bed," he said, rolling over. "But you're just going to have to get used to it."

*Fat chance, buddy.*

I decided to bail out—but not before I opened his Sub-Zero fridge and swiped a very nice bottle of Bollinger champagne. I don't condone theft, but at that point I figured he owed me one. Not to mention his poor ex-girlfriends, who doubtless deserved an Oscar.

I stumbled down the stairs as dawn was breaking, then realized that for once I had no money and would have to stumble several blocks further in my four-inch heels to find a cash point. Nigel was still asleep.

But despite the fact that my feet were bleeding, I knew I had made the right decision. I felt proud that I had stood up for myself, especially when he texted me a few hours later: "R u cold? Am drinking tea by the fire... Want 2 come over? xxx."

I smiled as I keyed in my response: "Sorry, will be washing my hair. FYI, the average woman needs 20 mins of clitoral stimulation to orgasm. Your exes were faking it. Take care."

# EIGHT

I've never believed in love at first sight. At university I read André Breton's surrealist oeuvre *L'Amour Fou* and thought that he sounded clinically insane. But now I was ready to carry a lobster telephone and grow a handlebar moustache, because mad love had happened to me.

It all started out so innocently, on a random Wednesday. I was out with Victoria, Mark (who was on best behavior as he'd just started seeing someone), and some of his work colleagues to celebrate his promotion to senior partner, and on the way back from a party at Pangea we decided to stop off at the Hempel Hotel bar for a nightcap. I was really proud of Mark, who, despite the fact that he is one of the smartest men I know and a virtual encyclopedia of scientific knowledge, has always felt self-conscious that he never attended university. This promotion put him ahead of several Oxford graduates, which I knew meant a lot to him.

Unbeknownst to Mark, Victoria and I were also celebrating the fact that her mystery infection was nothing more serious than thrush, which she'd passed on to her man. He'd been showering her with flowers, and invited her to dinner with his parents.

"So did he admit he'd been an idiot?" I asked.

"I told him that his behavior was disgusting, and was ranting and raving, and then he got teary-eyed and said that the reason he freaked was because he was really serious about me—then he told me he wants me to move in," she blurted out.

I raised one eyebrow. "And?"

"And I'm going to seriously consider it," she said, coolly perusing the bar menu.

But I could tell that for her this was a big deal. I was really delighted for her because, despite his genuine ignorance on the sexual health front, I knew Mike adored her.

The place was almost empty, and I was completely engrossed in conversation with Victoria when I saw a guy sitting across the bar: He was about my height but with broad shoulders, reddish blond hair, and cheekbones that could cut glass. There was something enigmatic about him. Usually the men I approach have an aura of arrogance, but he initially struck me as fragile.

"Hey, Andrew!" Mark called, waving as he came back from the loo.

"Who is that guy?" I hissed.

"Oh, that's Andrew. He has this company that makes these really intricate, futuristic, *Star Wars*–type surround-sound systems for the super rich. He's done stuff for the Oval Office and all the casinos in Vegas."

"He's really cute. Do you know if he's taken?" I had managed to sneak a glance at Andrew's left hand, but have learned the hard way that the absence of a wedding band means nothing in this country. Though I'm not sure that it's a deterrent: Some of my male friends swear they get more attention *avec* ring. As Mark always says, "The only thing that works better is a puppy!"

"I think he's divorced," he said. "But I'm not sure what the story is there. And I think he has kids. Way too much baggage, if you ask me."

"Whatever," I said. "Commitment-phobic men can have way more baggage than the ones who have tried and failed. No, I have to be careful," I said, waving away the glass as Mark slid the shot in front of me. "If my head in the toilet last time was any indication, Jose Cuervo's no friend of mine."

"Come on, liquid courage," he said as we clinked glasses.

I felt my face crumple as the ball of fire hit my guts, and knew that I was ready to make my first move. So I smoothed down my puffball miniskirt and sauntered across the bar.

"Hi." I shook his hand, plopped myself down on the stool next to him, and crossed my legs. "I'm Cat."

"Andrew," he said, amused. He smiled, and the crinkling at the corners of his blue eyes told me that he was approximately in his late thirties. "I noticed you first thing. Are you with Mark?" Translation: *Are you sleeping with Mark?*

"Mark is a very good friend of mine," I said. "But we're not together—in that sense." *At least, not lately.*

I read somewhere that it takes less than ninety seconds to determine if you have chemistry with someone, and the rest of the conversation is just filler. I can't remember much of that first conversation that had me so enamored—but I remember the way he looked at me like he was in awe, asked loads of questions, and put his hand on mine when stressing his point.

Everything about Andrew was just so, well, earnest. He was enormously successful yet self-deprecating, which I find irresistible. He referred to his multinational corporation with businesses on four continents as "my little project." Incapable of sarcastic banter, his humor was silly and good-natured, and very endearing.

He explained that he normally lived in the Hempel one or two days a week and spent the rest of the time in Dublin or traveling on business. He had three children and, from what I could gather, had married very young and was now separated. He was raised Catholic but after having an out-of-body experience when he had almost drowned seven years ago became more of a non-specific, spiritual agnostic. I found out all this in the first half-hour.

"I haven't had a girlfriend in a long time," he admitted when we were on our fourth cocktail. "I'm away four days a week, and I'm not really into the whole dating thing. I hate playing games. I tend to wear my heart on my sleeve." Usually this would sound like a line, but my relationship radar told me that he was being sincere.

"Sounds like my ideal man," I said. "I usually end up getting really frustrated because I need my own space in a relationship. Mentally and physically."

"But you're a sex columnist. You're telling me that you aren't high maintenance?"

"I'm emotionally high maintenance. And I'm brutally honest. But if a girlfriend was a pet, in terms of upkeep I'd be a gerbil, not a pony."

We all decided to move the party to the outside cabana, where candles and portable heaters kept the chilly night from encroaching. Victoria smiled and winked at me from the other side of the giant silk sofa. The room had a Moroccan theme, so Andrew and I sat on gold and red pillows on the floor.

"Cat just wrote an opinion piece on the female orgasm," Mark said, out of nowhere.

"Really?" Andrew looked amused. "And what is your expert opinion on the subject, Miss Townsend?"

I shot Mark a dirty look. "Yes, well, it was just about how Freud has a lot to answer for. He said that the clitoral orgasm was an 'adolescent phenomenon,' and when women reach puberty the 'mature' woman changes to vaginal orgasms. He had no evidence, but that didn't stop him from making entire generations of women feel sexually inadequate. And since the clitoris is largely inside the body and a lot larger than it looks, there's a theory that they are all coming from the same place anyway—" I cut myself off, determined not to talk about sex the entire night. "Bottom line is, Freud sucks and the clitoris rocks." It seems that no matter how much I try to avoid the subject of coupling, I keep coming back to it.

I guess it's futile to hope that, after hearing what I do for a living, a man, no matter how well-mannered and buttoned-up, will suddenly say, "So, tell me your opinion on the refugee crisis in Darfur." Instead, it's always, "Can men have multiple orgasms?" (They can, but that's another story.)

Victoria took another belt of Cuervo, this time straight from the bottle. "Wasn't he also the one who said that women are all bummed out because they don't have penises?"

"Yeah, it's a very phallocentric worldview." I glanced at Andrew. "Not that there's anything wrong with phalluses. I just don't want one. I mean, I want one—but not on me. You guys know what I mean!"

Everyone laughed, but I blushed, worried that I had embarrassed Andrew. But he seemed to take everything in his stride.

Victoria stood up. "Cat, we should go," she said gently. "Like, before it starts to get light outside. After all, it's a school night."

As Andrew pushed himself up, I noticed the muscles under his shirt flexing against the cotton and wondered what his bare chest looked like. I felt light-headed and the pulse of heat that was warming my stomach began to move further south.

We all said our goodbyes, and Andrew mentioned that he was about to leave on a two-week jaunt to Moscow to kit out some billionaire oligarch's pad. He walked Victoria and me to a cab, and said, "I'll call you from Moscow," as his lips brushed my cheeks.

I wanted to kiss him, but we were in company. But when the cab pulled away, I began to panic. Suddenly, the thought of not seeing him for weeks was unthinkable. The combination of tequila, some kind of inexplicable nostalgia, and sheer horniness made me want to turn back. I stopped the cab and jumped out.

"Cat, what are you doing?" Victoria said.

"I can't explain it, I've got to go back!" I said, slamming the door. "Get home safe." I ran before she could argue.

It was sleeting, tiny droplets of freezing rain that clung to my body, and yet again I'd left my umbrella at home. So, freezing, I ran through two garden squares—and couldn't find where the hell I was. How many squares with the same name could there be? After walking the streets for fifteen minutes, teeth chattering, I was ready to give up—and then I saw the distinctive pattern of lights shining from the top window of the hotel.

By the time I got to the lobby I was soaked to the bone, my beige Christian Louboutin heels covered in caked-on mud.

Still, I strolled purposefully through the lobby, head held high, and returned to the basement bar. It was empty.

"Looking for Mr. Brennan?" the bartender said, polishing a brandy glass. Was that his last name?

"Andrew? Yeah, I guess I am," I said sheepishly.

"He just went to take a phone call," he said, giving me a half smile. "But I know he'll be pleased that you're back. Can I get you a drink, miss?"

I tried to steady myself and look like a lady, even though my vision was blurring and I was on my way to some guy's hotel room whose surname I did not know. "I'll have a Southern Comfort on the rocks, please. Maybe it will help warm me up. Oh, and where's the loo?"

He directed me across the lobby, towards a massive lacquered white door that seemed to have no hinges. There was no door handle, the portal simply disappeared seamlessly into the stark white walls around it.

The bathroom seemed to be unisex, with doors that reached to the floor and a motion-activated sink that drained over smooth stones in each stall. Decorated with floor-to-ceiling mirrors, the loo was the same size as our living room. It would have been awe-inspiring while sober. But drunk, it was a bit disconcerting. Then again, I find escaping a regular cubicle a challenge once I'm past my third cocktail.

After washing my hands, I stepped in front of the full-length mirror and tried to dab at my raccoon eyes. "You know you look hot," I said to my reflection, sucking in my cheeks and pursing my lips until I burst out laughing. With my mud-streaked legs, I looked like I had just crawled out of a crypt. I tried paper towels and warm water, but they just dissolved white blobs into the dirt and added to the mess.

I pushed on the right side of the door—and nothing happened. Panicked, I tried the left side, pushing with all my might, and it still didn't budge. I squeezed my eyes shut and willed the door to open, but despite my best intentions I was locked inside the goddamned bathroom.

Then I banged on the door, hoping that someone would hear me. Suddenly, the door flew open, knocking me in the forehead. It was Andrew, and he didn't look the least bit surprised. "I was just about to call you after you left," he said, pulling me inside and looking down at my head with concern. "Are you okay? I thought you got lost."

"I don't—I mean, I just suddenly thought that I might not see you and—"

He kissed me, hard, and before I knew it we were pushed against the wall, his hand sliding up my skirt as my left leg twisted around him.

What had I been planning to say? That I wasn't that kind of girl? That I'd never done anything this crazy before? That would be an insult to both our intelligences.

Once in his suite, I grew a little disconcerted. Normally, I turn into a mini Miss Marple while making the rounds of a man's flat, because it gives me clues to his personality. But all he had in his stark suite were two dress shirts, two bottles of water, and a laptop. He was a blank page. My friend Charlie, a comedy writer, has a theory that we project a Matrix-like illusion of what we want onto our potential partners in the heady first flush of infatuation. I think he's right.

"Do you want some water?" Andrew asked, throwing his jacket over a chair.

"No," I said, "I'm thirsty for something else right now."

Yeah, I said it, though I knew at the time how cheesy it sounded. And I wasn't even being ironic.

We fell onto the bed and he started to unbutton his shirt. "Wait," I said, "let me do that." I slid his shirt off and began kissing my way down his muscular chest, then took one of his nipples and started sucking on it lightly, and running over it with my teeth. "Are your nipples sensitive?" I whispered. I heard him suck in a breath.

"They are now," he said.

We lay down next to each other and slowly peeled off our clothes. He slid his hands up my thigh, inside my knickers, and started to masturbate me. "Show me what to do," he murmured, putting my hand on top of his. "I want to learn exactly how to touch you. I want to give you both kinds of female orgasm."

Giggling, I moved his hand to my clitoris and guided his index finger, feather-soft at first, then more rapidly. I could feel my insides beginning to swell as he slipped the first two fingers of his other hand inside me. We went on for five minutes, and he kept alternating hands, taking his time, with me moaning and thrashing until I felt my muscles tightening around his fingers. "Oh, God, I'm coming," I said, then he slid his middle finger even further inside me as I spasmed around him.

When I caught my breath he was already kissing down my stomach and opening my lower lips, giving my pussy an affectionate kiss before starting to lick me, building his rhythm perfectly so that he didn't overstimulate my super-sensitive clit—until he made me come again. After so many drinks, a first-time orgasm from oral sex with a guy is, for me, about as likely as discovering a unicorn in the closet. This guy was a keeper.

"Oh, my God," I said, biting my bottom lip, and I held my arm out. "That was fucking amazing, my hands are shaking." I flipped him over and straddled him. "Time to return the favor."

I slipped his underwear off and flicked my tongue over the head of his cock before I took the entire shaft in my mouth.

"Stop," he whispered, pulling my head up.

"What's wrong?" I asked him.

"I'm serious," he said, "I'm so turned on right now from tasting you that I'm going to come straight away if you keep doing that—and I don't want you to feel short-changed."

I love guys who get that turned on from going down on me. Just thinking about it made me re-lubricate.

"Don't worry," I said, "I think we've both had a lot to drink and this whole thing is overwhelming, so why don't we just forget about the penetrative sex for tonight and concentrate on making each other feel good." The corner of my mouth turned up in a smile. "Surely mutual pleasure is the point?"

"God, darling, you are going to kill me," he said as I ran my tongue over the ripples in his stomach.

I wetted my lips and consumed him, all the way to the back of my throat like a porn star, pushing my hair behind my shoulders with one hand so that he could see me, while sliding my other hand between his legs to probe his bum gently. He moaned and leaned into me, so I slid one finger inside, gently, teasingly. When he came he flung himself back on the bed, chest clenched; his entire body looked like he was convulsing in an epileptic seizure. I've seen men in the throes of passion, but this was like something out of *The Exorcist*. For a horrible second, I thought he'd had a heart attack.

I was worried about his health. But, selfishly, I was also a bit panicked about myself. Shit, I thought, what am I going to say to his children, when they look up at me with little tear-streaked faces and ask me, solemnly, what their daddy's last words were and I have to tell them they were, "Oh, God, I'm coming"?

"Andrew? Andrew? Are you okay?" For about ten scary seconds when time seemed to stop, I really thought I'd killed him.

Several seconds later he caught his breath. "That was, without a doubt, the most intense orgasm I've ever had," he said. "What are you doing to me, Miss Townsend?"

"Whatever it is, we're doing it to each other," I told him. Then I asked, "Have you ever heard of the 'male G spot'?"

He shook his head, smoothed my hair, and held my hand.

"Well," I breathed, kissing him lightly on the lips. "You have now." Then I stood up and began to dress.

"What are you doing?"

"Well, darling, I have to be up in about two hours, and if I stay another five minutes I'm going to fall asleep."

"Stay," he said, sitting up on the edge of the bed. "Please. We can order room service for breakfast. And I want to sleep next to you."

I fell asleep in his arms, but left before he woke up. I didn't want our first "official" time to be in the morning, avoiding each other's kisses because of morning breath. I kissed him goodbye and left a note: "Had a fantastic time last night and don't worry. I still respect you. xxxx"

Perhaps the reason why I was able to click with Andrew was because I'd finally laid the ghost of Patrick to rest—along with a lot of other random guys—by spring cleaning my love life. Two days before my fateful meeting with Andrew, I was cleaning out my closet when I got a message from Martin, a suave and sexy professional ballet dancer with whom I had had two dates a while ago. He was lean, rangy, and hot—kind of like George Clooney on a hunger strike.

"Hey, sexy," he said, "it's been a while since we hooked up, and I've always wondered why we never took things further. I was wondering if you felt the same, and if you would be interested in catching up some time. That is, if you still remember me…"

Normally, I'm wary of recycling exes. But he was gorgeous, charming, and super fit—and for the past two weeks the closest I'd gotten to a dirty afternoon was scrubbing the rings off my bathtub. So I decided to give him a call.

Ten minutes into the conversation I was starting to remember why we hadn't clicked the first time around.

His opening gambit was to update me on his manic health regime. Finicky tastes freak me out a bit since men who are incredibly regimented in the kitchen aren't likely to let go in bed.

I know that mixing food and sex can go horribly wrong. Once I drizzled honey on a hairy ex and ended up having to cut it out; and a friend of mine still can't talk about the time she "lost" a banana. But nothing had prepared me for Martin's reaction that night when I sprayed whipped cream over my naked body. Everything was okay until the fateful moment he surreptitiously glanced at the can.

"You're checking the fat content, aren't you?" I said. He had looked sheepish and licked tentatively, but I could tell his heart wasn't in it. At the time I'd felt sorry for Martin because he wasn't able to let go and revel in the moment. For me life without a few vices would be boring and repetitive—much like our love-making that night.

Meanwhile, the phone call droned on, "So I do a hundred press-ups every morning, then pull-ups if my tennis elbow isn't acting up," he was telling me. "Of course, I have to stick to the low GI diet, which is a lot better than the low carb diet because you have to balance your protein and complex carbohydrate intake. That's what most people can't comprehend."

I needed to kill the conversation, so I couldn't resist winding him up by admitting my dirty little "secret single behavior": That sometimes, really late at night, I find myself drunkenly crawling through the aisles of Tesco's like a creature out of *Night of the Living Dead* in search of powdered chocolate cake mix.

"I take it home, and mix it with raw eggs to make the batter," I told him. "Then I start licking the spoon… and I can't stop!"

"I wouldn't do that if I were you, Cat," he said. "Your metabolism may be fine now, but in a couple of years you'll regret it." The only thing I regretted at that point was not having hit the delete button on my phone sooner.

And that's when it dawned on me: Every year, I religiously spring cleaned my closet, but wasn't it my little black book I should be blowing the cobwebs off? Finding a man with the same longevity as my wardrobe staples presented a serious challenge: The vast majority of my relationships went out of fashion quicker than that season's platform heels.

So I decided to apply the same ruthless logic to my mobile phone that I use with my moth-eaten garments: Anyone I haven't used—or missed—in the past year gets deleted from my life. Once I began to consign my outdated relationships to the same fate as my acid-washed jeans, I found that I couldn't stop. In two minutes, my vacation fling, my surfer shag buddy, and someone labeled, simply, "Random Guy From Amsterdam" were all erased from history.

It was incredibly liberating to get rid of my emotional clutter. I questioned my wisdom because I'd always believed that hanging on to the numbers gave me a sense of security—but I hadn't realized how much they were holding me back.

And if I couldn't bring myself to chuck out the things I'd outgrown, how could I expect to have room for anything new? I might have felt a bit naked and vulnerable without my fallback flings, but springtime was the perfect excuse for a sexual shopping spree.

Ironically, no sooner had I done my spring clean than I'd met Andrew. So now there was a new caller I was eagerly anticipating.

After two tense days, he finally rang to give me the dates he'd be back in London. I aimed for a sexy, sultry voice that sounded like I was filing my nails while speaking to him, while really I was sitting cross-legged on the sofa, my heart pounding wildly as I chewed on the phone cord.

My *Independent* editor had just assigned me to do a story on male vs. female approaches to wild spending before a date, so I had a perfect excuse to obsess over my upcoming evening out with Andrew.

I started mentally sketching out my outfit a full seven days beforehand. Sadly, I realized I had no suitable underwear. I have a rule with lingerie. I never wear anything for the first time with a new man that I've worn with a previous lover. I don't want bad panty karma. I find it hilarious when male friends complain that it costs them a three-figure sum to take a woman out to dinner, because women take the hit when it comes to pre-date preparation. All the boys have to do is show up and smile sweetly in the same suit they wear to work, having showered and perhaps applied a dab of aftershave. The cost for women is far higher, in time and cold, hard cash.

Five days before D-Day, I headed to Selfridges desperately seeking suspenders, plus killer heels. I brought Michael along for second opinions. My eye was immediately drawn to the Gina stilettos with a rhinestone buckle, very dominatrix-chic. "Do I look hot or scary?" I asked Michael, modeling them.

"This is scary," he said, pointing to the £365 price tag. "Jesus Christ! That's practically your entire rent."

Hyperventilating slightly, I asked if he thought that splashing out on lingerie would be a better investment. Could I justify spending £80 on a bra?

"Are you kidding? If you play your cards right he won't even think about looking at your feet. Definitely go for the underwear."

So I focused on a pink satin and black lace Agent Provocateur bra and underwear set, teamed with fishnet stockings. I handed over my credit card and felt my knees turn to jelly when I spotted the total: £203.

"It's going to be worth it," Michael said. "He's going to have a heart attack."

"Um, that's kind of what I'm worried about." I laughed. Still, I justified the expenditure by telling myself that had I bought the Gina shoes, I would have spent twice as much. So, really, I saved £162.

In Selfridges' sex toy emporium, I picked a mini bottle of Edible Mint Lube for £4.99. Being prudent, I also grabbed a three-pack of condoms for £3.55.

Visibly sweating, Michael bailed out. "I have to go to grill a very tough cabinet minister," he said. "Frankly, your guy isn't going to care what lingerie you have on as long as he likes what lies beneath, so I think this whole thing is a bit insane. But good luck."

But I was in a full-on shopping frenzy, and since I had decided to go for the smoky-eyed temptress look, I bought some Benefit Bad Girls black eyeliner and shimmery body powder from Boots to pat on my push-up-bra-enhanced cleavage. Total cost: £32.

With two days to go, I trekked to the salon to have the obligatory £30 Brazilian wax, since previous DIY attempts on my nether regions had led to blood, sweat, and many tears. There was also the matter of my feet, which due to my heel habit seemed to have morphed into something befitting a *Lord of the Rings* character. So I opted for a pedicure (£28), but did my fingernails myself, thus "saving" another £15. I was so nervous about seeing him that I'd been biting them all off, anyway.

Before I left the house I tallied up everything for my article.

*COST: skirt: £29.00; Agent Provocateur bra, knickers, suspenders, and fishnet stockings: £203.00; completely unnecessary makeup: £32.00; bedroom accessories: £8.54; pedicure/Brazilian bikini wax: £58.00; taxi: £15.00; emergency umbrella/breath mints: £6.00*

The total? A cool £351.54 in the name of hot sex. I must really like this guy.

# NINE

I was counting the days until Andrew's return, and I'm ashamed to say that I measured the time between phone calls. Fortunately, my evening trying out sugar daddy speed dating for an assignment was that week and would provide some distraction. Which was how, with visions of a Donald Trump–style comb-over dancing in my head, I attended my first—and hopefully last—such event.

When I got the assignment, I tried to put a positive spin on the experience. After all, since I put so much pressure on myself to succeed financially and professionally, I don't see any problem in requiring the same of a man.

Apparently, a lot of high-flying career girls these days feel the same way. Despite the fact they are more than able to pay their own way, they are looking for love—and a fat wallet.

SpeedDater, the website that brought us endless themed dating events such as dinner in the dark, text dating, and quiet dating, was the first company to cater for the growing trend by offering sugar daddy nights. The rules are similar to regular SpeedDater events: Women meet the men for three minutes each and tick boxes on a scorecard next to the names of those they want to see again. In this version, in a bar close to Piccadilly Circus, a group of twenty-three to thirty-five-year-old women were paired with men aged thirty-five to fifty who had to earn at least £50,000 per year.

I got chatting to Michelle, a thirty-five-year-old travel agent and veteran of several speed-dating events, over the complimentary champagne. She claimed to be looking for someone who could offer her financial stability, not full-length furs. "I'm not a gold-digger, but London is so expensive," she said. "My last boyfriend was unemployed, always talking about the 'big property deal' that would set him up for life. The truth is that I ended up supporting him for six months because the deal never came off. So these days, I would probably be less likely than I was ten years ago to agree to a date with someone who described himself as a writer or independent filmmaker." She laughed. "I know, that sounds terrible."

I felt a bit uneasy about being in a room where the barter system of youth vs. money was quite so blatant. But fifty grand isn't exactly sugar daddy territory—if I were Barbara Amiel, it would probably just about pay the petrol for the Gulfstream. I sat down at my table, pencil poised, and was introduced to my first date, Mike, a forty-year-old IT consultant with clammy hands. "I was afraid there might be loads of lecherous men here, but everyone seems quite normal," he said, adding that he met his last girlfriend at another SpeedDater event. He claimed to earn "a fortune" (though I didn't ask him) but his suit looked more Marks and Spencer than Mayfair.

Ding! Suddenly I was confronted with a balding man in a tie dotted with jaunty-looking miniature frogs. His sweaty forehead threatened to dislodge his very obvious-looking toupee, in a frightening shade of auburn that does not exist in nature. It looked like a piece of wispy red cotton candy.

"So, you are a very attractive young lady," he said, scratching his head and moving his hairline about a quarter of an inch to the left. "What brings you here?" he asked.

"Actually, I'm doing a piece for the *Independent*," I said, smiling. "But don't worry, I'm not using real names or taking any photos. It's more to get a feel for what these events are like, and I'm single so if I'm lucky I get a date out of it."

His eyes darkened. "Well, you're not writing any personal information about me! I'm a lawyer, and I will sue you if you print one word of our conversation."

Married, I thought, shifting uncomfortably. "Look, I'm not here to get anyone in trouble, it's supposed to be a fun piece about finding love, so if we could just chat for a few minutes…"

"I'm not saying a word. I'm too afraid of having it used against me. Women always use things against me. They always want to screw me over." Scratch. The rug was now perched at a precarious angle.

Jesus Christ, this guy was uptight, and my usual charming smile and short skirt combination wasn't working. The next two and a half minutes seemed like an eternity.

My next dates were Richard, a charming, impeccably dressed entrepreneur who claimed to be in his mid-forties, and Jay, a fifty-five-year-old who, bizarrely, insisted that I should recognize him because he was famous and had written books on skiing.

Throughout the evening, no one after the first guy mentioned money. A quick scan through the men's online profiles later suggested that many of them worked in the computer industry, the City, or property, and had incomes hovering around the £100,000-a-year mark, but there was no telling for sure. In my experience, there are two reasons why men hide their income: Either it's so big that they fear attracting the wrong type of woman, or it's much smaller than promised. To be fair, most of the men were polite and well turned-out, with no gold chains or Peter Stringfellow clones in sight.

Next up was Jack, a property developer, and clearly a fellow Charles Darwin fan. "I've always dated women who are ten to twenty years younger, because I think that it's the natural way of things," he said.

"Women are biologically programmed to look for someone who can provide for them, and it's normal for men to be attracted to younger, attractive women. I see myself with someone in her early twenties." He directed this biology lecture at my cleavage.

"I love Darwin, too. Actually I'm a big fan of the theory of sperm competition, where women who take multiple lovers have the evolutionary advantage; ever heard of it?" I grinned, showing teeth.

Ding! The buzzer sounded and he vanished into the night.

During the break, I chatted to a few women in an effort to understand why they were looking for a sugar daddy. A lot of them complained that their potential dates were closer to a hundred than fifty. "Some of these guys are clearly lying," said Anna, a brunette PR consultant and chain-smoker in her mid-thirties, as she stealthily puffed on a clove cigarette. The sickly sweet cloying smell reminded me of a funeral parlor, which was rather apt given that a lot of these men seemed to have one foot in the grave.

In my final round of dating, I discovered that some of the men had egos cashing checks that their bank accounts could clearly never cover. "My checklist of ideal qualities for Ms. Right is ludicrous, and I admit it," said Neil, a forty-six-year-old. "It's strange, because I'm right-of-center, over forty, and a voracious carnivore, but I only date women who are staunch vegetarians, incredibly left-wing, and usually much younger." And they said women had unrealistic expectations?

Still, no one seemed to think that money could buy happiness, and the women stressed that they would not pick a rich man at the expense of a nice, entertaining guy with an average income. They all said that if the chemistry wasn't there, then no amount of money would ever be enough. But I guess they would say that.

The next afternoon I got a call from Andrew, saying that he couldn't wait another forty-eight hours to see me, so he was flying back through London en route to Moscow and "needed to talk" to me. I arranged to meet him in the Hempel Hotel garden after lunch at the Ivy with my editor.

One reason why my freelance existence feels so surreal is because I spend most of my days alone and rarely get feedback. But that day, over flaky sea bream and a single glass of sauvignon blanc, I negotiated a raise for myself. I was so proud, especially when the editor told me how much he liked my writing. My column may not be Woodward and Bernstein, but I'm providing entertainment and helping people dissect what, for many of us, is one of the most important decisions we'll ever make. I couldn't help thinking that, corny as it sounds, being taken to the Ivy was a signal that I'd arrived in the London media world. Take that, Patrick.

Andrew stood up when I approached the table, and took my hands when I sat down. They were ice cold.

"So," I said, crossing my legs and leaning back. "What's the bad news, then?" Although I was wearing my pink satin and black lace Agent Provocateur lingerie set with fishnet stockings and suspenders, just in case the news was good.

"What makes you think I have bad news?"

At that moment a waiter appeared and served us two vodka tonics with a flourish.

"Two things," I said. "First of all, I just got a raise, and the universe has a way of evening things out. Second, in my experience, 'We need to talk' is something that detectives say on crime shows. Right before they tell the relatives that someone is dead." I tried to keep my tone light, but I'm sure he could hear the tremors.

"It's just that… we've only known each other for a short time, but I really like you. So I need to be honest with you about my situation."

I felt sick. "You still live at home with your wife, don't you?"

Then he uttered the two words that strike fear into the heart of every single woman. "It's complicated."

I yanked my hand back and felt my eyes fill with tears. "Wait, let me guess. You've 'grown apart,' and your wife doesn't understand you, right? I suppose next you're going to tell me that you haven't had sex in years?" I shook my head. "Look, when you told me that you were separated I thought you were living apart. I didn't know you meant 'separated in your head.'"

"Cat, please let me explain. Look, if you want to walk after today, I'll totally understand. But at least hear me out."

The next twenty minutes were a blur as he gave me the marital monologue.

"I left for six months and got my own flat, but it was horrible for the kids," he said. "Then last year my business got into trouble and I had to liquidate the flat to put the money back into the company. So I live in one wing of the house, and we're essentially co-parents. I'm away so much, and in the rare moments when I'm in Dublin I get to spend time with the kids. Anyway, she is away loads with her boyfriend in Spain."

"Wait," I said, my head spinning. "She has a boyfriend?"

"Yes," he said, looking me directly in the eye. "We have separate bedrooms. Because I was away so much and focused on the kids when I was there, the situation was tolerable until I could find another, smaller flat." He sighed. "And then you walked into my life, and feeling about you the way that I do…"

Despite myself, I smiled. "And how is that?"

As I looked around the garden on that bright, sunny day, I couldn't help thinking that if this relationship were a horror movie, this would be the beginning where the girl hears a strange noise. Does she call the cops? No, she descends into the basement, because at that point the illusion of maintaining control and having a happy ending is stronger than the fear. So when the bogeyman jumps out with a knife, she's terrified—but not entirely surprised.

In the first flush of infatuation, warning anyone about their lover is about as useless as screaming, "Don't go in there, girl, he's got a knife!" at the hapless horror film protagonist. When it comes to love, people suppress any niggling doubts and become masters of self-deception.

After he'd murmured his sweet nothings, we went upstairs. I pushed him against the wall and unbuttoned his trousers to slide his cock into my open mouth. I read in a women's magazine that blow jobs are most intense when men are standing, because the blood rushes downward. I put his hand in my hair so that he could grip me and pull me towards him.

After a couple of frantic minutes, he pushed me away and started tearing his clothes off, getting momentarily caught with his shirt over his head. By the time he got it off, I was sitting on the bed, adjusting my stockings.

"Do you like my surprise?" I asked shyly, letting my hair fall over one eye as I looked up at him.

"I'm thirty-seven years old, and I could come in my pants just looking at you," he said, walking towards the bed. I reached for him, but he pushed me back. "Not yet," he said. "Not until I've tasted you."

I lay back and felt him gently tonguing the inside of my thigh, and I could feel his hot breath through my knickers when—BRRRING!

My mobile was ringing. It was one of the editors on the features desk and she sounded stressed. "Cat," she said, "for some reason we didn't get the column through this morning. Not your fault, our email is screwed up," she added hastily. "Are you in a position to re-send it?"

"Um, well," I said, as he pulled my panties off, slowly, leaving the stockings, "I suppose I can try to get to a computer, I'm kind of in the middle of something though..." I bit back a moan as he spread my legs and started running his fingers down my thighs.

"We need it in the next ten minutes, or we'll have to hold it for a week. We just don't have any choice."

I sat up with a start. "Okay, I'll get it to you. Don't worry. I'll call you in five."

I hung up and looked at Andrew. "Honey, I know this isn't the most romantic first time, but can I borrow your laptop?"

"I let my colleague borrow it, sweetheart, since I took the afternoon off to be with you."

"Shit!" I said, feeling the panic set in. "I've got to re-send my column. I'm totally screwed."

"Don't worry," he said gently. "Didn't you say you had a printout with you?"

"Yes, I always carry one if I'm not in the house."

"So use my BlackBerry," he said, fishing it out of his jacket. "How long can it take you to type 600 words?" He smiled mischievously. "I promise to make a very tedious exercise interesting."

For the next ten minutes, he knelt at the end of the bed, my legs draped over the edge, tonguing my lower lips and gently slipping his fingers inside me.

Somehow, breathing heavily, I managed to finish with only two spelling errors. Then I called my editor back.

When she picked up, Andrew mouthed, "Sit on my face," and pulled me up to the top of the bed.

"So," I said, lowering myself on to his mouth, "you got everything okay?"

"Yes, we did, sorry to bother you but we would have hated to have had to cut it. Did you manage to finish that thing you were in the middle of?"

I bit my bottom lip to keep from gasping as Andrew pulled me down onto him, and I ground my hips against his face. "I'm working on it," I replied.

"Well," she said cheerily, "bye then."

I hung up just as he increased the lapping—his thumb was inside me now, pulling me down onto his insatiable tongue. I could feel my climax building as he licked me. Then, a few seconds after he said, "Baby, I want you to come on my face," I felt myself let go completely, gushing all over him as I clenched my white-knuckled hands into the headboard.

When he pulled me down on the bed and started fucking me, our gazes locked. I felt like he was looking into my soul. It dawned on me that I should probably protect myself from this onslaught of emotion. With Andrew I found myself opening up parts of myself that I'd kept hidden, even during my time with Patrick. He was seeing the real me. It was scary.

But by then, I was too far gone.

After our amazing sex, I stared at the digital clock on the wall for hours. I've never been afraid of the dark and can pick up a spider without batting an eye, but I do have one irrational fear: Instead of wanting to cuddle after sex, I have a fight-or flight reaction when staying overnight at a new man's house. When I see the sun rising, I feel like a werewolf panicking about an impending full moon, even though, for such an occasion, I would no doubt have shaved my legs.

What puzzled me is that this was happening with Andrew even though I adored him.

Part of my problem is physical: I'm a really light sleeper who just can't deal with snoring. I've always found it a bit strange that, even though it's socially acceptable to have casual flings, staying overnight seems to be viewed as mandatory.

In fact, I can count on one hand the men I've felt comfortable waking beside. With the right person, that brave post-coital chat and the ensuing Sunday roast are amazing, but it doesn't come naturally to someone who craves her own space.

That's why I have learned never to invite a man back to mine: I relish the freedom of an instantly accessible escape hatch—or at least a minicab. If you are already at home, it's tough to come up with an excuse. "I've got an early meeting" sounds a bit lame when the guy in question knows that a) it's Sunday and b) I work from home. Calling him a cab seems a bit mean. On the rare occasions I've let people stay in the past I've suffered through—and got zero sleep.

But maybe there's a more complex reason why the line "your place or mine?" has become a purely rhetorical question for me. A tumble between the sheets is one thing, but letting a man see my barefaced, pre-coffee, at-home self? That's real intimacy.

However, instead of doing another disappearing act, I decided to be honest with Andrew about my sexual sleeping disorder.

"I totally understand," he said. "Then again, if you're already up…"

Five minutes later, I wasn't the only one tossing and turning.

Maybe there's something to this intimacy thing. But then again, maybe I just needed to find a man who could go all night!

Since I'd found myself in a monogamous relationship, I decided to work my experience with Andrew into that week's column, "The Allure of the Taken Man." How appropriate.

Most of my girlfriends have had run-ins with philanderers at one stage or another, and we all realize that the guy who doesn't give us his home number, speaks in hushed tones on a mobile phone, or keeps boxes of Tampax lying around for his "sister" is probably shady.

I always knew that my first love, a gorgeous French guy, would be a nightmare. One night, at a Mexican restaurant with friends, I caught a brunette giving him evil stares. I had a burning sensation in my gut, and it wasn't down to the enchiladas. "You spent the night with her, didn't you?" I asked him later.

"No, no," he said, "it was only fifteen minutes in the bathroom."

He wasn't even being ironic.

There may also be a scientific explanation for what scientists call "mate copying." Researchers have found that female quail prefer a male they have just seen copulating, and female guppies go for the most popular male even if he is a bit of a wimp.

Even subconsciously, it's easy to succumb to flock mentality. It's the same logic that compels us to buy a vest we thought was hideous until we saw Kate Moss wearing it. This could also explain why Pete Doherty had so many groupies, despite the fact that he hadn't had a shower since about 1998.

*But sometimes,* I wrote, *cheaters can be hard to spot.*

I stared at the space after the blinking cursor for a full ten minutes before logging off and hitting the sack. The bogeyman might still be lurking in the closet. But for the moment I wanted to maintain the illusion of a happy ending for a bit longer.

# TEN

For most people, meeting a new lover's parents is the relationship's first big hurdle, but since my extended family lives on another continent, it was my friends who administered Andrew's baptism of fire.

The prospect of meeting my friends also caused our first verbal sparring match, since he thought I shouldn't mention the fact that he was married.

"Look," I said, "my friends mean a great deal to me, and while I respect your privacy I can't not tell them something so important. It makes it look like we have something to hide, which we don't, right?"

He took my hand. "Of course not. By all means, tell them what you want to. And they can ask me anything they want."

I left out the obvious subtext: I would have told them anyway. Because, as most men correctly surmise, women talk—about everything. Any man in a relationship with a girl who has friends can be assured when meeting them for that "getting-to-know-you" drink that they already have the lowdown on his erectile dysfunction, intimacy issues, strange birthmark, and fear of spiders. They know that he cried when his grandma died, and that he once unknowingly kissed a drag queen. Luckily for the boys, girls' one saving grace is that we are usually more tolerant of flaws.

Andrew and I met for a late dinner in the downstairs lounge at Roka, and in the five minutes before my friends arrived we became one of those obnoxiously tactile couples in a dark corner that I normally hate.

"Hello, lovebirds! We hate to interrupt," Amy said.

Andrew removed his hand from my hemline and kissed her on the cheek. I did the introductions, then the girls squeezed in next to me on the banquette as Andrew ran to the bar to get us a round of drinks.

"Well, darling, he's just as cute as I remember. I'm glad I wasn't wearing beer goggles," Victoria said, squeezing my hand as he returned, precariously balancing three cocktails on a silver tray.

"Here you are, ladies," he said with a flourish. "I didn't want you to have to wait another ten minutes for libations."

Amy and Victoria seemed charmed by Andrew, and conversation was flowing smoothly, interrupted only by his trips to refill our drinks. I was getting a warm, fuzzy feeling that wasn't alcohol-related, and, for once, everything just felt easy. They liked him.

I was basking in the moment when I glanced behind him and realized that I was sitting across from a guy I recently had sex with—and, unfortunately, he wasn't my boyfriend. Sitting directly in front of our table, facing us and staring, was Nigel from the horrible one-night stand several weeks ago. I could still see his horrified reaction to my impending masturbation: He had actually pulled the sheets up to his neck, as if he were afraid that a monster was going to jump out of the closet. God, what had I been thinking?

I shook my head, hoping that this was a hallucination. But I knew that the men my subconscious conjured up all had better fashion sense.

He was wearing, inexplicably, a puffy vest over a short-sleeved shirt, and what looked like blue Converse. Frankly, he looked like a child who should be taking the special bus, not a thirty-something professional.

"So, Andrew, I have to ask, what are your intentions with my friend?" Victoria challenged him. "Because I have to tell you, the fact that you still live with your wife makes us all very suspicious."

Here Amy cut in, "But we understand that situations involving children can be complicated." Amy's boyfriend had a son from a previous relationship so she had a more tolerant perspective than Victoria and me.

Andrew looked unfazed, and smiled. "I totally understand, and if my friend was dating someone in my situation I would have the same concerns." When he paused, presumably to elaborate, I deduced that I had one of two choices: Either look through Nigel and pretend he didn't exist, or be woman enough to approach him—leaving Andrew alone with Victoria, who I nervously noted seemed to be on the warpath.

"Excuse me for a second, honey," I said, squeezing his hand. Since Nigel and I were sitting in each other's direct line of vision, I took a deep breath and headed over the next time his gaze met mine.

"Cat, hey, you're looking hot as ever," he slurred. He took a long drink from his bottled beer and grabbed my hand, then mumbled something like "great tits" as I leaned down. I quickly deduced that he and his sartorially challenged posse were all hammered. Fortunately the hip-hop muzak playing in the background meant that he was out of earshot to Andrew.

"Hello, I just saw you, and wanted to come over and say hi." I looked down. He was still holding my hand, trying to focus his gaze. "So, um, hi."

"That's a lovely blouse," he muttered as I straightened up and retracted my hand. "I believe the last time I saw that blouse, it was crumpled on my bedroom floor." He cackled hysterically, while his friends looked really uncomfortable, and shrugged.

"Yes, well, anyway I've got to get back. I don't want to be rude to my friend—so have a great night," I said brightly. I was starting to sweat.

I wish I could say that it was the first time that I'd had an awkward encounter with a former one-night stand that I'd rather forget. But I was already thinking of that week's column when I went back to rejoin my friends. The truth was that in a sexual slump, sometimes the boys who got me the hottest were the ones I never took out in public. There was the tedious corporate lawyer who only became interesting after four beers, and the ex I continued to drunk-dial for booty calls even after he told me he didn't want a girlfriend. They were my late-night, clandestine encounters that my girlfriends and I called our "Happy Hour Hook-Ups" because they only started looking good after a few two-for-one specials.

Sometimes, channeling my secret slut side feels like the 3 a.m. trip to the kebab shop that leaves me bloated, with lamb juice all over me—deliciously satisfying, but slightly guilt-inducing and definitely not appropriate in public.

When I sat down at the table, the three were toasting, so I guessed that their little tête-à-tête had gone well.

The next time Andrew excused himself to go to the bathroom, I quietly pointed out Nigel to my girlfriends and filled them in on our misadventures.

"It's so embarrassing, because he's acting so juvenile," I said, desperately trying to avoid his gaze as he waved and launched a menu folded into a paper airplane our way. "I'm just hoping he'll leave without saying goodbye, because I really don't want Andrew to have a close encounter with that repressed freak."

"Don't worry, *he's* the one who should be embarrassed," Amy said.

"By the way, I think Andrew is completely sincere. He seems like a great guy."

"But just be careful," Victoria added. "Even when they mean well, guys with complications can still end up screwing you over. Anyway, subject change—we've all had our coyote shags," Victoria admitted. "There was the accountant that I took home after two bottles of vodka at the office Christmas party. He told someone at work we kissed, and I totally denied it and laughed. I know, I'm a horrible person!" she said, peeping out from between her hands. "But I didn't want people asking me questions about something that I knew was a one-off. Ooh, shut up, here comes your boyfriend!"

Andrew slipped his arms around me. "Did I miss anything?"

"We were just discussing embarrassing one-night stands," Amy said. "Have you ever had one?"

"I can only think of one that was truly hideous," he told us, smiling slyly. "There was this totally stunning girl that I went on a date with before I got married, and she kept referring to her cat as her 'baby.'"

"That's not so bad," Victoria said. "Amy does that with her cat all the time!"

Amy punched her on the arm and giggled.

"It gets worse." Andrew smirked and set down his drink, leaning forward for dramatic effect. "Right before the appetizers were served, she asked if I wanted to see a picture. I said sure, imagining a cute little photo of a cat. And then she pulled out"—he sighed and closed his eyes, pressing his hands to the side of his temples—"an accordion wallet, filled with about thirty different photos of the cat in various custom-made outfits. There was the cat as a ballerina with a tutu, chef, and I swear to God she had a pirate outfit with booties. It even had an eye patch."

We all convulsed with laughter, my martini shooting out of my nose so that I had to blot it with a cocktail napkin to stop the stream.

"It all comes down to that fine line between hot sex and guilty sex." I took another big gulp, even though my nostrils were still burning. My friends claim to stay quiet because they don't want to be judged, but often they are much harder on themselves than their friends would be. I adore organic eggs Benedict, but at a pinch my friends would think nothing of it if I wolfed down the occasional McDonald's Egg McMuffin. The same principle applies when I'm sexually ravenous.

"What is up with those guys back there?" Andrew said, turning his head as one of them launched another paper airplane at the back of his head. It missed.

"Remember my friend Charles's ex-girlfriend? The one who once tried to attack him with a claw hammer?" Amy quickly changed the subject.

"Apparently she was a bit pissed off that he lost her mobile after a drunken night out," I explained to Andrew. "But don't you think men have a different attitude towards stealth sex? They don't feel bad about keeping dodgy hookups to themselves."

"I think you're right," he said. "Girls have this thing about confessing everything and being honest. To a man, telling you about the time he woke up at some girl's house and her boyfriend popped out of the closet is just too much information."

Later, when Andrew and I walked back to the hotel, I casually mentioned the table behind us again. "Hey, so the reason those guys were acting so weird is because I slept with one of them awhile back," I blurted out, stopping to look up at him. "Not exactly my finest hour—but I want to tell you everything."

He took my hand and laughed. "Well, he certainly seemed fixated on you," he said. "So am I going to be pining for you years from now?"

I smiled and kissed him. "Shall we go upstairs and find out?"

# ELEVEN

Even before I tentatively opened one eye the morning after a marathon date with Andrew, I knew I'd gone too far.

The previous night, we'd been in bed after a two-bottle dinner followed by several snifters of hugely expensive brandy, when I accidentally blurted out: "I love you." He froze, like a deer caught in headlights. Then, total silence.

Okay, I might have done the verbal equivalent of premature ejaculation, but he's the one who'd been pursuing me, and telling me about the inner workings of his mind. So why did I feel so guilty?

My total honesty can lead to verbal diarrhea in social situations, so I'm not surprised that I admitted my feelings so readily. I guess that makes me an "emotional slut." I know I should probably be more mysterious, but the truth is that I have no interest in changing my personality. If a man can't handle someone who's feisty and direct, it's probably better to know sooner rather than later. My honesty is ultimately positive, because it stops me from getting stuck in false situations and gives me a fantastic sense of freedom. When I told him how I felt, I was euphoric, and had the same sensation I'd had when jumping from a plane while sky-diving. All too soon, however, I had the suspicion that my chute had failed to open and the ground was racing up to meet me. I don't sleep around looking for love. When I fall into bed with a man, I'm looking for sex—pure and simple. Emotional intimacy and physical intimacy are two completely different animals.

I was also panicking because part of me was having flashbacks of my experience with Patrick, and the first time I realized that "Freak Out!" was not just the chorus of a 1970s disco anthem. After our ill-fated encounter at the Bleeding Heart, I never heard from him again—despite the fact that he had said the L-word numerous times, and told me repeatedly that he wanted to marry me.

Most of my girlfriends have had run-ins with drama-queen men, and some are cynical as a result. Because chances are, the guy who talks spontaneously in the future tense about going away together on the second date will probably never show up for the third.

So I met Michael for a drink, and asked him what I should have done. Since he spent so much time charting the love lives of tabloid regulars (he calls Westminster "showbiz for ugly people"), he's astute at guessing people's motivations. He'd also been a serious commitment-phobe lately, so I knew he'd level with me if I'd gone too far with Andrew.

"What the hell was I supposed to do?" I said, sucking on a honey-glazed peanut from the bar. "Said, 'Just kidding!' or acted like I do in a new relationship when one person farts, and pretend it never happened?"

"You probably scared him," he said bluntly. "So don't be surprised if he runs like hell." He raked his fingers through his dirty blond hair and signaled the bartender for another round.

"But he was the one going on and on about intimacy," I protested.

"Yeah, but you have to remember that men are the weaker sex, even if they do try to be control freaks. You've got to be careful how you handle it. He's now in the power position, and it's going to be tough to turn that around."

Call me a hopeless romantic, but I just can't bear to think of love as a zero-sum game. Besides, with all my neuroses, I don't have to play hard to get. I am hard to get. Michael is a notorious serial dater, so his reaction caused me some serious distress.

Victoria, on the other hand, advised me not to panic. "You were in bed!" she shouts over the clamor of revelers in the background at her boss's birthday party. "That's an automatic get-out clause. Just pretend that it never happened."

In the end, I decided to take my mum's advice, "Just be yourself," to heart, and kept telling myself, "If it's meant to be, it will be."

I then wrote about the entire incident, which was probably a stupid idea. Now he'd know how much I was bothered by my vulnerability; it'd be like he'd read the CliffsNotes to my brain patterns.

So later, when we met for cheeseburgers at PJ's in South Kensington, I was determined not to be overemotional, and to try to make light of the situation. I saw him, wearing the blue sweater that he knew I loved, with a rolled-up newspaper under his arm. I couldn't help but think, *He's my boyfriend.* I felt a surge of proprietary pride. Then I saw what he'd been reading: my column. My heart flipped.

"Sorry for the other night," I said offhandedly, as he clumsily embraced me. "I blame the brandy. And remember, sweetie, I reserve the right to use poetic license."

"Well, I hope that what you said wasn't fictional," he said, taking my hand and tilting my chin up, so that he could gaze into my eyes. "Because I love you too, Catherine."

When we finally got back to the hotel, we didn't even make it to the bed. I can only hope the downstairs neighbors were understanding.

"I'm going crazy!" I yelled at Mark, who was admiring the bare butt cheek of a bottle-blonde Asian girl named Cristal—"like the champagne," as she'd repeatedly emphasized.

"Sorry, I got a bit distracted there, sweetheart," he said, turning back to me as she blew him a kiss. "What were you saying?"

We were at an upscale "gentleman's club," and as the pneumatic brunette gyrated in my lap to the strains of "Hungry Like the Wolf," her pert D-cup breasts hovering inches from my face, I began to wonder what I'd gotten myself into. Curious about men's fascination with strip clubs, I had agreed to accompany Mark on one of his boys' nights out.

"I said, I'm going crazy waiting for Andrew to figure out everything with his life. I want to know where I fit in. I really feel like I'm in love, and I just want to—" I raised my head over a pair of massive silicon mounds— "shout it from the rooftops! But all I can think about is who we could end up hurting. I don't get the honeymoon period, because he still hasn't dealt with the consequences of his last honeymoon."

"Look," he said as he put his hand on my knee. "Like I said before, I'm not sure that this situation is healthy for you. This guy is able to have his cake and eat it too right now, so why should he change anything?"

I started to protest, and he shushed me with his hand.

"I know what you need, a lap dance!" he said, and summoned yet another blonde over.

After he paid, my heart raced as the dancer snaked in and out between my legs. I was an emotional wreck. And yet I was seriously turned on. But I was also a bit embarrassed, like when I'm at the gym and a nude woman is blocking my locker, with her privates at eye level. I just didn't know where to look—but I couldn't look away. I definitely don't consider lap dances cheating, because strip clubs are all about fantasy, not reality. After all, I doubt that any man I date would run off with Bambi from Lithuania.

I've been to the occasional Chippendales show with my girlfriends, but just because I have a laugh while stuffing £5 notes down a fit man's pants doesn't mean I want to be oiling his torso backstage later. I've had several friends who have worked as strippers, and they were all savvy businesswomen who assured me that at the clubs my man is just another dollar sign. Which is also why I find the idea that strip clubs exploit women ridiculous—the women earn truckloads of cash. So as long as guys are honest about their nights out, I have no problem with them paying for surgically enhanced girls to straddle them.

My male pals agree. "It's sort of a cheesy male-bonding experience," Mark said. "I think it's better for the guys in relationships, because they can go home and take the sexual tension out on their girlfriends. Otherwise it can feel like going to a restaurant, smelling the food, and then having it yanked back before you've taken a bite."

However, most of their girlfriends don't agree. So tonight I'm one of the boys. If seeing naked women whets a man's appetite for a night of passion with me, so be it.

Of course, I would be wary of any guy who dropped thousands at clubs, uttered the phrase "She really likes me" about a dancer, or had a four-times-a-week habit, like Victoria's ex. "I'm totally cool with the occasional visit, but he was there constantly," she said. "When we went together, he whipped out his loyalty card! I ran out after he suggested we eat at the hot food buffet where there were loads of naked girls running around."

As for Mark and me, the voyeuristic thrill started to evaporate after shelling out loads of cash for a few watered-down drinks.

"You want my opinion?" he said. "Women overanalyze everything.

The bottom line is, you need to base your decisions on actions, and ignore his motivation. Who cares? Is he leaving? That's what you need to ask yourself before you decide 'Should I stay or should I go?' You need to make a list of the pros and cons in this relationship, and be really logical about it."

Five minutes later, I found myself in the bathroom, talking to one of the performers, a girl in a bunny costume, about my problem. She was drying her white fluffy halter top under the hand dryer because some guy spilled a body shot on her.

The dancer's perspective was different than Mark's: "I think that if you really love this guy, you need to be able to be honest with him," she said, fluffing her hair and scrubbing a club-soda-covered napkin over the light pink stain. "Go home and talk to him. That's my advice." She smiled and patted me on the shoulder. "Of course, my last boyfriend just got out of prison. So I'm probably not the right person to ask."

"Thanks, that really helped a lot," I said. "You know what they say, it's always a lot easier to give advice than take it yourself."

But my lap dance had definitely acted as an aphrodisiac. Because when she kept telling me how gorgeous I was, the illogical part of my brain started thinking, *Wow, it's not just about the money!* Now I knew how the blokes felt.

So, even if I hadn't got any further on the Andrew conundrum, at least I'd learned a thing or two about strip clubs. In the end, I decided to keep an open mind: Maybe these clubs really can enhance a relationship. Just so long as your romance doesn't begin and end at the hot buffet dinner!

I went back to Andrew's suite, woke him up, and ripped my clothes off. After a night of being teased, the sex was exhilarating.

A week after my strip club outing, I decided to follow my intuition and discuss my situation openly with Andrew. If that meant our romance had to end, so be it. I was sick of walking around feeling anxious. That morning, en route to my usual cupcake run at the Hummingbird Bakery where I would scalp the icing off exactly three pink ones, I openly wept after seeing a married couple holding hands in line ahead of me. It was time to stop the madness.

Andrew kept promising to "sort himself out," but I was starting to think that his promises to move out of the family home were empty. Much as I wanted to believe him, the only baggage I saw him carrying was emotional.

"Look," I said to him later, while we were walking back to the Hempel hand-in-hand in the rain, "I'm feeling really uncertain about our relationship. I know that you have a lot to deal with right now, but I told you from the beginning that I couldn't be involved with someone living in the same house as his wife. And I know that the end of your marriage has nothing to do with me, but I need to know where I stand."

He sighed and stopped abruptly. "But you know where you stand. I love you, and I belong to you as much as a man can belong to a woman. But I don't want to leave my kids, and it's just going to take some time."

Then I dropped the bomb. "But, Andrew, how long? It just feels like there is always going to be another birthday, or business deal. I need some reassurance from you that I'm not going to be here in a year's time with everything exactly the same, feeling like an idiot for having trusted you. There's no way for our relationship to move forward while you are stuck in this situation."

He brushed my fringe out of my eyes and looked down at me. "I will sort everything out. I promise." We strolled back in silence, as rain drizzled down around us.

But later, after we made love and were lying in the dark holding each other, he turned to me and whispered, "What will happen to us if I can't ever leave?"

I freaked out, ran into the marble bathroom, and burst into tears; he tried to comfort me—but the damage had been done. I understood at that moment that the only thing worse than the lies he was telling me were the ones I was telling myself. My stomach heaved and I leaned over the toilet where I vomited a stream of vodka tonic and bile.

Afterwards we both cried and held each other, and I realized exactly what I was giving up: Someone I actually wanted to call my boyfriend, felt proud of whenever he walked into a room, and, unlike anyone I'd ever met before—even Patrick—could share anything with. But despite Andrew's many attractive qualities, I had discovered the real downside of "taken" men. Because of their complicated living situations and the stress of deception, they are the focus of the relationship. Everything has to follow their timetable, and if you make the decision to stick around, there's nothing you can do about it. That was never going to work for a control freak like me. I've worked too hard to make a life for myself to let someone else tear it apart.

I spent the next two days crying my eyes out. But by losing him, I'd like to think that I gained something in return. I learned that I had to be strong enough to walk away from someone I really loved, because I believed that I deserved something better: a truly committed relationship. Now I knew, more than ever, that this was what I wanted.

Something had happened that night. I learned how to detach myself from my emotions in the interests of self-preservation. I couldn't control Andrew, but I could control my choices. I was growing up.

# TWELVE

S o," Victoria said, "how are you holding up?"

We were waiting for the Northern line on a packed King's Cross platform, en route to Camden to buy platform heels for her, slutty underwear for me. No matter how crap the state of my love life, somehow shopping for lingerie always gives me fresh hope that a fine-looking man will be taking it off with his teeth at some stage.

I smiled. "I'm fine. I just feel really stupid, like I should have known better. After Patrick and I broke up it was radio silence. This…" I could hear my voice trembling. "This is something different."

"Is he still texting constantly?"

"Every day. It's hard to ignore him, because I really want to talk to him. But it won't do any good. I told him to give me a call if and when he ever sorts his situation out. Until then, I'm hoping we can be friends."

"Sweetie," she said, "that's really brave of you."

"Well, he's a good guy. That's why I miss him so much." Tears filling my eyes, I tried to change the subject. "So, which Tube line do you think has the hottest men?"

We came to a few conclusions on the ride home:

1. *The Piccadilly and Circle/District lines are best for morning and evening rush hour, because of the high proportion of men heading into the City.*
2. *The Hammersmith and City line is best avoided in the afternoons, because the huge delays mean that anyone attractive is probably going to be seriously annoyed by the time you chat them up.*
3. *The Northern line is dodgy, and bereft of prospects. At any hour. Unless you want to buy pot.*

It had been almost a month since my split with Andrew, and other than a few morale-boosting shopping trips with Victoria I couldn't seem to break out of my listening-to-Joy-Division-while-wandering-around-the-flat-like-the-living-dead-in-my-dressing-gown phase, so I decided that the time was perfect to blow the dust off my porn stash. I needed some inspiration.

Given that pornography has become so ubiquitous in popular culture, I'm often surprised that boys seem shocked when I mention my personal porn collection. My first experience with adult films was seeing a Ron Jeremy flick, featuring his legendarily enormous member, at a university party. Since then, I've often thought that the protagonist's werewolf-like body hair should be used in birth control campaigns, because it was scarier than any horror film. In fact, the whole experience turned me off porn for years.

But these days, girls aren't limited to watching submissive women in naff outfits servicing gold-chain-wearing guys with milk-white paunches. Female directors such as Candida Royalle and Petra Joy have created an entire genre out of girl-friendly porn that has some semblance of a plot and the emphasis isn't always on the "money shot." On the other hand, too much of a storyline can be distracting. I don't want to have to wonder what the characters' motivations are when I'm watching a scene between the half-naked pizza delivery boy and the horny housewife.

There's also the logistical difficulty to overcome: It's hard to imagine popping in cult classic *Edward Penishands* with my flatmate on the other side of our paper-thin walls. And the last time Michael and I hit a seedy Soho sex shop, we headed out five minutes later after a creepy guy with a ponytail started following us around.

When I recounted that experience to my girlfriends, I was surprised to hear that porn was still a bit of a taboo subject. Amy always quotes Naomi Wolf, who argued that porn ultimately turns men off real women. I find her argument a bit simplistic: I've never met one for whom a pixilated image wasn't secondary to the real thing.

Besides, I always try to keep politics out of the bedroom.

In the end, Amy admitted to a penchant for skin flicks after a few drinks, but was adamant that she prefers late-night soft porn on cable TV. "It's less embarrassing. Although the downside is I can't record it on Sky Plus, because then I'll definitely get busted by my flatmate," she laughed. I agreed with her about the importance of finding a good hiding place, which is why I put my last porn DVD in the case for *Maid in Manhattan*, the atrocious Jennifer Lopez vehicle. There was no danger of it ever being discovered there!

In the end, I found a shop online and chose *Sinful Rella*, a parody of the fairy tale reworked with three lusty stepsisters, a pimped-out fairy godfather, and two hunky guys masquerading as "horses." I watched it, alone and feeling pathetic, and started to laugh. But, finally, the tale of the prince searching the land for the perfect blow job began to turn me on. The only drawback was that I had to keep one hand down my tracksuit bottoms, and the other poised on the remote in case I heard Victoria's key in the door.

I'm pleased that porn has become a small but integral part of my sex life, either with a partner or when I'm biding my time between boyfriends. After all, they may come and go, but I'll always have *Hard Love in High Heels* to tide me over. It's perfect when recuperating after a breakup because you miss the hot sex but are in no state to get back out there and engage emotionally. The only remedy I know better than *Ass Masters IV* is some quality time with Mum.

I'd just spent five days with her back home in the States and loaded up on a lot of hugs, chicken soup, and relationship advice—even if I had to avert my gaze slightly when she asked to read copies of my column. We got into a rhythm: Every morning she would brew a pot of coffee strong enough to put hair on my chest, which we drank by the swimming pool where we smoked our one clandestine cigarette of the day while her pug and chihuahua danced around our feet (she has five dogs so there's always loads of action). On the third day, Sophie, Mum's fifty-pound bulldog, dived into the pool and sank like a cannonball, so I had to jump in fully clothed to save her. My bulldog *Baywatch* rescue was by far the most exciting adventure of the whole trip. Mum and I watched loads of trite Danielle Steele TV movies on Lifetime, billed as "television for women," and I slept ten hours a night, which for me is pretty unprecedented.

"I'm proud of you," she said as she dropped me off at the airport. "And you're much stronger than you know."

I love Mum, but after several days with Super Wal-Mart as my most exciting outing, I was definitely ready to get back to London, and back in the game.

Before boarding the flight—Orlando to London—my intention was to use frequent flier miles to bag an upgrade. But when I started talking to Nick, the tall, fit, Australian insurance investigator seated next to me, I decided that I could bag something better than an upgrade. I've sampled the single-serving peanuts and vodka bottles, so why not single-serving sex?

I joined the Mile High Club several years ago, during a flight to Martinique with my French boyfriend. A recent survey found that 4 percent of Londoners have flown the friendly skies in more ways than one, but I've never hooked up with a stranger, because I'm usually sandwiched between the fat guy and the screaming kid.

After Nick asked, "So do you come here often?" talk turned to work and families. Our flirtation was starting to feel like a relationship: After nine hours, I'd learned more about his life than I'd managed to find out about some of my exes in six months.

Three mini-bottles of champagne later, I was trying to think of a good way to make the first move when we hit some serious turbulence. I'm a nervous flier, so I gripped the armrest as the plane lurched through the clouds. "This is going to sound so cheesy," I said, "but I'm really scared right now. Is it okay if I hold your hand?"

"Go ahead," he said, squeezing reassuringly. "It's just a few bumps in the road, nothing to worry about."

About the time that people started crossing themselves I was petrified, vaguely nauseous, and horny as hell. So I grabbed Nick and kissed him. We made out for a full ten minutes, until the rollercoaster dips mellowed to a gentle rocking.

Fear can be a serious aphrodisiac. It has a physiological effect—thumping heart, quicker breathing, and adrenaline rush—that mimics sexual arousal. That's why terrified people often experience a parallel increase in sexual intensity, and horror movies are such a popular first date. Meeting strangers when physiologically aroused increases the chance of having romantic feelings towards them.

In the "shaky bridge study" carried out by psychologists Arthur Aron and Don Dutton in the 1970s, men who met a woman on a high, rickety bridge found the encounter sexier and more romantic than those who met her on a low, stable one. But they warned that while someone attractive becomes more so in a tense setting, the unattractive appear even less appealing.

Nick and I had bonded after the turbulence, and somewhere past Greenland we decided it was now or never. So he put a blanket over my lap, I unfastened his trousers, he slipped his hand up my dress—but every time we tried to get a bit friskier, the flight attendants came by policing the cabin. It was a bit like being high-school rebels at 37,000 feet.

Our options for going all the way were pretty limited, because a) the "fasten seatbelt" signs were on and b) the attendants hung out outside the toilets. So we held hands, and I drifted off to sleep.

By the time we'd crossed the Atlantic, Nick and I had eaten together, shared toothpaste, had a (sort of) near-death experience, and discussed childhood fears and life after death. After all the intimacy, I was starting to feel like I needed some space.

When we landed in London, he gave me his number.

"You're really nice, but… well, you live in Australia, and as you know I just got out of a relationship," I said. "Anyway, I think we'd struggle to top the drama of our first date."

"I understand," he said, helping me with my coat. "Well, it's been one hell of a ride. You are an amazing girl, Cat."

"Thanks," I said, feeling my heartache lift, if just for that moment in time. "And Nick?"

He turned around, pausing for an instant.

"Whatever happens, we'll always have Greenland."

He walked down the gangway and out of my life, though I did keep sight of him until we filtered like cattle into the passport lines; he was

EU (apparently he had a relative born in England or something), I was in the dreaded "All Other Passports" queue.

It had never occurred to me that I was in serious danger of overstaying my tourist visa until I found myself face to face with a sinister-looking sixty-something immigration officer. Her cold, lifeless blue eyes bulged slightly behind tiny gold spectacles on a chain. Under her chin she had a huge black mole with a hair protruding from the middle, and several long chin whiskers. I couldn't take my eyes off them.

"So you're here on a tourist visa then? How long have you been in the UK?"

I answered her questions honestly but could feel panic rising. I was technically only allowed to be in the country for six months in any twelve-month period, and I was flirting dangerously with the limit.

With sweat oozing out of my pores from the stale air of the flight, I focused on the mole and directed my responses to it. Did this woman look in the mirror in the morning? Had she never heard of tweezers?

"Miss Townsend? I asked if it was your intention to find permanent employment in the UK?"

"No," I said, "I'm just visiting."

She scratched her chin. The hairs bristled. "And what sort of work do you do?"

Tweezers. A razor, for Christ's sake, I wanted to say. It's not that hard. "I'm, um, a journalist."

"Who are you working for?"

"Well, no one full-time, I'm sort of freelancing right now." I realized how weak this sounded even as the words passed my lips and had flashbacks of my disastrous conversation with Patrick. Suddenly, I felt like some kind of criminal. "I'm hoping to write a book as well."

She glared down at me, and just when I thought they were going to take me into one of those interrogation rooms and put me through a full-body cavity search, she stamped my passport.

"I'm going to let you through, Miss Townsend," she said. "But before I do, I'm going to tell you that an immigration officer like myself might have serious cause to question your motives for staying in the UK next time you come through. Best to keep that in mind."

Heart racing, I swallowed, nodded, and dashed through customs.

# THIRTEEN

Though the calendar said it was the first official week of spring, London was bleak, gray, and horribly unpredictable. Or was that just me?

Ever since my split with Andrew—my second painful breakup in less than a year—I'd started to feel cursed. So I was following my mum's advice and treating the breakup as bereavement.

Apparently, I had to move through the Five Stages of Death: Denial (He'll change his mind!); followed by anger (How dare he do this to me! He'll regret it!); followed by bargaining (I'd do anything if he would just take me back...); then depression (beating pots and pans around the kitchen in time with death metal tunes—or, worse, Céline Dion!); and, finally, acceptance.

At that point, though, acceptance of death seemed somehow easier and cleaner than dealing with the aftermath of an ex. It sounds frivolous, but at least I wouldn't have to worry about running into a corpse sipping a mojito with his arms around a supermodel.

I instant-messaged Mark, whose eight-hour time difference meant that he would be at work on the trading floor in Hong Kong.

His response was: "You guys always feel that you have to learn a life lesson. Just stop obsessing over why it happened and move on. The guy was a loser. End of story."

"But to move on, I think we need to understand our behavior," I mailed back. "Otherwise, we're doomed to keep repeating the same patterns over and over again."

With Mark on the other side of the world, I called Michael and Victoria for a lunchtime summit meeting. But if I had planned on being a typical girl and digesting my entire relationship along with my miso soup, Michael stopped me overanalyzing by starting up a titillating debate about bedroom technique.

We were having this discussion at a very crowded Wagamama restaurant near Bank station. I was beginning to feel much more positive and hopeful about the future, despite my precarious visa situation.

I'm often amazed at how little men know about women's anatomies. My friends and I spend a good percentage of our lives poring over ridiculous articles in women's magazines about "How To Give The Perfect Blow Job" and "The Top Ten Things He's Thinking in Bed," and ages agonizing about whether we look better in demi-cup bras or a corset by candlelight. We dissect our blow job technique, and whether rimming should be a regular item on the sexual menu or a one off à la carte for a serious boyfriend.

Meanwhile, men seem to think that just showing up and getting hard constitutes an effort. Which is why I consider the ubiquitous availability of Viagra a blow for female sexuality, because as Victoria always says, "Just because they can get it hard doesn't mean they have the first idea what to do with it!"

"Look, I try, but it's so damned complicated," Michael said, taking a bite of his tofu/chilli noodle soup hybrid. "And would it kill you guys to give us a little guidance? Half the time, I'm flailing around down there with no idea what I'm doing, and she's moaning, so she sounds like she's getting off on it, but really, who the hell knows? She could be checking her nails."

"Women are to blame, too!" Victoria squealed. "I can understand faking as a one-off, if you're tired or whatever, but doing it on a regular basis gives the guy the idea that whatever crap technique he has is working for you."

"I totally agree with you," I said, then drained the last of my beer and smiled at a guy who was staring from the booth behind us. "Hey, Michael?" I asked shyly. "Have you ever faked an orgasm?"

I told him about a long-ago liaison with a guy who convinced me that women aren't the only fakers. We just have an easier time because of the lack of physical evidence.

It began when my date, an artist who specialized in video installations and was a brilliant conversationalist on every subject from obscure Spanish cinema to theoretical physics, suddenly turned deathly quiet when we got into bed.

I tried talking dirty and asking what he liked, but elicited only monosyllabic grunts in response. Then, after an hour and a half—right at the point when my mind started wandering to brands of soya milk at Tesco—he suddenly shouted, "Oh, God!" and stopped.

It's hard to explain, but something about his reflexes seemed a bit too voluntary. Afterwards, he immediately jumped up and ran to the loo to get rid of the condom. I gave him the benefit of the doubt that night, but after the next time I guessed that his "stealth orgasms" might have been staged for my benefit. But why?

"We do it for the same reasons as women: Usually we're drunk, too stressed or tired or whatever, or sometimes we've started to sober up and realize, to coin a horrible phrase, that we're just not that into the girl. And we suspect that she's getting sore and fed up," Michael said.

I paused. "I guess since I'm used to men worrying about coming too soon, it never really occurred to me that taking too long could be just as much of an issue. In fact, it sounds like a dream."

"It makes sense," Victoria said, taking a sip of her carrot juice and ignoring the stares of the family of four next to us. "Sometimes a guy will be going down on me and I'm thinking, 'Will you just get this over with? It's so not gonna happen,' but I don't want to hurt his feelings, so I'll do a few 'involuntary' contractions and that's the end of it. He's happy, everyone's happy."

"Involuntary?" Now Michael put his chopsticks on his plate, transfixed. "Can girls really fake the contractions?"

I rolled my eyes. "Of course. We all know how to do our Kegel exercises."

I told Michael and Victoria that the whole experience with the artist reminded me of my early days as a conscientious schoolgirl, when I lived to count the gold stars next to my name for tasks accomplished. In some ways, I guess I felt that, without positive feedback, I wasn't "woman enough" to make him come.

"I'm sure he was probably just trying to spare your feelings, in a nice way; it's nothing to do with you," Michael said. "I remember with one ex, who was gorgeous and totally amazing in bed by the way, that after I'd drunk half a bottle of Scotch and knew there was no chance, it was just easier to throw my head back, grunt, and be done with it than carry on."

"But can't girls tell?"

"Not with a condom," Michael insisted, "so long as you get rid of it without her seeing it. Or pull that whole tantric 'I orgasmed without ejaculating' line, though admittedly it's probably not going to work with a drunken one-night stand."

"I think that lying in bed is like lying on a CV: You may get away with it for a while, but it's so much worse when you get found out in the end," I told him.

"Yeah, well, you girls never know what you want. The last time a girl said, 'Tell me your fantasies,' I talked about watching her with another girl. She freaked out, then got up and left. So these days, I tend to stay quiet!"

I laughed.

"No wonder!" Victoria said. "She probably felt totally inadequate. God, you can be crass."

"To change the subject, Cat, tell us about your date with the S and M guy," Michael said.

"It's nothing, really. I just met this very hot man for a drink—a very straitlaced banker, by the way—and he keeps talking about how he wants me to spank him."

"Isn't that a bit freaky?"

"No way!" Michael said, coughing into his napkin. "There is no hotter thought than putting a gorgeous girl over my knee!"

"No, Michael, he wants *me* to spank *him*."

"Oh, well, that could be hot, too. Though I must confess that I'm not really into pain."

Victoria signaled for the bill. "Are you going to do it?"

"I think the power play element could be interesting. The only problem is that he's clearly done this before, probably with professionals, and it involves a serious level of organization. I have to go shopping this afternoon for supplies. What do you guys think: cane, ruler, or paddle?"

# FOURTEEN

When I was younger, picking up a man in a bar for a one-night stand was like sucking down half a box of Krispy Kreme doughnuts at 4 a.m.—satisfying at the time, but liable to leave me with a slightly sick and guilty feeling afterwards.

These days, I relish every second of my encounters: the good, the bad, and the bizarre. Women who engage in casual couplings are often accused of "acting like men." But if men can get their chests waxed and be "in touch with their feminine sides," I see nothing wrong with aspiring to emulate them in some respects. After all, my male pals can shag on the first date without regret—hell, they are lauded for it. So why shouldn't I?

From David's shy, affectionate nature, I'd expected that ordinary vanilla sex—not BDSM—might be on the menu. But on our first date, I teasingly bit his ear when we kissed in the taxi, and it quickly became clear that the more I clamped down, the more excited he got. By the time we made it back to my flat, he was begging me to break out the bullwhip. So I ended up going upstairs alone.

I'm really a submissive at heart, so I've always found dominating a partner a bit difficult. A couple of years earlier I had a boyfriend who asked me to use nipple clamps on him. I was so panicked about hurting him that I couldn't relax. Instead he asked me to spank him, but we were pretty drunk and I ended up using the only implement I could find—a kitchen spatula. It wasn't exactly *9 1/2 Weeks*.

But the ultimate aphrodisiac for me is making someone's fantasy come true. Guys usually ask to spank me, which is why I've spent more than one evening donning a "naughty schoolgirl" kit. Though it's always fun at the time, I would pick a tongue-lashing over a riding-crop-lashing any day.

Still, I was intrigued by the prospect of unleashing my dormant dominatrix. So I headed to an underground boutique in Covent Garden.

The salesgirl showed me an acrylic ruler that promised "more bite than bark for a stinging spanking" and a rubber tassel-whip. A bit daunted, I decided to stick with the wooden paddle I had unearthed from an unused "Spank Me Santa" kit someone sent me last Christmas. "You may also want some aloe vera gel, in case you break skin," she told me.

I was so far outside my comfort zone that I decided to role-play with a different persona to make the transition easier. David is a public-school boy, so I became the stern headmistress disciplining an unruly pupil. We met on the top floor of a bar with a panoramic view of the City, and I wore a black power suit rather than my usual jeans and sexy top. He could barely contain himself as he paid the bill, but I would not let him touch me—yet.

Back at his flat, I tried not to giggle as I put a thirty-eight-year-old professional over my knee. I started out gently, and began to administer some discipline. At first, I kept nervously asking, "Harder? Faster?" I repeated the spanking mantra with a Jedi-mindset intensity: "Build-up is essential. Starting out too rough right away can quickly wear out your bottom."

He started to writhe and redden, so I picked up the pace—and the paddle. I realized how thrilling it was to find the key to his sexuality that made him lose all inhibition. As it was his birthday, I made him count down from thirty-eight. "But if you miss one, I'll have to start all over," I warned. He slipped up twice—on purpose.

In the end, I relished the feeling of being completely in control. So when he asked me if I would mind caning him next time, I told him I was game. In fact, I was rather enjoying my dalliance as a dominatrix. Maybe next time I could order him to clean my flat afterwards.

When I told Victoria about my spanking session, she told me that I needed to find a man who challenged me.

"Hey, David was a challenge. Do you know how difficult it is to balance a fifteen-stone man on your knee?"

"I mean challenges you mentally, not just physically."

"Well, I don't know where I'm going to meet him. I just read that 30 percent of people meet their partners through work, and I work from home, so unless I start a torrid affair with the pizza delivery guy I thought I'd better branch out."

Victoria responded by begging me to go as her "date" to a black-tie dinner thrown by a friend of her company's CEO. She was helping organize the guest list and had managed to wangle a place at the table for me, though I think the gratis press passes were really meant for journalists who write about finance rather than fetishes.

I picked up Victoria at her office in Knightsbridge en route to the Park Lane Hotel.

"Wow," Victoria said when she saw the pink and white lace fifties-style vintage prom dress I'd bought at a cheap outlet store in the States. "You look very angelic."

"Yeah, well, we both know that it's an illusion. You look very chic and elegant, while I look like the top of a wedding cake!"

"Don't be ridiculous," she said. "Anyway, I have a surprise for you." She opened her gold clutch to reveal our place cards, our names embossed in an elaborate silver sans serif font.

"What are you doing with those?"

"I'm doing a switch, and putting us next to Grant—"

My heart lurched. I was in awe of Grant, who had a medical degree and also ran a hedge fund, which he used to sponsor charity medical groups in Africa. He was about my height, solidly built, with dark hair whose immaculate coiffure I'd always found a bit suspicious.

Nevertheless, I'd been secretly Googling him for months, ever since I'd read a piece about the rise of green capitalism, which described how to pay for children's face transplants with corporate profits. He was engaged to a "stylist" (Grant used his connections to get his celeb friends to use her) who constantly antagonized Victoria at her job in fashion PR.

"We can't!" I hissed. "We'll get caught."

"Don't worry, darling. It's just like walking up to a nightclub; it's the people with confidence who breeze past the doormen. We'll fake it, no one's going to say anything."

"What about his date? Don't you think she might get a bit suspicious?"

"She's horrible! That woman is constantly coming into the office to borrow free clothes and treats everyone there like shit. She tells everyone that she's a size 0 and was so freaked out about us coming back there with fours and sixes that my boss made us cut the labels out of the back. I hate her. So, I want you to flirt with him and make her life hell. If you get him away from her, maybe she'll get away from me."

Now I knew why Victoria wanted me as an ally in lieu of Michael.

He would not have been able to see past the stylist's flirtation, whereas I would be Victoria's ally against her barbed remarks. Women are much more calculating in their turn of phrase, and can transform a seeming compliment into a verbal acid burn for the recipient. I had heard that this woman was a nightmare from other sources too, and figured that anyone who referred to herself as "a socialite" would probably be pretty obnoxious. Still, I was determined to try to be friends.

I could feel my palms sweating as we weaved our way through the champagne reception to the table. Victoria accidentally-on-purpose dropped a napkin and pretended to rearrange it while slyly swapping the place-names.

I hate banquet dinners because I always wonder how long the food has been sitting out. No matter how posh my surroundings, it makes me think of the post-church brunch at Denny's in Florida, where massively corpulent women would load their plates with waffles the size of serving platters coated in runny strawberry-flavored corn syrup.

Besides, I like my meat raw. That's not a euphemism; I'm a steak-tartare-eating chick who is as ravenous a carnivore in the kitchen as in the bedroom. The food at these functions is always lukewarm and slightly overcooked, with no nod to adventurous palates.

We sat down and started chatting to the three other couples at our table, including Grant and his business partner, a German guy wearing an expensive-looking gray silk suit in lieu of a tux.

I struck up a conversation with Grant during the appetizers, and was thrilled to discover that he liked my column. "I always read the *Indy* for the environmental coverage, and I think your columns are hilarious," he said, pouring me another glass of sauvignon blanc. "But what happens when you meet Mr. Right and settle down? Will you stop writing?"

I attempted to cut into my steak, but the knife made no progress. "Actually, I think that having someone I was that crazy about would be an adventure of a different kind," I said, smiling.

"Are you planning on evolving your writing into anything else?" His fiancée, her face somehow hard despite the aquiline nose and perfect blonde up-do, raised one eyebrow. At least she tried, but her lack of expression made me suspect her forehead had been Botoxed into submission. "I mean, I'm sure that chick lit stuff sells, but it's not exactly Hemingway, is it?"

Suddenly furious, I felt myself flushing. "Look, I'm not claiming to be a literary great," I said, "but it is slightly annoying that if a man writes a book about feeling alienated or unsure about relationships and his place in the world, it's automatically really deep and everything is suddenly a metaphor. When a woman writes about depression, people are like, 'Get that bitch some Prozac! She's probably just got PMS!' At the very least, I hope that people get a good laugh."

Grant laughed. "I think I'm going to be very bad and go for a cigarette," he said as the waiters cleared our main course plates. "Does anyone else want one?"

"I'll have one," I said, raising an eyebrow.

"No, thank you! Those are disgusting, and I don't want to get wrinkles." His fiancée crossed her arms over her chest.

"No danger of that," Victoria whispered in my ear. "Her face is shot so full of toxins that she looks like a stroke victim!"

I laughed, which I disguised as a cough, and followed Grant and the German.

"I have a confession to make," I said to Grant as we went to the outer bar, which allowed smoking. "I loved the idea of the sea as the metaphor for life in *The Old Man and the Sea*. I really, really wanted to like it because I think that Hemingway is a great writer. So I told everyone I did. But secretly? I was thinking, I am so bored, when is this guy going to get out of the goddamned boat already?"

"I suppose that's the difference between women and men," he said. "For us it's about the journey, not the end result. About living outside your comfort zone, and taking chances."

"Well, Hemingway and I are definitely on the same page there," I said, reaching for one of Grant's Marlboro Lights. "Lately, I feel like I'm in a canoe in the ocean with no life jacket."

"Wait, you have to try one of these." The German guy was offering me a miniature cigar.

"No thanks," I said, "I don't really like the taste of cigars."

"No, seriously, these are different, they taste like clove cigarettes," he said, passing me one. "Why don't you light it, and if you don't like it I'll take it back."

"Well, okay," I said, as Grant turned to speak to someone we'd seen inside—I think she was a writer for the *Daily Mail*.

While their backs were turned, I dipped my head down towards the candle. Suddenly, I heard a crackling sound and saw a flash of orange light in front of my eyes.

"Is something burning?" the woman next to me at the bar asked her companion. At that moment, I saw a thin wisp of smoke emanating from my singed hair. I smoothed the burning strand flat against my forehead with my palm, raced past Grant and the German, who was now hitting on a tall blonde, and swiftly announced, "I'm going to the loo."

Panicking, I patted my hair down, and it wasn't until I was standing in front of the mirrors that I realized that the front section of my hair was blackened and crispy. At that moment, I saw Victoria approaching in the full-length mirror behind me.

"Oh, my God," she said, covering her mouth with her hand. "What happened to you?"

"How bad is it?" I said, my voice breaking. I smoothed the front section, but the charred ends broke off neatly.

"Calm down, honey! Look, if we move the parting a bit…" She ran her hands through my hair, which by now was sticking straight up.

"I can't believe it! And we were getting along so well. Now I'm going to have to sneak out through the back door," I wailed.

"No way. Look, we can fix this," she said, whipping out a pair of manicure scissors from the bottom of her handbag. "Okay, so we just have to cut out the burned part," she said, gently snipping the frazzled ends. "Then find something to calm it down a bit…" She pumped a bit of liquid soap out of the dispenser and used it as hair gel. "And we need to improvise. Voilà!"

I looked at myself, at the front clump of sticky, burned hair that she had somehow managed to freeze into place behind my ear. I looked like a porcupine in an evening gown.

"Now," she said, "we're going back out there. You have to talk to Grant."

"I don't date taken men." Even if he did seem perfect on paper.

"But she insulted your book!"

"He's still taken, and I've definitely learned my lesson there," I said, fluffing the back of my hair and hoping that I didn't smell like burned rubber. "Besides, I don't believe in cat-fighting unless it's carefully supervised in Jell-O and/or mud. If he likes someone like her, he's clearly not the guy for me."

# FIFTEEN

Cut it." I laughed, sinking down into my trendy, new east London hairdresser's chair. "But nothing too drastic—if I end up with a mullet, I'll really be depressed."

After two days of hiding in a head-scarf, my gelled hair looked like a Barbie doll's plastic mane that someone had cut through with a hacksaw. Anyway, my singed locks were the perfect excuse: I'd had the breakup, now it was time for the break-over.

In any case, being newly single is one of the few times when it's socially acceptable to revel in complete narcissism. I especially needed a pick-me-up after getting loads of hate mail in response to that week's column, about breaking up with a hairdresser. One missive in particular really got through to me. I knew it was obviously written by someone who a) did not understand ironic comedy or b) did not believe that articles about genocide and glitter nail polish could coexist inside the same newspaper, but still—this time, it was personal.

*Oh dear! I've just read your article in Thursday's* Independent.
*I hope to God that me and you never meet. How can someone*

*use more than 500 words about THEIR HAIR when there are millions of people dying of STARVATION, GENOCIDE, and easily curable DISEASES? You are a SHALLOW, VAIN, MATERIALISTIC, HORRIBLE, STUPID little girl.*

*I can't believe you even have the sheer audacity to put your name, PHOTOGRAPH, and contact details to such a disgusting piece of writing. I am sure anyone with any shred of MORAL DECENCY will be equally repulsed.*

*I hope your mother is proud!*

Another irate reader wrote: "If I wanted to read about the sexual conquests of a filthy gutter whore, I would visit a backstreet in Soho. You obviously have no morals."

The piece that caused such outrage?

*After months of being secretly dissatisfied with my hairdresser, Sam, I've found someone else who knows just how to touch me. But when I'm with her, I feel like I'm cheating on a lover. Sam has helped me through a lot of scrapes. My hair was in a fragile state when I first came to him wearing a knit cap. A disastrous, drunken DIY dye session had resulted in my hair turning a green-black hue, and I was practically in tears.*

*"Don't worry," he said with authority. "We're going to fix this, even if it takes all night." I plopped into a chair and put my hair, the symbol of my femininity, into his hands. Four hours and a few hundred pounds later, I walked out with my natural medium-brown hue blow dried to a glossy shine.*

*Since then, Sam has become my friend and confidant. And since I tend to change hair color as often as men, our relationship has outlasted several of my boyfriends.*

*But one night, after loads of red hair dye (I was going for a Rita Hayworth look) and even more red wine at the restaurant next door, we ended up in bed. It turned out that the chemistry between us was much better in the shampoo bowl than the bedroom. And although our friendship has remained intact, Sam seemed rushed the next time I came in for a trim, and failed to lavish his usual care and attention on my irregular cowlicks. On another visit, he gave me so many layers in the back that I practically had a mullet. So I've started playing away.*

*Was it worth it? I was hooked the first time I felt the cold pressure of my new stylist's scissors on my neck. I emerged with long layers and a perfect fringe, and felt sexier than I have in a long time.*

*With so many crises in the world today, it seems crazy that a few strands of keratin can wield such power over me. But, with the exception of the musk ox, humans are the only mammals with almost continuously growing hair (scientists point to grooming rituals in primates as evidence that something in our very DNA compels us to coif) so maybe it's okay that I'm a little obsessive over my locks.*

*I hadn't had the heart to tell Sam that I'd found someone new. I managed to stall for a couple of months by using the old "you were on holiday" and "it was only a few highlights!" lines when he called. But the final straw came this week, when I ran into him at a bar near his Soho salon.*

*"You've been avoiding me," he said gently.*

*I decided to come clean. "You know that I loved the way you did my hair, but I just decided that I needed a bit of a change," I said, looking him in the eye. "I felt weird about it, but I hope that we can still be friends."*

*He laughed and bought me a drink. "This new cut really suits you, Cat," he said. "But I bet you'll be back eventually." He could be right. But for now, the hair wants what it wants.*

So in addition to my sexy new come-hither fringe that fell over one eye, my narcissism had extended to a Brazilian wax, manicure, pedicure, some type of aluminium body wrap at Bliss spa that made me feel like a Christmas turkey, and a gold corset that cost more than my rent—all guilt-free.

The next step in the recovery process was to embark on a dating detox. I had to quit cold turkey; so I deleted Andrew's phone number, email address, and photos from my inbox, erasing all my hopes for our future along with him. I still wanted to be friends in future, but I wasn't ready yet. I'd also decided that, in the meantime, all men would be referred to in code names, because I didn't want the commitment of learning surnames and backstories. I just wanted to have some fun.

"Keep an open mind, and don't rule anything out," Victoria said. "When one door closes, another always opens."

In the spirit of detoxing my dating and moving on to enjoy myself, I arranged a night out at Soho House with Amy and Victoria, where we fell to discussing our worst sex ever. On this one I usually side with Woody Allen, who said, "Sex without love is an empty experience, but as empty experiences go it's one of the best." Besides, bad sex tales are great fodder for my column, since the most cringe-inducing encounters often make the best stories. I had many contenders (the guy who accidentally gave me a black eye during a fellatio-induced muscle spasm springs to mind), but all in all the worst sex award went to a man I had met recently online.

We met up twice, and though he was cute and affable, I didn't see any long-term potential. And yet, somehow we ended up sleeping together, after too much Jack Daniel's. At first it was a perfectly pleasant experience—the assembly-line, pre-packaged, fast-food version of a one-night stand.

Except that... I've always found aural sex a huge turn on, from the initial make-out moans to the screaming-while-hitting-the-headboard finale. But the next time I urge a lover to "talk dirty to me," I'm going to be careful what I wish for. Despite being witty and articulate by day, Jonathan was stone-cold silent in bed. He was so quiet that I could hear the traffic outside, and in the run-up to orgasm he reminded me of a lion stalking an antelope on the African plains. His idea of talking dirty was telling me he had a penis.

So, in an attempt to spice things up before our next time, I told him in explicit detail exactly what I wanted to do to him. I even downloaded an adult podcast to his iPod—the noughties version of a cheesy 1980s phone-sex line—for some inspiration. Our second date, over candlelight and a bottle of Bordeaux at a French restaurant, was more sexually charged than ever. I got so turned on listening to him tell me during dinner what he had planned for later that he got me to slip my knickers off and hand them to him under the table.

My master plan worked brilliantly—in fact, maybe a bit too well. Jonathan went from eerie silence to never shutting up. His monotone play-by-play accounts of our sexual encounters became so detailed that I felt like I was listening to a football-match commentary. "I'm caressing your right breast, now I'm touching your right nipple... I'm going to score in a minute, baby!"

"That's awful!" Victoria cried, shaking with laughter.

"Yeah, it was," I said, blushing and hiding behind my napkin. "But then it got so much worse."

Although I'm a huge fan of filthy banter, his stream-of-consciousness rants were turning into a serious passion-killer. However, he was clearly making such an effort that I didn't want to hurt his feelings. But the final straw came when mild-mannered Jonathan shouted mid-coitus: "Who's your daddy, bitch?" By then, the only involuntary muscle spasms I had were from laughter.

"But the worst happened when he was behind me, grinding away, and then…" I cringed. "You know how I told you he was a bit pissed off when he discovered that I speak fluent French and he doesn't, even though he lived there for, like, three years?"

"Yeah?" Victoria said, raising one eyebrow.

"Right, so he started talking dirty in really bad, heavily accented French, and starts going, I swear to God, '*J'aime votre chat*' over and over!"

Amy covered her mouth. "Oh. My. God. That is mortifying. So what did you say, Cat?"

"Well, I tried to ignore him, but he just kept repeating it, so finally I turned around, sat on the bed, and said, 'Look, dude, if you are going to insist on talking dirty in French there are a couple of things you should probably learn. First of all, since you are, after all, fucking me you can probably use the familiar *tu* form. Second, you are saying "I love your cat," masculine, not "I love your pussy," the feminine form.'"

They both cracked up. "What happened then?"

"Then he started this long conversation and told me that I had intimacy problems, which he could be right about. Anyway, that was the last time I saw him."

Amy took my hand. "You do not have intimacy problems. You certainly didn't have any problems committing when someone you adored came along. And look how close we all are!" She reached over and gave me a half hug.

"I just wish I could meet someone I really like—who doesn't have any complications," I added.

"Meeting someone and having a relationship won't solve your problems, Cat," Amy said gently. "You know my guy has a six-year-old and an ex-wife, so even if you are madly in love with someone it has its ups and downs. It's easy to think that once we find a 'soulmate' all our problems will disappear, but it's just not true."

I knew that she was right—she's always been the most measured of all of my friends, with loads of common sense. She's always telling me that there's no winner or loser in a given situation, while Victoria is much more competitive.

"Yeah," Victoria grumbled. "I would never have thought this time last year that I would seriously be considering moving in with a boyfriend—into a house in the country, no less, with cats!"

"You're moving into a house in the country?" Amy said.

"You're getting cats?" I screeched. I was thrilled for her, and not that surprised that after careful deliberation she had decided to take her relationship with Mike to the next level. Still, I couldn't help feeling that everyone around me was coupling up, and saw settling down as the natural progression of things. But to me, it felt like the end of an era. Despite our rodent problems, I'd gotten very used to living with a partner in crime.

Thinking back on past New York flatmates, I despaired at the thought of sharing with strangers. It rarely worked out well. There was the Korean roomie at university who moved her non-English-speaking mother in with us after a month. She cooked Korean food constantly, so the smell of kimchi permeated all my clothing. As one then-boyfriend put it, "Boiled cabbage is so not sexy." There was the flatmate who found religion and would be leading Bible study groups when I came home from Saturday night dates, and the guy whose regular "dates" all turned out to be hookers. I dreaded having another one.

At the end of the evening, with Victoria going back to Mike's and Amy going home to her man, I toyed with the idea of ringing Jonathan. Despite our cringe-worthy encounter I could feel a bout of late-night insomnia coming on, which sparked a craving for misadventure. But I figured that it was either a night in bed with him or scarfing down the half jar of Nutella resident in our cabinet while watching old *Simpsons* episodes. *The Simpsons* won. They have way better one-liners.

# SIXTEEN

Twenty minutes after cracking one glitter-eye-shadow-encrusted eye open, I was waiting in line at Starbucks, eyeing the Classic Coffee Cake and its 630 calories and 10 grams of saturated fat.

I knew these amounts because I once had an interview with Gwyneth Paltrow's macrobiotic nutritionist. For my background research, he gave me a fact sheet that contained the calorie count of every dessert containing sugar, thus ensuring that he destroyed every ounce of pleasure that I would ever get out of eating them.

My Starbucks habit is a symbol of my life: I know that if I want to save loads of money in a year, the way forward is to forgo my daily soy latte and drink instant coffee from a Thermos. After a year of sacrifice, I could save more than a grand.

And yet I'm a sucker for instant gratification. In the same way that perfumers cleanse their olfactory palates between scents by smelling coffee beans, each new encounter in Starbucks provides a clean slate to the disastrous night before—a chance to start a new day.

But there's another reason why Starbucks makes me nostalgic: Every major moment of my life has happened while I was sipping a cup of coffee. Starting with the first time I ever drank a cup, at my aunt's house, the autumn that my entire family imploded.

My aunt and my mum are incredibly close, so our families always celebrated the holidays together in one big boisterous group.

Until Uncle Will didn't show up for Thanksgiving dinner one year. I remember how my mum raised her eyebrows when he called from the road, where he was supposedly "driving around the back roads, lost in a bunch of trees." Of course, the only topiary he encountered that day was the pubic mound of May, the town's blondest—and most surgically enhanced—aerobics instructor.

Three days later, he told my aunt that he was leaving. And she lost it. After hurling his stuff on the lawn, much to the bemusement of neighbors, she became catatonic. Her days were spent hanging around the house in her tracksuit watching old VHS movies of family vacations and her wedding. It was scarier than any horror movie.

When the tape ran out, her favorite pastime was to drag each and every member of the family one by one into her living room, where she would insist that we "have coffee and talk." When even my seven-year-old sister ran out kicking and screaming after my aunt asked her to look at her breasts to "feel and compare" them to May's, she realized that she had to find another innocent victim for her vitriolic tirades. In this case, it was the saleswoman behind the counter at Macy's department store.

We were in the Atlanta mall, and she was—for the fourth time that month—returning a dress, still with its tags on, that she had already worn once. She didn't need it, she told me, because she had already bought one in every color.

Most people get counseling, but my aunt relied on retail therapy.

Normally she picked a twenty-something, gum-cracking sales associate who would prove to be an easy target. But today, the only person behind the counter was the manager, who had her black hair pulled back into a severe bun that made her eyes bulge slightly. "I'm sorry, miss," the beehive brunette told her, "but we cannot accept returns after seven days—it's store policy."

"I don't believe that you understand," my aunt said, spittle flying from her mouth as her voice broke. "I purchased the dress to attend a *function*. The *function*"—every time she said the word her immaculately manicured hand slammed on the countertop, which I watched in horror—"was a party for my twentieth wedding anniversary when all of my family and friends would celebrate our *beautiful* and *sacred* union."

People pulling items from shelves hesitated slightly, watching peripherally while pretending to examine scented candles a few aisles over.

"Miss, I'm sorry but I really don't have any—"

"But I'm not going to be going to any party, because my shitbag husband ran off with that silicone-tit whore!"

I twisted away from her as a scented candle clattered to the floor.

Ten minutes later we walked out, cash in hand. She was smiling and humming Neil Diamond show tunes.

"Do you want to go get some ice cream?" she asked brightly as we went into her house. Despite her sartorial victory, Uncle Will had left her with no job, no money, and three children to raise on her own. He had become that middle-aged cliché, the guy zooming around in a red sports car wearing suspiciously tight tank tops, saying things like, "You know you guys are the most important things in the world to me, right?" while screeching his tires in a desperate attempt to get them back to Mum's.

I remember looking at the photos of their happy family on the shelves, and thinking how unfair life was. All the vows they took and the steps she took to add to their family should have strengthened her position, but really the kids and house were open flanks that left her vulnerable. She put too much faith in someone else, and she got screwed.

When I got home, I poured myself a glass of milk and asked my mum if my aunt and Uncle Will's fate could ever happen to us.

"No, darling," she said, hugging me. "We're a family, and we're all in this together!"

Less than two months later, my dad walked out. He never came back.

My mum and happy families were on my mind when Victoria and I met at a leaving do for a colleague in her office, which, this being London, translated into "get raging drunk and stick your tongue down the throat of that guy from accounting."

I wasn't complaining. After suffering the masochistic Manhattan CV-swap that passes for a dinner date, dating in London is like being a kid in a candy store. On some level, even the mishaps feel like permanent vacation.

"Bella is leaving to become a novelist," Victoria told me, severing an olive from her martini toothpick. "Have you seen the book?" She handed me the paperback, its cover an illustration of a woman in a lab coat and an Indiana Jones caricature guy wearing a hat and khakis.

Looking for the dirty bits, I flipped through to a pivotal scene near the end.

*Kate had been waiting for this moment since two months ago, when cut-throat negotiator Brad Stone first walked into her offices at the Chicago gorilla sanctuary. Despite his strapping build and matinee-idol looks, Brad's brusque manner had alienated everyone in her office. But it was his idea to pitch the documentary to the television production company, which, even Kate had to admit, would generate enough revenue to last until the next decade. Now the two black gorillas, Coco and Harold, could be released into the wilds of Kenya. Brad had saved the sanctuary.*

*Standing in her robe and looking up into his gray eyes, Kate felt that it was her own heart that was being set free. Because the tough business executive who left a trail of broken hearts behind him had taught the gorillas sign language—and she was melting.*

*"Harold signed 'I love you' this morning," she whispered.*

*"He's not the only one," Brad growled as her robe slipped to the floor.*

I burst out laughing.

"So, what do you think of our budding novelist? Pretty impressive, huh?"

"It's terrific, I'm really happy for her," I said sincerely.

Victoria and I made our way toward the open bar and downed several Love Bird Specials (some pink concoction heavy on the Cointreau) while discussing how women's emotional expectations are raised to unrealistic levels by a diet of romance novels.

"You know what I think?" I slurred, as Victoria made frantic throat-cutting motions with her hand. "I think Kate should save herself a lot of time. I can give her the real ending right—" I hiccuped, "right now. She'll give up her promising career as a researcher to stay at home and have Brad's children, at his insistence—then boom! The end of Brad and Kate." I failed to notice that Bella, the author, was standing right next to us.

Victoria took me by the arm. "Ha, ha, you're so funny. I'm sure she's just kidding," she said, leading me out.

"Give Brad five years," I said. "I'll bet he won't even pay child support!"

When I got home, I continued my tirade against Bella's protagonist.

"Let me save you some time, Kate," I said, pouring myself a shot of vodka and sinking on to the sofa. "Brad was obsessed with you because you resisted him. But give it a few years and a few kids, and suddenly he won't recognize you as the spunky career girl you were before you had his children and took responsibility around the house. He'll start telling you that you've changed, and that you two have 'grown apart.' That's right about when he'll start screwing the twenty-three-year-old biologist in his lab—because she reminds him of how you used to be. But it won't be his fault, he'll blame you for it! Why don't you just save yourself a lot of time and get out now?"

I realized then that I'd been talking to fictional characters much more than real ones lately, as Victoria brewed us a cup of tea.

"You have to stop worrying so much about the future that you sabotage the present," she said. "You have to trust yourself."

"I have absolute faith in myself," I said to her, "it's just men I'm not so sure about."

# SEVENTEEN

A few days later, I had an emergency drinking session with Victoria and Mark at our flat. Apparently, when I moved to London, my hasty relationship with Patrick wasn't the only thing I neglected to think through. There was also the pesky matter of getting a work visa. Which, as it turned out, is extraordinarily complicated for someone in a competitive profession.

"Right. We need to think outside the box and come up with a strategy," Victoria said as she poured me another shot of vodka and handed me a sugar-crusted lemon wedge for my favorite, a lemon drop shot. "Most of my friends who have moved here either have a grandparent or parent born here, or they already had their jobs when they moved over," she said, patting my hand. "I've asked around."

Mark was less sympathetic. "Didn't you think about this before you moved?" he asked, putting his head in his hands. "I can't believe you could be this impulsive."

I stared at him, saying nothing.

"Okay, so I can believe you're that impulsive," he said. "Go through your options again."

I sighed and told him about my research. I didn't have a contract, and being freelance didn't give me any right to stay in the country. Normally, when a company in the UK wants to hire a foreigner, they do all the paperwork and you get a four-year work visa. But a lot of companies don't want the bother—and expense—of sponsoring an alien unless they have to because they have to jump through so many hoops.

There's something called the Highly Skilled Migrant Program, but you have to earn points on a system, and it helps to have an MBA or earn lots of money, neither of which applied to me. I'm not a native of a Commonwealth country, so couldn't do the working holidaymaker visa.

Between shots, Victoria and I Googled the list of skills in demand, and my heart sank. If I were a nurse or IT specialist, I wouldn't have a problem. But journalists were a dime a dozen. "Let's see if you could fit into any of these skill sets," Victoria slurred, scrolling down. "Hmm, structural bridge engineer? Geoscientist? I don't see any openings for sex writer. I don't suppose you could pretend to be a surgical dentist?"

"Let's face it," I told her, "I'm screwed."

"So you've done everything so far in the wrong order," Mark said, pouring me more vodka, this time into a tumbler. "You know, Cat, there is another way."

"What do you mean?"

"Well, we have a pre-existing relationship, of sorts. My mum is English and I was born here, so you know I have a British passport as well as an Australian one . . ."

"Oh no," I said, shaking my head, anticipating what he was about to say.

"I'll marry you."

Despite myself, I was seriously touched and felt tears welling up. "You're not serious." I stared at him, and our eyes locked. "You would do that for me?"

He shrugged. "Why not? You're one of my best friends and you need help. I bet you would do the same for me."

I started to cry. "But what if you meet someone you want to marry?"

"Well, I'm figuring that with my track record, anything that could help me dodge the marriage bullet for a couple more years may be a blessing in disguise."

I reached across the table and took his hand. "But it's such a big deal—and you wouldn't get anything out of it," I said.

"I think it's a great idea!" Victoria said, handing me a tissue. "The way I see it, you guys spend most of your time a continent apart, rarely have sex, and fight like cat and dog. It's a match made in heaven!"

"This is serious, Mark," I told him. "It means that you couldn't marry anyone for the next couple of years. And how do I explain this to a guy I'm dating? 'Hey, baby, I'd love to go out with you. Oh, by the way. I have a husband'? They'll freak out!"

"Think about it," he said, grabbing a bread roll. "If you decide to go down that road, I'll be there for you. I'm serious. It's me or the guy with the foot fetish, right?"

"We've only been out a couple of times, and frankly it's getting a bit tedious," I said. "It's not that I mind indulging a fetish once in a while, but he's obsessed with my feet. We were watching a movie last night and he asked if he could massage them, which I'm fine with, but then he started sucking my toes."

"That's disgusting!" Victoria said. "Still, I wouldn't mind a bit of maintenance. Can he do pedicures?'

We all laughed, breaking the serious mood and allowing me a breather from thinking about Mark's offer. I was still reeling, and unsteady and emotional from all the booze.

"Okay, you guys, I'm hitting the sack," I told them.

I didn't sleep much because I kept tossing and turning. On the one hand, tying the knot would solve all my visa problems in one fell swoop. On the other hand, what if I wanted to get married in a church ceremony later? If I met Mr. Right, I would have to tell him honestly that I was a divorcee. Even booking a ceremony with Mark and facing all the well-wishers made my stomach turn, because I would feel like such a fraud.

But I had to admit that Mark was by far the best candidate. He was my friend, there was no unexplored sexual tension, and on the off chance that we ended up having to live together, at least I wouldn't catch him at 2 a.m. sniffing at my insoles.

# EIGHTEEN

I wondered if Victoria and Mark had a point: The other evening when we discussed my work visa problem, they both agreed that it was difficult to see where my professional life ended and my personal life began. I was picking dates based on their relative degree of weirdness, like the trader with the foot fetish. Was I attracted to him, or seeking anecdotes for my column? I loved my work, but the lines were becoming blurred.

The trader and I emailed for weeks before our first meeting, when I asked him about the genesis of his particular fixation. He explained that his obsession started at the age of ten, when he saw his fit teenage babysitter painting her toenails with her legs up on the coffee table while wearing a short skirt.

"I think that a woman's feet are the hottest things in the world," he said on our second date, shyly rubbing my calf. "How would you feel about me sucking your toes?"

Later that night, I watched in fascination as he tried to fit my entire foot into his mouth. Never one to shy away from a bit of adventure, I got a very pricey pedicure the next day. I have always prided myself on my open-mindedness when it comes to sex: With past boyfriends, I have learned to avoid accidental candle-wax burns, perfected the art of tying a square knot, and squeezed into a seriously uncomfortable white PVC nurse's uniform.

The trader and I headed off to Selfridges, where he watched me try on seven pairs of shoes before I picked out some red glitter Gina peep-toe stilettos. My palms were sweating at the thought of spending more than £200 on shoes. But I handed over my credit card.

And, for a couple of weeks, I was in heaven. I loved the idea that I was fulfilling his deepest fantasies, he seemed to adore me, and he gave a mean foot massage. But it wasn't long before I started to wonder if his obsession with my size eights was eclipsing everything else in our relationship. He couldn't get aroused unless he was in direct contact with my feet, and my sex drive was shrinking at the same rate as my shoe collection was expanding. Hot sex took a backseat to hot baths, with him wielding a pumice.

Our stormy relationship ended—literally and figuratively—after a fight in a bar when he told me that he had sucked another girl's toes at a fetish party. I ditched the strappy sandals, tended to my blisters, and lived in flip-flops for weeks. It was probably for the best, since the constant pressure to perform was getting pretty exhausting and I had found myself uttering the phrase: "Were her arches higher than mine?"

I remember running out in the rain after our fight, catching my Christian Dior stiletto boot heel in a street grate and realizing that my relationship, and my shoe collection, were both broken.

So it seems that there is someone for everyone. After that, I was hunting for a guy whose sexual tastes were a bit more in line with mine. But I definitely gained a lot from the experience—and I'll always have the trader to thank for expanding my killer shoe collection.

Awhile after my row with the trader, I got a call from Victoria telling me that Grant was in her office talking to her boss. "I asked him when the big day was, and he told me that they've broken up!" she squealed. "Get down here now!"

I remembered back in high school when we used to do "drive-bys," cruising past the object of our affection's home while pretending to be out shopping. So I decided to orchestrate a "walk-by" in the downstairs lobby of Victoria's building. I bought a soy latte and took my laptop, perching myself outside Starbucks between the elevator and the front door.

With my glasses on, laptop humming, and papers artfully disheveled, I crossed my legs and waited for him as Victoria texted that he was coming down. But five minutes passed, then ten, and I never saw him. I was packing up my laptop when I spotted him—already out the door and about to cross Sloane Street. The lights were changing, so I raced after him.

I tried to follow him discreetly while crossing the street, but my new haircut meant that I couldn't see a damned thing and ended up crashing into him—and splashing coffee on his very expensive-looking suit.

Fortunately, we laughed about it, and he casually mentioned that he'd broken up with his girlfriend since we last met, which I took as a very good sign. Then he invited me to a swanky summer party at the Orangerie in a few weeks' time.

I told him about my heartbreak, and the freaks I'd been dating since. He stepped closer and looked down at me. "If that guy didn't see that you were a once-in-a-lifetime catch, I would forget about him," he said.

My hands started to shake, and I blurted out, "Yeah, um, see you at the party," before jumping into a cab—headed the wrong way. I could only hope that I'd be kicking the giraffe cuddly toy currently sharing my bed to the floor very soon.

In the meantime, I had an assignment to undertake: Writing about "nonsexual" male escorts.

When I went online and started browsing the listings, my eyes settled on Adam. Online he looked gorgeous, and claimed to be well over six feet tall. It turned out that the "nonsexual" escort agency Adam was registered with had thousands of clients on the books and, not surprisingly, about 90 percent were career women. The owner assured me that they had a rigorous vetting procedure for all escorts, including references and career background checks. "There's no legislation in the UK for agencies, and the majority sell sex," he told me. "Our escorts use their real names, give you their mobile numbers, and meet you at a public place."

I did a bit of Internet research and found out that my "date" had been working part-time as an escort for a year on top of his day job as a consultant, and averaged two outings per week. He charged £65 an hour, with a three-hour minimum.

But I've had enough blind-date horror stories to last me a lifetime, and I couldn't shift the image of a gold-chained gigolo from my mind. My palms were clammy as I entered the restaurant to meet Adam. I had no doubt he could handle work functions, but could he convince one of my closest friends over lunch that we were a loved-up couple? I was starting to panic.

When I saw him, I was genuinely shocked because he was so gorgeous. Adam was tall, with broad shoulders, white teeth, and thick black hair that fell over one eye and gave me the inexplicable urge to push it away. He bought me a drink immediately (he told me that he pays the bill to maintain the image, then expenses everything later).

Good manners score major points with me. Then again, that's the least I would expect from someone who I'm paying for by the hour. I wanted to stay professional, but I knew within ten minutes of meeting him that I would be tearing his clothes off within forty-eight hours—at least in my dreams.

With Andrew, sex was linked to the love I felt for him. With Mark, it was physical compatibility honed by multiple encounters—but this was something else. It was raw, immediate, and unconnected to love. I'm not sure if it was the symmetry of his face, biological determinism, the fact that I was ovulating at the time, or a serious case of pheromones, but I knew I had to make a play for him no matter how dire the professional consequences.

I had told everyone I was writing an article about introducing a new boyfriend to some of my colleagues and friends in the same day, to see how he coped. They thought Adam and I had met a few weeks ago. Given that my longest relationship in three years lasted six months, this was major news. My friends were desperate to meet—and question—him.

We had five minutes to cobble together a story before Amy arrived. "I usually just say we met in a bar," he said.

I was worried that he was drastically underestimating the nosy nature of my friends. Amy will want to know how he wooed me, when we first kissed, and definitely how serious he is about me. No light interrogation, I warned him.

Unfazed, he simply said, "It's going to be fun."

His cavalier attitude caused a nasty, nervous rash to prickle its way up my neck.

It was time for the first challenge.

When Amy arrived, I could see how impressed she was when Adam stood up and pulled out a chair for her. He immediately ordered her a drink and was incredibly effusive about her choice of restaurant. He was charm personified, and she was melting in front of me.

"So," she said, skimming the menu, "how did you two meet?"

"I sort of picked him up in a bar, playing pool," I said, taking a gulp of my drink to buy some time.

"Yeah, she is extraordinarily bad at pool," he added smoothly, touching my arm. This guy was seriously convincing. She teased him about the pressure of meeting so many of his new partner's friends so soon, and he gazed at me shyly and said, "She does put me in some strange situations, but she's definitely worth it." Christ, he was smooth.

I started sweating when she asked about his career, but he batted back answers like a real pro. Since Adam worked a day job, his comments were all plausible. I kept staring at his hands—beautifully manicured despite his insistence that he had hidden calluses.

The wine flowed and he slipped his hand into mine—very sweaty and, dare I say it, also very welcome. An hour later, the meal was over and within minutes of us parting, I received a text from Amy saying, "He's amazing!" I felt bad so I confessed the truth to her, but she was having none of it. "I don't care if you hired him, you can't fake chemistry like that. He's totally into you."

Next up was Mark, who was in town on a two-day conference. He took to Adam straight away, taking great pleasure in recounting a few stories that demonstrated my drama-queen tendencies. Adam even looked interested when we started talking about old friends who he, of course, had never heard of. Adam was also buying all the drinks—I couldn't help thinking that my tab was really going to add up at the end of the night.

After Adam and I left, I called Mark from a cab and 'fessed up to our ruse. "Really? I would never have guessed that you weren't together, especially since I caught him looking at your chest." Mark then questioned me about how to become a male escort. "I would be totally up for it," he said. "Wait, wait, ask him if I would have to sleep with fat chicks!"

I hung up and Adam and I went to our last stop of the evening, a perfume launch. After my largely liquid lunch, I was feeling seriously merry. By the end of the evening I was beginning to see the advantages of an escort. There were no awkward pauses in conversation and none of the tension that goes with trying to impress a genuine date.

Adam and I turned to congratulate each other on a job well done and I felt confident enough to ask him if he was attached—and he winked at me. Or maybe he just had something in his eye?

"No, I'm single. I joined the agency because I thought it would be an adventure," he said, "but if I had a serious girlfriend that would be another exciting chapter in my life."

Was he flirting with me? I think so, and I was flirting outrageously back. "I have to tell you, you're a very sexy girl," he said, smiling down at me. But was he being sincere? Or just visualizing the new mountain bike he'd buy factoring in his fee? Actually, I didn't care. I was already plotting my next move.

"So, come on," I said, taking a sip of my vodka tonic, noticing that he stuck to sparkling water. He was probably afraid that I'd try to take advantage of him. Which, at that point, was a valid fear. "Girls must hit on you all the time. And you're telling me that you never hook up with any of them?"

"No, I don't," he said. "Two reasons: Number one, I don't mean to sound arrogant, but I don't have any problems getting a 'regular' date. And two, these women know my last name and where I work. What if one of them got upset, or wanted to see me again? At the end of the day, this is a job for me; what if they paid for something and I got scared that I couldn't deliver?"

"I have a feeling that you wouldn't have a problem delivering anything," I countered, purposely licking my lips.

He told me that more than 50 percent of his clients, who include teachers and even a policewoman, are regulars. During the last year he has escorted women to everything from work functions to evenings at the theater and even the Chelsea Flower Show. "And yet, I've never gone further than a kiss on the cheek," he said.

"So, do you have a strategy for dealing with unwanted advances? Because I'm sure that women must try to get 'extras' at the end of your dates."

He laughed. "Not as much as you might think. But I usually walk them to a taxi, then immediately go for their cheek and shake their hand at the same time, so there's no opportunity for them to go in for the kill."

"And I suppose fear of rejection must be a pretty powerful deterrent for them?"

"Exactly."

"So if I was to try to kiss you, would you block me?"

I knew I was being unprofessional, but the combination of pineapple mojitos, a recent breakup, and perfume fumes were making me hallucinate. I knew that I was pushing my luck, since he could have knocked me back and humiliated me both personally and professionally. But our physical connection was too strong to ignore. I had to give it a shot.

I moved towards him and he responded, first by kissing me gently, then by wrapping his arm around me as our tongues grew more insistent.

On the rare occasions when I'm that attracted to someone, it feels like there is literally a force field pulling us together, and the inevitability of us fucking furiously is much harder to resist than giving in.

"Take me home now," I whispered insistently.

"Yes, ma'am," he said, taking my hand and pulling me down the dark stairwell.

But when we got out to a cab suddenly I had second thoughts and pulled away. "Look, I really want you right now," I said, sliding his hand up my thigh, "but I need to write this piece in a semi-professional manner. So I should probably head home alone. But I hope to see you again soon."

I went home and unearthed my trusty Rabbit, and slid it inside me, picturing his long, lean, and muscled body moving over me in the dark. I came in record time, biting the pillow to muffle my moans.

The next morning, I woke up to find a voicemail, which he'd left while he was driving to work. "Hey, sexy, I had a great time last night," he said. "And once you finish your article, I was wondering if I could have the pleasure of taking you out on a real date?"

# NINETEEN

I stumbled in, bleary-eyed, after my second evening with Adam. I tried to maintain interest while he talked about his family and hobbies, but the chemistry was so intense that I asked him to take me back to his place before we were halfway through the second bottle of wine.

He lived in a shared house in North London, with two mates he'd had since university. "But they're out tonight," he said, with a mischievous gleam in his eye. "So, can I offer you a ride back to my place?"

I ended up balancing myself on the front handlebars of his bike, laughing and holding on for dear life, while we careered through rainy Belsize Park. We were singing show tunes, loudly and off key. By that point, I was too pissed and freezing cold to worry about falling and breaking my neck.

He took me up to his room, and as soon as we shut the door his hands were everywhere. After taking off my top, he pulled the cups of my bra down to suck lightly on my nipples. I've never understood why so many men insist on biting them—probably yet another porno casualty. But his gently lapping tongue felt fantastic.

"Take off everything, but leave your knickers and shoes on," he whispered, wrapping his hands around my waist. They were so huge that they almost spanned the not inconsiderable circumference. "Then I want you to put your hands on the wall, and keep them there, no matter what," he said.

Slick with anticipation, I followed his instructions as he dimmed the lights. I wondered if he was going to re-create the Ellen Barkin/Al Pacino cop scene from *Sea of Love* that got me so hot when I was a teenager staying up late to watch it on Showtime.

He started kissing my ankles, sliding his tongue upward over my calves and spreading my legs with his wrists. When I moaned and tried to lean down into him, he straightened and warned me: "Don't move your hands, or I'll stop!"

I bit my lip to keep from screaming as his hands moved higher, cupping my ass through the thin silk of my black knickers. Then he pulled them down, slowly, lightly biting the back of my neck, then slipped his fingers inside me, working me into a frenzy as he parted my thighs further.

I heard him unzipping his jeans and, flexing my arse muscles, I looked around to get a glimpse of his cock. It was average length but incredibly thick, and my first fleeting thought was, *Will it fit?* I licked my palm, reached for him, and guided him inside me. "Put. Your. Hands. Back on the wall," he told me.

I gasped with pleasure, and we fucked furiously for about five minutes, him grinding against me while fingering my clit until I came, hard, bucking against him, and he followed soon after.

Then he pulled out, gently, and led me to the bed. Our second time was more tender, with him looking down at me, our eyes locked the entire time, so intensely that his beautiful green eyes morphed into one giant Cyclops eye.

After a few minutes, my mouth was getting parched, so we retired to the kitchen to grab a glass of water. Seeing a Belvedere vodka bottle on the counter, I poured some over ice and slugged a bit down, giving him a shot—from my mouth. He slid his hands up to my arse, naked underneath his oversized baby-blue cotton shirt, and propped me up on the counter. I sucked in my breath. "I'm cold," I said, putting my hands on the back of his neck and pulling him towards my mouth. We kissed hungrily and I could feel his massive hard-on as he scooted me to the front of the counter. "Is it safe?" I asked as he lifted me up on to him. This was a rhetorical question at that point, since I wouldn't have cared. In fact, I found it very erotic to think about who could be watching us. That's a common fantasy of mine while I'm fucking, imagining that flatmates could hear how hard I'm being fucked through the walls, or seeing us through the garden window.

"God, you have the most amazing body," he said. "I would so love to fuck you in the arse right now. Have you ever done that?"

I took his hand, lightly biting the tip of his index finger and sliding the first two down the back of my throat, hoping that he would anticipate later pleasures. "Not really," I muttered sweetly, batting my eyelashes. "I mean, not often. But the thought of doing it with you makes me really hot. One thing, though—do you have any lubricant?"

He gave me that blank stare that told me he had no idea what I was talking about. He'd probably never thought about the fact that the anus produces no natural lubrication, unlike the vagina, and somehow I thought that the phrase "anal tear" would be a bit of a buzz kill, so I nudged him towards the cabinet. "Vegetable oil? Olive oil? Anything that would make me… slicker."

He broke away from me and frantically hauled basmati rice, pasta, and some unidentified spices out of the cabinet. "I think we have—no, wait, that's syrup. Um, how about this?" he said, triumphantly unearthing a bottle of henna-colored liquid.

"Sesame seed oil? I don't really want my skin to smell like chicken teriyaki. Maybe we should leave that particular kink for next time, huh?" God, men are clueless sometimes.

"Whatever you say, baby," he said, wrapping my legs around his waist and carrying me to the kitchen table. As he looked down at me, he said, "Or would madame prefer the pool table?"

Lying in bed, blissfully, afterwards, I told him about a scheming co-worker's Machiavellian tendencies, and he said, very politely, "What does that mean?"

After Adam and I had gone out four times, I was beginning to feel like I was coaching a spelling bee from his bed. Since our first real date, I had explained "marginal," "verbose," "salacious," and "cunnilingus" (though fortunately his lack of Latin did not impede him in the bedroom). In most of my relationships, I have spent hours debating everything from the English translation of *L'Amant* to Patrick Swayze's mullet. This time, I'd shamelessly chosen sizzling sex over sarcastic banter.

I've always maintained that the brain is the sexiest muscle for seduction, so I felt a bit shallow admitting that, for now at least, a perfect set of abs seemed to be doing the trick.

I didn't know what genre of movie he liked, his views on politics, or even his middle name. But I could write volumes on how he liked his neck kissed, and knew how tightly I could bind him to his bed's headboard without causing wrist abrasions.

Perhaps pillow talk doesn't need to involve discussions about string theory. After years of dating self-centered "artists" whose endless phobias and issues needed to be explored in depth over dinner, dating a guy whose main priority in life was playing football felt like a vacation.

"When a guy is that gorgeous, you don't need to spend a lot of time talking," said Victoria, who had counseled me through several exhausting post-mortems with neurotic creative types. "What you need now is a semi-literate fuck machine."

Anyway, it wasn't that Adam was stupid: As a graduate who ran his own company, he was an expert on car parts and woodwork. While he might not know Nietzsche from Nabokov, he was charming and had an incredibly kind heart.

But was I seeing more to the relationship than there was just because the chemistry was so fantastic? Sex has always been a huge priority for me, so in a way I was a victim of my own success. I asked Adam if it bothered him that he had no idea how my mind worked. "That will come in time," he said, winking at me.

In fact, most of my girlfriends admit that their most unforgettable nights of passion were not with their boyfriends; instead they immortalize the nights they copped off with "a Greek guy whose English was basically limited to 'You. Bed. Clothes. Off,'" as one girlfriend of mine succinctly put it. Alas, none of these sexually supercharged flings lasted very long.

Meanwhile, my male friends failed to see the problem. "Just chill out and enjoy it," Michael told me after I admitted to him that Adam and I didn't really talk. "You want literary conversation? Join a book club."

Were Adam and I adopting the guise of a semi-steady relationship as an excuse to use each other shamelessly for sex? Lacing up my corset for another night out, I decided that I could live with that. Later, in bed, I apologized to Adam for being jaded. He looked down and ruffled my hair. "What does 'jaded' mean, honey?" Maybe with someone this beautiful, it really doesn't matter.

It didn't make sense. For the first time in a while, I was sharing my bed with a gorgeous man whom I fantasized about constantly in my waking life. And yet my subconscious was getting seriously out of control.

I'm not particularly interested in politics, so it came as a bit of a shock when I first started having graphic sex dreams about Gordon Brown. While I welcome the idea of dreaming about public figures, I was expecting my subconscious to conjure up Daniel Craig or Clive Owen—not a jowly Scotsman whose chin seems to have no bounds.

The dream begins on an Orient Express–style train. I am on a book tour, wearing 1920s clothes. Our eyes meet across a dinner table, and soon we are stumbling to my cabin, kissing passionately. By the end of the dream we are cuddling and talking about our future. I wake up, usually in a cold sweat.

I am, very definitely, not attracted to Gordon Brown. It's a different story, perhaps, with Tony Blair. I had the chance to meet Blair a few months earlier at a charity event in London, and when I told him that I wrote about sex and relationships, he really turned on the charm. "That sounds a lot more interesting than politics," he said with a laugh, before putting his arm around my waist to pose for a photograph.

Desperate for answers about my dreams, I called in an expert. Ian Wallace is an Edinburgh-based dream therapist. He reassured me that having dreams about politicians was a common phenomenon and did not mean that I was destined to do a Lewinsky. He told me that many of his clients had vivid sex dreams involving people they felt they were not attracted to in real life. He pointed out that, like Brown, I'm ruthlessly ambitious.

But why had my subconscious not picked someone more charismatic, like Blair or Bill Clinton?

"As Gordon Brown is the public official recognized as in charge of the national economy, your dream suggests that you are beginning to formally recognize your own self-worth and the unique value of your journalistic explorations," Ian said. "This dream is a message from your unconscious, urging you to be more aware of your inimitable value in waking life and to celebrate your creativity."

And, apparently, the train is some sort of "metaphor for an intellectual journey" in the dreamer's own profession.

Then again, Gordon is dark and brooding, qualities I have found irresistible since I read *Wuthering Heights* at school. And I do find Scottish accents seriously hot.

It was all a bit weird, and enough to make a girl leave the night light on. But since he was helping me deal with unresolved issues in my psyche, I wasn't sure I was ready to kick Gordon out of bed just yet.

Since the relationship with Adam was raising all sorts of questions in my mind, I rang him to broach the possibility of writing about him.

"What are you going to write about?" he asked.

"Well, that we don't really talk about much, but have great sex, and our different, um, approaches to literature and stuff…" I made a face at myself in the mirror, realizing how lame I sounded.

"So basically saying I'm an illiterate idiot?" He laughed.

I knew I probably sounded like a complete bitch. "No, it's really supposed to be funny and cheeky. But if you don't want me to write it or it makes you uncomfortable, I won't, I swear."

He paused. "But you said I was good in bed, right?"

"Absolutely." I closed my eyes and imagined his hands running up my bare legs.

"In that case, no problem, sweetheart. I'm proud of whatever you write."

"Well, I thought it was important because I think we both know that, amazing a time as we have, this relationship isn't really going anywhere."

"Do you want to come over to talk about it? I wanted to take you to dinner, because there's something I've always wanted to try. But it's a bit naughty."

"Really?" Although it was warm in my bedroom, I could feel my nipples getting hard. "And what would that be?"

"Watersports," he blurted out.

Despite myself, I was rather shocked. "You mean that you want me to pee on you, or you want to pee on me?"

"Um, I'm not sure… Both, I guess."

I thought about it for a second. "Okay, but just so we're clear, we are only talking about urine, right? You don't want to put on a nappy or anything? Because I'm not down with that."

"God, no! That totally disgusts me!"

I sighed, relieved. "Okay, baby, well, I guess the final question is, is your bathroom clean? Because the last time I checked the tiles, it seemed that I wasn't the only living organism using the shower. And you boys have definitely punished that toilet."

That afternoon before our "date" with deviancy, I did some research. Readers often ask what my limits are, and I give my standard answer that anything between two consenting adults that feels good should be encouraged.

But there are a few things that have always been, for me personally, off the menu:

1. *Nappy fetishes. (I don't like changing children, much less adults!)*
2. *Body piercings. Watching I'm A Celebrity Get Me Out Of Here, all I can think about is how I would much rather sip a cockroach-and-worm milkshake or plummet from a bridge than encounter a nipple ring. Though I think they look*

*great on other people, I have an irrational fear of them that*
*completely kills my sex drive.*
3. *Threesomes with a serious boyfriend. Always the guest star,*
*never the main attraction is my rule.*

Other than that, I'm pretty open-minded.

Overall, I think the allure of watersports has something to do with the moral dirtiness of sex in general combined with the perceived "hygienic dirtiness" of waste. But contrary to the belief that urine is an icky toxic spew loaded with germs and poisons, human urine—when fresh—is virtually sterile. It's actually antiseptic enough to be used in cleaning wounds (in the absence of more conventional agents).

As for toxicity, many humans and certain animals regard human urine as a perfectly acceptable and even highly desirable beverage. This seems less surprising when you consider that human urine is actually 95 percent water.

I was also curious for another reason: Although most women's magazines advise us to void our bladders before sex, I've actually noticed heightened sexual sensitivity when I drink just a bit of extra water about an hour beforehand so that I'm roughly half full, because the extra pressure feels amazing. But it's a delicate balance, because sometimes my urge to come is overwhelmed by my urge to pee.

I wanted to find out if I could do both at once. So during our evening out, I eschewed coffee and drank passion fruit martinis, because I'd read that the juice could dilute the taste of urine. I also learned a few random snippets, like "Never ever urinate in a Singapore elevator, since apparently they have sensors that detect such actions!"

Planning for a close encounter with urine is actually a pretty nerve-racking experience. Though I stroked his ankle with the arch of my foot during dinner, I was nervous about my food choices. The steamed asparagus was definitely out, as was the Caesar salad with prawns (I didn't want to risk anchovies), so I settled for the raw oysters, which are supposed to be an aphrodisiac anyway.

I also drank water, because I wanted clear urine, but not too much—I didn't want to give him a golden shower until I was good and ready.

By the time we got to his place and started stripping each other off in the kitchen, I was seriously turned on. The pressure on my bladder heightened every sensation, but was still slightly uncomfortable.

He led me into the bathroom, where I straddled him on the toilet, facing him and sitting on top of his hardness. "Does this hurt?" I whispered. "Maybe we should move it to the bathtub."

"Actually, this feels amazing," he said, kissing me passionately. "I can't wait to feel you gush all over me."

So I held my breath, bore down on my bladder, and—nothing. No matter how hard I tried, I could not make any liquid come out. Now I knew how men with hard-ons feel, because my engorged and aroused insides just would not cooperate.

Suddenly feeling rather self-conscious, I began to giggle and then he cracked up, too. When we'd recovered we decided just to take a bath together instead. In the morning, we said our goodbyes. We had experienced our erotic story arc, finishing with a grand finale. So I was ready to let the credits roll.

# TWENTY

I had my long-awaited first date with Grant, who had stressed that he could only handle going out on a "nonexclusive" basis since he'd just got out of a relationship. This suited me perfectly. I was so stressed out about my visa situation that a little escapism was just what I was looking for.

Unlike most of my previous flings, the anticipation of hooking up with him had been building for months, and I was ready for action as I dressed for the party at the Orangerie.

"Wow," he said, when he saw the slinky, semi-transparent gown in iridescent gold that I'd borrowed from Victoria's office (tags tucked in because I had to return it the next day). "You look beautiful."

He made sure that my champagne glass was constantly refilled and guided me around the room with his hand on the small of my back making introductions. When we finally left he put his jacket over my shoulder and I tingled with anticipation at his touch.

The outfit did the trick. Back at his Knightsbridge house, he carried me upstairs and we started stripping each other off. Unfortunately, in his eagerness to ravish me, he tore the strap of my gown. I felt an almost physical pain as I heard that rip—the dress cost more than my rent.

Over coffee the next day, I tried to explain my clothing addiction to Grant. Lingerie being my particular weakness. I told him how buying my first La Perla bra was a bit like losing my virginity. I remember the trepidation of trying it on, and how turned on I was in the dressing room when I saw how the silk hugged my skin. I remember the rush of handing over my credit card and how, after all the anticipation, the transaction took only two minutes.

I now have four massive drawers full of gear. There's the "nice" drawer, filled with high-end French lace balconette bras and silk side-tie knickers, the "naughty" drawer, with its corsets and suspenders, and the "miscellaneous" section where I store themed outfits like Naughty Nurse, French Maid, and my trusty rhinestone-studded bullwhip. Last of all is the rapidly dwindling "normal" drawer.

My friends think I'm insane, as most of my purchases never see the light of day, let alone a handsome stranger. But lingerie makes me feel that the possibilities for hookups are limitless, even if I'm just going to Tesco. I may be buying loo roll, but the fact that I'm wearing a corset while doing so is my sexy little secret.

It wasn't always this way. In my teens, when I was still worried about appearing to be a good girl, I used to wear horrible underwear as a way of guaranteeing no sex on a date. It didn't work. I still went to bed with the guy, but I had to apologize for my frayed knickers before doing the deed.

Nowadays, I don't mind being caught out in a pair of ratty jeans, but the thought of a paramedic having to cut off my clothes after a car accident and finding a pair of big gray pants is too much to bear. That said, I've had my share of sex-related sartorial disasters. I once wore a PVC cat suit that gave me a head-to-toe rash. Another time, a pair of too-tight hold-ups left me with thighs that looked like two servings of broccoli.

After we'd finished our coffee, Grant took me to Coco de Mer. As I tried on a black and white push-up bra with stockings and suspenders, he slipped into the changing room. "God, you look sexy," he said. We both got so turned on that I sat on his lap while he "helped" me unhook them.

Running his hands over the demi-cups, he said, "Whatever we spend on this, it's definitely worth it."

We went back to his flat and I unwrapped the box, then let him unwrap me.

"Okay, so it's been two days, and he hasn't called!" I told Victoria later when we met for Starbucks at Whiteleys. "But he's mentally stalking me. I knew that fourth 'x' on my last text message was overkill."

Victoria smiled knowingly. "He'll call. I would put money on it."

"I must have been an idiot to believe that 'I don't play games' line. It's been a full seventy-two hours since we shared a profound sexual connection—"

"That's for sure." She laughed. "Look, he's probably just doing the three-day-rule thing, and trying to be cool. He's playing the game, so you have to stay one step ahead. Do not call him," she said firmly.

"The three-day rule doesn't apply if you've slept with anyone. It gets truncated to twenty-four hours. God, I thought everyone knew that!"

"Cat—" Victoria said.

But I was on a roll. "You know what really annoys me? We sit here and tell ourselves that men are agonizing over whether to call, saying, 'Maybe it was his childhood, or maybe the fact that his dog died when he was ten makes him afraid of intimacy.' When the reality is he's probably just not into me. Or fucking someone else," I said miserably.

"I saw the way he looked at you," Victoria said, shredding her maple nut scone and taking tiny bites. "Believe me, he'll call. But you cannot call him," she repeated sternly. "Speaking of commitments, have you spoken to your potential fiancé yet?"

I sighed. "Not yet. But I'd better make up my mind soon. In the meantime, I'm going for a bit of retail therapy. I may have no control over my destiny, but I've decided that whatever happens, my future is going to unfold in hot underwear."

I walked home via Boots and Agent Provocateur on Kensington Park Road, where I tried on several bras. The coldness of the dressing room made my premenstrual nipples hard, and as I watched them spilling over against the silk cups I thought about bringing myself off right then and there. Only the absence of a locked door and presence of an over-attentive salesgirl held me back.

Getting horny in the middle of the day presents a quandary for women: Dirty public restrooms don't lend themselves to fantasy, and most changing rooms have a long line and/or no locks on the doors. If I had to get down and dirty in a changing room, I would probably pick the Gap. They have a laid-back staff, adjustable lighting, and nice-sized rooms.

Looking for an outlet later that evening, I broke one of my own rules and called Andrew. Despite having deleted his digits, the number was burned on my brain. He picked up after the third ring, and my fourth dirty martini. "Andrew, it's me. Listen, baby, we haven't spoken in a long time, so I'm going to be blunt," I slurred. "I know that we still have a really intense connection, and you feel it too, don't you?"

"Actually, I don't," he said. "And, um, I think you have the wrong number. My name is Tom."

Call it my dirty little secret: I'm a closet drunk-dialer. By day I'm clever and logical, but after a drink (or ten) I morph into the girl who once woke an ex at 2 a.m. singing an eighties love ballad, thinking it would be cute and ironic. It wasn't.

My drunken logic after an evening of partying is as follows: I haven't been able to work out my differences with the guy who dissed me through adult discussion, but now, after liquid inspiration, everything is crystal clear. So why shouldn't I call to let him know what he's missing?

The consequences of the call don't hit me until the next morning. I find myself reaching under the pillow for my mobile to figure out who I've called even before I scramble for painkillers.

I've done them all: The cheesy, nostalgic greeting that usually follows an overdose of Richard Marx lyrics at weddings; the "accidental" dial from the bottom of my handbag so that he can hear what a great time I'm having; and, yes, even the booty call.

At least I'm not the only one. These days, dialing while drunk has become a social phenomenon. Back in the pre-mobile era, having to locate a phone booth or landline usually killed the urge. But like caller ID and texting, drunk-dialing now plays a central role in modern courtship.

Mobile phone firms have been scrambling to come up with deterrents. Virgin Mobile has offered its Australian customers the option of blocking certain numbers until 6 a.m. Another firm has launched a "Breathalyzer" phone that bans certain digits when blood-alcohol level is above a certain point. It has already sold 200,000 in Korea.

My girlfriends and I have developed our own strategies. During post-breakup periods, we adopt a "friends-don't-let-friends-dial-drunk" policy, which means swapping phones with a designated dialer. The repercussions of the two-minute "cathartic" call, such as being labeled a bunny-boiler, can be mortifying. Worse, the object of our (drunken) affection might just take us seriously.

A girlfriend of mine from New York was alone one night when she began to get curious about her ex-boyfriend, a postman whom she'd dated for two weeks at university. After several shots of schnapps, she let her fingers do the walking. He showed up on her doorstep the next morning. "He said that he'd always dreamed about marrying me, too, and I had no idea what he was talking about," she said.

As for my ill-fated tête-à-tête with Andrew: I finally reached him, only to proclaim loudly, "I'm over you!" followed by, "Can I come over?"

Fortunately I made it home alone and slept soundly as evidenced by the drool on my pillow. But yikes. Maybe there is something to the Breathalyzer. Now if they could only come up with an anti-drunken hook-up feature…

It's not the first time I'd found dating and technology to be an uneasy mix. Even though I'd like to consider myself fairly adept at both, I just hadn't got the hang of the texting obsession. In the States the text is considered a mere rest stop on the superhighway of love—a check-in point between phone calls. But in the UK, some of my friends have had entire relationships that started, bloomed, and were finally extinguished via a two-inch screen.

Case in point: My recent first date with Edward (since Grant had asked for nonexclusivity I had thought I'd better take him at his word). Edward was a short but achingly fit writer with piercing blue eyes, was one of those ones that made me regret going home alone.

He sent a message later to make sure I got home in one piece, which I thought was very sweet. But then he texted again the next day, and again later that week asking "Where r u? Do u wnt 2 meet again?"

In the entire week of back-and-forth midnight missives, he never actually called me. We'd had amazing face-to-face conversations, but instead of letting his fingers doing the walking, he was relying on his thumbs.

I typed out polite, perfunctory replies at first. But when I got his next messages asking for "another d8," I confess that I hit the delete button.

I've had my share of Internet hookups, and have largely accepted the role that emails play in modern courtship. Long emails can show the nuances of a man's personality and his sense of humor. But I've always believed that if a man wants to pick me up, he'll have to pick up the phone first.

Maybe my attitude is anachronistic.

It's my male friends—never known for being great communicators—who are most enamored of the seductive power of SMS. Michael swears by texting, since he says that it lessens the sting of rejection when his overtures are ignored. "Edward is probably just shy," he said when I took him out for an Indian meal. "I often do the same thing, because sending a text is much less of a risk then going out on a limb with a phone call."

I can understand his logic, but if he risks nothing he shouldn't be surprised if the relationship that develops mimics the pattern of the text messages: short, sweet, and noncommittal.

Not that I have anything against texting—it's great for work, noisy locations, and confirming addresses. I also love sending flirty messages (except when I've had three tequila slammers at a party and end up sending a very graphic note to Mum instead of Mark!).

But in the smorgasbord of communications, text messaging should be a piece of naan bread at best, never the main course. And they should never be used as substitute for conversation. Otherwise, you risk depersonalizing the important interactions that should be made face to face, like the first dates, the first "I love you," and breakups.

So I decided to give Edward a ring. I left him a voicemail saying that I had a fantastic time with him, but that I didn't accept dates through text messages. He never called back and later told our mutual friend that he feared I was "too high maintenance."

Perhaps our fledgling relationship fell victim to simple miscommunication. Then again, maybe he was a serial texter, like a guy I met once who used to cast his net wide by sending texts to loads of girls, always late at night while drunk, in hopes of an electronic booty call.

I'll never know. Either way, I expect a guy who genuinely likes me to do more than send a few badly punctuated, half-arsed blurbs in horrific, abbreviated text lingo. But at least I'm not sitting around waiting for my handbag to vibrate.

After all, technology may change, but thoughtfulness never goes out of style. In other words, Edward: "C u wen hell 3zz ova!!"

# TWENTY-ONE

The first thing I saw when I opened my eyes in the morning were the ten crisp £50 notes on the bedside table. After a night of long hard sex, Grant had taken an early morning flight for a work trip to Johannesburg.

Our long-awaited third official date the night before was amazing. His driver picked me up at home, then we headed out to an intimate Italian restaurant, followed by a load of cocktails and champagne. At some point I had told him that earlier in the day the cash point had eaten my bank card, and the branch told me it would take five days to replace. "The irony is, I'm wearing £120 knickers and have £7 in my account," I said with a laugh.

I didn't mean this to be a pickup line, but it worked. We went back to his flat and did it everywhere—the bed, the sofa, the floor, and even the shower. Since Grant traveled constantly, I had no idea when I was going to see him again. Was this supposed to be payment for services rendered? In a daze, I dressed, took the cash, and found myself wandering through Hyde Park to New Bond Street.

I felt I was in a moral gray area. But even though I knew it was wrong, my knees went weak and I felt a surge of desire when I entered the

Christian Louboutin boutique and tried on the black leather stilettos.
I was falling in love—with the shoes.

I called Victoria, who viewed sticking endless bar tabs on anyone
with a Y chromosome as her right, to ask if taking the cash would
make me a hooker.

"If you take the money you'll change the whole dynamic of the
relationship," she said. "And, yes, it's prostitution."

I've been on both sides of the money equation with men, and braved
every mode of transportation from private jet to the front of a bicycle
because we didn't have enough change for the Tube... I could almost
feel the devil on my shoulder, urging me to shop on. But if money is
power, then pocketing the cash at this early stage could give him the
edge, and I'd been taking care of myself for way too long to let that
happen. So I reluctantly put the shoes back on the shelf.

When he called the next day, I told him that I appreciated the gesture
but would be giving the money back. He laughed when I told him
how much I'd been obsessing over it.

"It's not a problem, sweetheart, I didn't mean anything sinister by it. I
just wanted to make sure that you were covered for the next week."

He asked me out again, and I suggested we go for a few beers when
he got back from South Africa. This time, I'd be buying.

Meantime, the matter of my potential fiancé loomed large. After many
sleepless nights, I was still debating whether or not to accept Mark's
drunken offer.

Over a cup of disgusting instant coffee at the flat, Victoria and I
were mulling over my options. I could stay indefinitely as a tourist,
but if I ever tried to return to the States I would run the risk of
not getting back in. And I loved my family too much ever to let
that happen.

I was paying taxes, I didn't want to leach off the benefits system, I spoke the language, and I really wanted to be a good citizen. Simple enough, right?

"You know, Cat, you don't have to go through with this," Victoria said after I called the registrar to enquire about booking the ceremony. "We could always say that we're lesbians—that way you wouldn't have to tie the knot."

"But we have to have been living together for two years, and I don't want to put you in that position," I told her, grimacing as I took a sip. "At least this way, technically, according to the legal definition Mark and I have a pre-existing relationship, which in this case means a horizontal one," I said.

I'd heard stories about illegally assuming a friend's identity while working in cafés, using someone else's National Insurance number to get paid and then getting the money from them. But it's going to be tough to pretend that I'm anyone other than Catherine Townsend, considering that I have a bylined column.

"This whole thing is pretty ironic, considering that my entire life is based on being single," I said.

"You're still single! If anything, a quickie marriage will give you street cred. After all, Britney's done it!"

"Great," I said, laughing. "So now I'm modeling my behavior on skanky celebrities. This is not what I imagined my wedding day to be like."

"Maybe it's meant to be," she said. "Just keep thinking of the end result, and everything you'll gain."

"I know I'm not exactly a model of morality here, but I really did think that my wedding was going to be sacred. Even if everyone secretly snickered at the fact that I'd be wearing white." Suddenly the room felt claustrophobic, so I opened the terrace doors. "I just wish there was another—more legal—way out."

"Why don't you ask Grant to step in and help you, since he's got the political connections?" Victoria asked. "Do you think he's The One? Would you tell him about your problem then?"

"I'm not sure that I believe in soulmates," I told her. "I mean, I know that you and Mike are happy, and I hope that I find that some day. But right now, I really don't think I can deal with anyone else's drama, because I have too much of my own." I smiled. "He's Mr. Sorbet Sex. Definitely not life partner material."

Sorbet sex is the palate cleanser between relationships, a close cousin of the Rebound Guy. But while the Rebound Guy helps get confidence back on the relationship front, sorbet sex allows me to recoup sexually and stop associating the sex act with my ex-boyfriend.

It also prevents me obsessing when I meet someone else I like, because I've got another point of comparison besides my ex, which stops me fantasizing about him. Even if this sex isn't technically that great, it helps me move on.

Equally, sorbet sex helps avoid the pitfall of recycling an ex-boyfriend. One of the hardest things to kiss goodbye has always been the ex sex, that amazing feeling you get when someone really knows you. But emotional connections like these can be few and far between, since it's hard enough to find someone I want to invite into my home, much less my superego.

I blame Plato. He introduced the idea of soulmates into popular culture when he said that in the beginning there was only one being, with both male and female parts. The perfect human then tragically split apart, and according to legend men and women have been looking for their "other halves" ever since.

This might have been a lovely idea in a time when people considered themselves lucky to reach age thirty and wore dodgy togas. But it doesn't really work for me.

"I totally understand," Victoria was saying. "I've always hated fairy tales. They are so masochistic to women. Cinderella was a house slave, Snow White got poisoned, and Sleeping Beauty was in a coma— all waiting for Prince Charming to come along. And what about Rapunzel? She was trapped in a tower until that guy climbed her hair to get to the top. If it had been me I would have had some fat bloke grab on and scalp me.

"It's not any better now. The first romantic movie I ever saw was *Splash*, when Daryl Hannah was the mermaid who grew legs. She was a mute nymphomaniac, and Tom Hanks fell in love. Then there's *Pretty Woman*, which I read somewhere is still one of the most popular DVD rentals for the eleven to fifteen age group. No wonder we're still waiting for Richard Gere to show up in a limo."

"I know! We rented *Love Actually* last night, and it was so funny—the Prime Minister and the tea lady and Colin Firth and the chick who didn't speak English."

I sighed dramatically. "Sometimes I think it would be better if I didn't speak the language. Simpler, anyway. That way, you could write your own dialogue and imagine that the guy was saying what you wanted him to say."

"If you're referring to Andrew, I'm not sure that it would have made any difference," she said. "He told you—in English—that he was married, but you were already so into him at that point that you continued."

"I've just had a string of bad luck. I'll meet the right guy."

"Are you sure you're ready?"

"What do you mean? I was 'ready' when I met Andrew!"

"Yeah, but from the beginning it was obvious that he wasn't really emotionally available. I think that if he had turned around and said, 'Okay, Cat, let's be together for ever, I've left,' you would have ended up dumping him in less than six months anyway." She paused. "Maybe you should worry less about whether or not you are right for them, and ask yourself whether they are right for you," she said gently.

I thought about what she said. On some level, I've always been attracted to a challenge. This was part of Grant's attraction. I didn't necessarily want to spend the rest of my life with him, but I wanted him to want me. Put simply, I wanted to win. I leaned back and closed my eyes.

"I, um, need to ask your opinion about something. I'm really in love with Mike, but in the past two months I've dreamt about sleeping with two other guys from work who I find revolting," said Victoria hesitantly.

My eyes flew open. "Anywhere interesting?"

"I'm serious, Cat. Mike's been really pressing me on this issue about buying a house together, so maybe I'm just freaking out. Anyway, these guys mean nothing, but I've actually caught myself flirting with them, too. Do you think I'm horrible?"

I put my hand on hers and squeezed it. "No, I think it's completely normal. It's like you said, in relationships like mine and Andrew's, things were always so volatile that I never had time to think about cheating. When I settle down and get comfortable, I usually start to get a wandering eye."

"But I chatted up Alan!" Alan worked in her IT department, and we'd recently debated whether the rather prominent bulges under his shirt constituted man-breasts.

"Yes, but maybe you're afraid of cutting yourself off from all those other possibilities that you had when you were totally independent. For me, the dreaded 'c-word' was never commitment, it was compromise."

"So you really think it's about the house?"

"That, or you're secretly attracted to Alan, and want to have his babies; maybe he could nurse them!" I ducked as she threw a cushion at me, laughing.

"I'm sorry, that was mean. Look, Alan is sweet. But winking at him is obviously a cry for help. You have to chill out. Mike is a great guy." I gave her a hug, then gathered my bag and walked out the door.

Afterwards, I thought a lot about infidelity. Men are always going on about evolutionary theory, and how they are supposed to spread their seed as wide as possible in order to perpetuate the species.

But are women so different? The moment I get comfortable and settled in a relationship—though admittedly those moments are few and far between—my confidence emboldens me. I could be having dinner with my partner, but secretly I'm imagining a threesome with the hot blond waiter and the guy at the table next to us. Maybe with girls like Victoria and me, after so many years of à la carte sexual encounters, the thought of a set menu for the rest of our lives makes us panic. Maybe it's not the men we don't trust: Maybe we don't trust ourselves to stick to the diet.

# TWENTY-TWO

That's it," I said, grabbing my clothes and mopping the sweat from my chest, "I'm out of here." Just after 2 a.m. on the fifth night I'd spent at Grant's house, I realized the late summer heatwave was driving me insane.

Grant had copious amounts of body hair. Normally I love hairy chests, but in a sweltering dark room it's like being covered with an electric blanket. I start to feel as if I'm being cuddled by a guy in a gorilla suit.

Summer is meant to be a time of unbridled hedonism, when sunlight stimulates the body to produce more serotonin to boost our moods. But this year my libido seemed to be falling as the mercury rose. I wouldn't go back to a man's place without obsessing over the size of his unit—his air-conditioning unit, that is. When tempers flare as quickly as the temperature, everyone gets a bit ratty and something as simple as an outing to the corner shop has the potential to turn into a meltdown.

But the heat does have its advantages. "Warm day, isn't it?" acts as a ready-made opening line for the notoriously repressed British male, although it sounds better in the sunny park than when I'm dripping with sweat in a sweltering Tube. By that point I'm feeling murderous, not horny. So that afternoon I headed to Holland Park in anticipation of spotting acres of bronzed, fit flesh.

Sadly, all I found were men with milky-white beer guts and numerous tattoos sunbathing alongside a guy in shorts who looked like a fat version of Frodo from *Lord of the Rings*.

I don't know any woman who would dare to bare all in the park without agonizing over her flabby bits and ensuring she had the perfect fake tan/wax/sarong combination. The builders near the park obviously do not subject themselves to the same level of scrutiny (many of the bare-chested horde have bigger breasts than me) as they enquire, "Do you want some of this?" while gesturing vaguely towards their genitals.

But it wasn't only singletons who were struggling—couples were resorting to desperate measures to beat the heat. "Last night Mike and I were half naked, eating ice in a bid to cool down," said Victoria. "It wasn't erotic; in fact, we fought over the last ice tray."

But things were looking up because Grant had just called to tell me that he'd booked us into a boutique hotel. "I thought we could have a dirty weekend in town," he said, adding, "It has amazing air conditioning."

I told him to count me in.

But first I had an afternoon encounter planned with a man who's got what I crave and knows how to satisfy me completely: He drives a Mr. Whippy van.

"You should enjoy the rush and not take things too seriously," Mark told me down a crackly mobile phone line. "Trust me. When you've been settled for years with some guy and cutting his toenails on the sofa, you'll look back and long for the thrill of these days."

Years? Most of my relationships crash and burn before the milk in the fridge has expired. I admit it: I'm addicted to the first flushes of love affairs, and I tend to bail out long before the steamy sex devolves into sock sorting. Anyway, how could I "relax" when my stomach was churning, though I had to feign nonchalance when he called lest he thought I was desperate? It was exhausting.

"By the way," Mark asked, "have you thought any more about my offer?"

"I have," I told him, "and if you're still up for it, I've decided to accept."

"Of course, sweetheart. Do you still want to meet for lunch?"

Was that hesitation in his voice, or was I just being paranoid? "If you don't mind, that would be great. We can talk about making the arrangements then. You know that you don't have to do this, right? I'll totally understand if you want to back down."

"I wouldn't dream of it, honey pie. For every problem, there's a solution. So let's just discuss the logistics, okay? See you outside my office at one?"

"Great. If you don't mind, I need to swing by the Agent Provocateur concession at Selfridges really quickly."

"Another date with Grant?"

I could hear the disapproval in his voice. I knew that he had written off Grant as a serious contender. He thought Grant should step up and offer to help me with the visa problem, but he failed to realize that I was still determined to play the role of Fantasy Girlfriend for Grant. Grant's idea of handling problems was to leave behind a wad of cash—just like my dad. Maybe that's why I loathed the idea of feeling that I "owed" him anything.

"Yes. I've really got to stop bankrupting myself before every outing."

Mark laughed. "Have you thought about the irony of this? You're going shopping with your fiancé for lingerie to wear with your lover? How very modern."

Unable to concentrate on anything else, including a rapidly approaching deadline, I Googled a medical website and came up with this: "The state of romantic love is often characterized by feelings of exhilaration and intrusive, obsessive thoughts about the object of one's affection." Apparently, scientists have discovered that the brain of someone falling in love—or at least lust—resembles those of people who snort cocaine.

I was high on dopamine, fueled by mind-blowing sex. Which would explain my conflicting feelings about Grant.

I read somewhere that women secrete oxytocin—the so-called cuddle hormone that makes us bond with babies—after sex. We crave whoever we're sleeping with because it chemically rewires our brains.

I sensed that Grant and I were ultimately incompatible. But I felt like the lab rat in the experiment where pressing a bar dispensed drugs. Studies showed that given free rein, they kept on self-administering hits until they died. Pleasure is addictive.

I met Victoria early the next morning at our gym near Ladbroke Grove, where I did almost an hour on the treadmill to clear my head. Afterwards, I filled her in on the gory details of my encounters with Grant while coating myself with body lotion. The endorphin rush felt fantastic but clearly wasn't enough for her: She popped three Nurofen Pluses.

"The problem is I genuinely can't tell if my infatuation is the sign of greater things to come, or just a chemical reaction," I told her.

"I know the feeling," she said. "The best sex I ever had was on holiday with this Greek guy. I met him, we spent the next ten days on the back of his motorcycle, and it was all so romantic." She flipped her hair over.

"Of course, that was before I realized that we were actually running from the cops during our romantic drives on the beach."

Having just taken a sip from my water bottle, I laughed so hard I almost choked. "Look, Cat, the reason that Mike and I work is because we were friends first," she said, hitting me on the back. "Just try not to get too carried away with this guy, okay? I set you up with him for a fun whirlwind romance, but you barely know him. And he's been on-off with this other poor girl for years. I hate to say anything, but you do tend to pick guys who are either physically or emotionally unavailable. Do I see a pattern here?"

I snapped her with my towel and laughed.

At that moment, I got a text. Grant was inviting me to his flat, in the middle of the afternoon. Probably not the behavior of someone who's looking for long-term love.

I should really have made an excuse about being too busy—or played harder to get. But it was a gorgeous day, the sun was shining, and I decided to live in the moment and headed off in search of my next hit. For the moment, at least, I was an addict.

# TWENTY-THREE

Sitting in the posh men-only salon, I swore I could hear a baritone scream over the piped Sade, and I wondered if Grant regretted the day he uttered the fateful words: "It's just waxing, what's the big deal?" It started with a dare. Grant was a huge fan of the Hollywood wax that leaves one completely bare (perhaps because he was follicularly overloaded himself). I also loved the look and heightened sensitivity.

After a long talk, we'd decided to keep things casual. He was constantly jetting off to Africa, and if I'm honest I thought it was too soon after Andrew to get serious about anyone. Our ambiguous relationship status was making our sex life even hotter.

But as he practically lived abroad and we saw each other only occasionally, I thought there was something unfair in his expectation that I maintained this nether-region grooming 24/7. Especially when he was so furry I was practically coughing up hairballs. So Grant and I did a deal: I'd continue the masochistic ritual only if he agreed to a one-off back, sack, and crack waxing.

Meanwhile, his hair removal was limited to swiping a razor through his unibrow occasionally. This is a lot easier than putting my ankle over a strange woman's shoulder while she rips off a piece of fabric from an area that only my gynecologist should really be inspecting.

I can understand Grant's aversion to pubic hair, though, because I feel equally obsessive about ridding men of all facial hair (except for three-day stubble, which is hot). The only thing worse than a retro seventies 'stache on a guy (which is the stuff of horror movies and resembles a caterpillar dipped in motor oil) is a goatee, because if a guy can't even commit to a full beard, it's not a good sign. Every time I talk to a man who has one, I'm secretly fantasizing about tying him down and plucking the hairs out one by one. (I could just shave them, but I guess I'm a bit of a sadist).

Ever since metrosexuals brought the female obsession with body hair to mainstream men, most of my male friends will admit to pruning their downstairs hedges occasionally. But it's as much for the illusion of extra length as pleasing their partners. "I started trimming down there after I read something about how porn stars shave," Mark once confessed after several Coronas. "It's like a fun-house mirror—objects look larger than they are!"

Like those scary women with eyebrows plucked so thin they have to be drawn back on, sometimes men go too far. One summer I went on a few dates with a cyclist whose chest was as smooth as a Mexican hairless dog. He admitted to shaving his legs, saying it helped aerodynamics, but he freaked out during a music festival with friends after he forgot his razor.

After twenty-four hours I began to understand why: His five o'clock chest shadow was razor sharp, and under the full moon his body hair was sprouting faster than a werewolf's. The final straw was the next afternoon, when he complained that his spray-on tan had started to get patchy and our day-long shagfest somehow morphed into an extended lecture on exfoliation.

I was thinking about him forty-five minutes later when Grant emerged sweating, dabbing at the corners of his eyes. "Dear God," he said, shuddering, "no one told me that they tweeze after the wax!"

Back at his flat, I soothed his tender areas in more ways than one by getting really creative with aloe vera gel. At some point, I'd tell him that I really preferred the all-natural look on men. Just not right now.

Finally, a long-term male presence in our flat. Unfortunately, he was a furry mammal, a mouse, and I'd dubbed him Ralph.

"I know I've got to get him out of there," I told Grant, "but I can't bring myself to put out a trap."

"Why don't you just put out some poison? Or call an exterminator? You've got the killer instinct." He playfully slapped my bum. "God, you have a great arse. Seriously, it's perfect."

I cringed. "The thing is, I don't want to kill him, I just want him to go away," I said. "I've tried reasoning with him. Twice I've caught him under a glass and thrown him outside, but he always seems to make his way back in."

"That flat is falling apart," Grant said, lighting a cigarette. "Why don't you let me help you out with a new place?" He smirked. "Unless you're planning to move in with your husband?" When I had told Grant about my situation he had been remarkably understanding; in fact, a little too understanding. I suppose I had hoped he would be a bit jealous. Instead, he found the whole thing amusing.

"What, you mean pay my rent? I can't accept that," I told him, folding my arms over my chest. "If a man helps with my rent, it's going to be because I'm living with him or married. Period. And right now the only man I'm sharing with has four legs."

He parted my thighs and looked down at my perfectly smooth pussy.

"So where are you off to this weekend?" I asked him.

"I'm going to my house in Lake Como."

"What, partying with George Clooney?" I teased.

He sighed. "Actually, I'm going with S. We've decided to go ahead with the wedding."

"What?"

I was momentarily stunned but after a second I sure as hell found my voice: "But you're not in love with her! You told me that!"

"Yes, but it's more complicated than that. We have a great friendship, and the same interests. I think we'll be a good match."

I jumped up and he put his arm around my waist, trying to pull me back onto the bed.

"Come on, don't be like that; this doesn't have to change anything between us."

"What on earth do you mean 'doesn't have to change anything'? You're getting married! It changes everything."

"Look, I thought you, of all people, would understand that sometimes you have to do what you have to do to give someone security," he said. "It's time for me to get serious and settle down, and after all this time I owe her."

"Mark and I are different—at least I'm not lying to him," I spat, pulling on my panties and bra. "Don't you think you 'owe' her someone who really loves her?" I grabbed the rest of my clothes.

"Darling, don't be so naïve. That infatuation, that 'in love' feeling, fades after a few months. She has almost no sex drive, so she has no problem with me going elsewhere. I thought you would understand. What about the prairie voles?"

He was referring to the piece I'd done on the nonmonogamy of most mammals. Prairie voles are a rare exception; most scientists believe that this is due to a chemical called vasopressin. Copious amounts of vasopressin receptors in the males make them much more likely to pair-bond for life. Humans aren't wired in the same way, which some use as an excuse to cheat.

"Don't you dare drag the prairie voles into this! Humans have free will, and respect and self-control, or at least they should."

"Wow, look who's talking. As I recall, your last boyfriend was married."

Stung, I backed away from the door. "Look, Grant, I know I'm not perfect. I've made my mistakes. But I'm not going to enter into a long-term adulterous affair with you. I'm not going to deceive anyone. I'm done with all that."

"But I thought this would be what you wanted. No complications, we're friends, you're an amazing lover…"

"You want to know what I think?"

He laughed. "As if I could stop you. Shoot."

"I think that, when it comes to women, you have a serious madonna/whore complex going on. You think that you need one woman for companionship, the glacial social ice queen, and a changing cast of characters for everything else. And you know what? You're wrong. Some day, I am going to prove you wrong. I am going to meet someone who I have amazing debates with over dinner and fuck senseless in the bedroom."

"Look, I don't doubt your sincerity. But you can't fight men's basic nature. They want variety." He sat up and pulled on his socks.

I put my key to his flat on the table and grabbed my handbag. I paused with my hand on the doorknob. "It's not about the nature of men, Grant, it's about respect. Haven't you heard the Latin proverb: *Quod me nutrit me destruit?* You have to choose to nourish your relationship with your partner. It's about sacrifice, something that you know nothing about." I opened the door and put one foot out into the hallway. "But

I'm not giving up hope of finding someone faithful, who I'm madly in love with." I omitted to mention that I'd gleaned that little nugget of classics from a blog about Angelina Jolie's tattoos!

"Maybe for a while, darling. But it won't work long-term."

"Then I'll stay alone. At least I'll be assured of spending lots of time with my soulmate. She'll be there every time I look in the mirror."

I stumbled into the night, and into a cab. This was one of those times when I was grateful to be a narcissist.

# TWENTY-FOUR

The split with Grant didn't break my heart. But even though I knew that he wasn't right for me, our separation still left a void in my life, because he was the perfect man on paper. It's hard to let go of the "résumé man," that seemingly perfect individual who ticks all our boxes. I couldn't help going over the "if onlys": "If only he'd met me before he met her," and "If only the timing had been different."

Victoria brought me back down to reality. "So what you're saying is, 'If only he was a totally different person, things would work,' right?" which made me laugh.

"I think it was deeper than that," I told her. "Everyone has always thought of this guy as the consummate player, so I think that I wanted to win. I know I wanted his approval, which is why I never asked him for his help."

"Well, that's a shitty basis for a relationship. If you can't bitch and moan to your partner, you're doomed. That's not reality."

"I knew that reality wasn't something that Grant wanted to deal with," I said.

On the surface, Grant and his wife will make the perfect power couple: They are the type that society will envy as they are photographed at masked balls in *Tatler*. But, morally, that man is rotten to the core.

I realized that my attraction to men who don't love me back was part of the challenge. When I was young I was told to work hard in school to get the best results; in New York the people who fought the hardest got the best internships and the most competitive position. So, by my own logic, why would I want a man who simply fell into my lap with no effort on my part?

To get me over him, I planned a girly getaway with Victoria and Amy.

We booked a weekend in a fabulous flat in Italy, and I had visions of a slightly dirtier version of *Roman Holiday* dancing in my head.

On the flight, Amy talked nonstop about how fiery and passionate Italian men are.

"My first boyfriend was Italian," she said. "I love them because they don't play games and aren't afraid to make grand gestures." Amy never dated English men because she found them cold and repressed. I thought that she was being a bit harsh. Her current squeeze is American and loves to talk about feelings, which suits her down to the ground.

It's wonderful that she has found someone with emotional intelligence. But I'm afraid that I'm just the opposite. I just need a glass of wine and a bit of space when I come home; I don't want to have interaction with anyone for at least an hour.

"Yeah, well, unfortunately they're probably making grand gestures to about twenty women at a time," Victoria said. "When I first start seeing someone, I don't want them to go over the top because I don't yet trust them. I just want to have a drink after work."

"I'm with Victoria. I prefer sincere men—even if they are slightly bumbling," I told Amy. When a guy asks me what I want to do I always suggest going for a drink and going on from there; "going on from there" meaning that I want to see how much I like them before committing further.

Our first evening in Rome was a breath of fresh air. We went to a gorgeous restaurant near the Piazza di Spagna and window-shopped in the cobblestone streets while throngs of immaculately coiffed women with rhinestone-encrusted jeans sauntered past talking loudly on mobile phones.

But my quest for *amore* hit a few snags when I met Antonio, a gorgeous Italian who caught my eye while I was dancing on a banquette at 3 a.m. Victoria was next to me chatting to one of his friends while Amy boogied on the dance floor in front of us. I kept wildly swaying back and forth, fighting to keep my balance as my heels dug into the puffy leather. Eventually I had to sit down, which is when Antonio made his move.

We stumbled outside and he mumbled something about building missiles for Nato. Actually, "I love to watch your hair blow in the breeze" was the most coherent English phrase he spoke all night. But he was hot and I'd had three Limoncello shots, so I didn't resist when, after walking us home, he stepped inside my lobby and kissed me.

The language barrier didn't seem to matter once we were speaking in tongues, but I don't have the vocabulary to talk dirty in Italian, and in this case thought the fantasy would be better than the reality. When I politely said I was going upstairs alone he seemed a bit offended.

Working out later that his sweet nothings translated to: "There's a party in my pants and you're invited!" gave new meaning to the term "romance languages." I find it strange that none of my foreign phrase books explains dating etiquette. Forget asking directions to a museum—I need to know how to ask for a condom.

The confusion with Antonio reminded me of the time I tried to break up with my French ex-boyfriend: English–French dictionary poised in hand, I tried to translate "We've grown apart."

Instead of leaving in tears, he tried to seduce me. Exhausted, I told him it was my time of the month. He left and came back brandishing a stack of envelopes—which is how I figured out that the word "tampon" in French has something to do with a date stamp. Anyway, at seven the next morning, Antonio texted to ask me out again and I thanked him for a lovely evening, but explained that I needed an early night before my flight home. In the next hour, I had four more texts and six missed calls. "You can delete my number because you were rude to refuse my invitation," he wrote. "If I were younger, I may have room for empty kindness, but I find your hypocrisy rather sad."

I guess I shouldn't be surprised by Antonio's aggressive behavior. After all, the Italian Supreme Court ruled as recently as 2001 that a man fondling a woman's buttocks is not sexual harassment as long as the act was "not premeditated."

Rome is fabled to be one of the most romantic cities in the world, but I'm starting to think that living at home well into adulthood stunts the men's growth in more ways than one. I'll take the drunken pub lunges and shyness of British boys any day: At least they seem sincere.

As I boarded my flight, I texted Antonio a brief response that I hope is pretty clear in any language: "*Finito.*"


When I told my mum about Grant, she was amazingly positive, as always, and assured me that I had done the right thing. Then she shrieked that her pug was chewing the carpet, and she put her next door neighbor Nancy on the phone.

Nancy rattled on and on about how her three girls were all married and expecting children, and then she asked what I had been up to.

So we had a five-minute conversation about my moving from New York to London and getting a national newspaper column. "That's nice, dear," she said. "But have you gotten serious with a man yet? You don't have forever to start a family, you know."

In my view, a functioning uterus and a wedding dress will never be my most important assets, but I suppose her attitude isn't that surprising. Her logic explains why men like Jack Nicholson and George Clooney (hot but with a penchant for live-in pigs) are still considered "catches," while single women in their late twenties and thirties are viewed with suspicion.

I want to meet someone who I can share my life with. But I hate the idea that destiny can be pre-planned.

And I couldn't bring myself to say, "No, Mrs. Carter, I haven't met that special someone yet—though I did nearly piss all over a male escort a couple of months back!" I politely said my goodbyes and allowed her to hold on to her illusions about the world.

Of course, some women meet the love of their lives at an early age. And there are some who are desperate to hold on to a man because a relationship gives them the validation they crave. But, increasingly, it's women, not men, who are afraid to commit. And finally, I had to admit that I was one of them. Though I would love to find someone amazing, on the whole I preferred short love affairs to monogamy. I crave the rush of the first three months.

Until I found my perfect man, I was choosing high-drama relationships on purpose because part of me wasn't ready to make a lifetime commitment. So I tended to gravitate towards men who were totally inappropriate. Either they lived on another continent, were older, involved with someone else, or permanently between jobs.

My first love was all four. I met Jean-Claude, a gorgeous Frenchman with piercing green eyes, when I spent a year studying in Paris at age seventeen. He told me he had a job with the government, which was all that kept him going after his wife died. We dated for eighteen months before I figured out that his entire persona, including his marriage, had been a complete fabrication. He broke my heart. But despite the pain and his duplicity, I learned a lot, and I am thankful I'm not preparing *boudin blanc* in the suburbs waiting for him to come home.

Over beers near Liverpool Street, Michael explained his theory that men have a more realistic expectation of commitment than women. "I get the feeling that women expect the guy to constantly bring them flowers and keep everything exciting. Men just want a pretty girl who is happy to see him most of the time."

He might have a point. Possibly, one day I will meet someone who makes me want to commit to something more than good conversation. Until then, I was enjoying the ride.

# TWENTY-FIVE

In my opinion Oscar Wilde had the right idea when he said: "A little sincerity is a dangerous thing, and a great deal of it is absolutely fatal."

To me, the beginning of any new relationship is like two cars playing chicken. I rush towards my new man at top speed, seeing how much I can get away with and putting everything out on the table. Then I start searching for signs that something is going to go wrong.

I think my fascination with men's deception began with Sherlock Dog, a plastic basset hound whose legs were attached to little wheels so that I could roll him around the house.

I went to my grandmother's every day after school, where I would watch episodes of *Murder, She Wrote*, a drama from the eighties starring Angela Lansbury as mystery-writer-turned-amateur-detective Jessica Fletcher. Despite being a world-famous author, Jessica remained a resident of a cozy coastal town in Maine and constantly visited a network of old friends who lived all over the world.

Jessica's one eccentricity was an insatiable curiosity, which she used to solve crimes. Everywhere she went, someone inevitably dropped dead. The bumbling local cops would always arrest the most obvious suspect—usually a friend of hers—and she would be left to weave the facts of the case together to prove them innocent. Her tenacity and attention to the tiniest detail always solved the case (though why anyone would invite Jessica along knowing that people tended to die in her presence was the one mystery they never quite solved).

The show fascinated me, though the plots were pretty predictable. She always had a startling insight about a seemingly minor fact some twelve minutes before the show ended. The real killer soon confessed, in exhausting monologue, exactly how they did it, while menacingly cornering her. Then the police would burst in to the rescue. They were always in awe of whatever factoid she had picked up on to crack the case, and she was so perceptive that she could always pick out the one lapse in judgment the characters made to prove their culpability.

But the best part was that the bombshell clue was always visible in the episode, so eagle-eyed viewers could theoretically solve the case as well. It meant searching every gesture, and examining the possible double entendre in everything that was said. Solving the cases took total concentration—I only ever managed to get a few right.

I think Grandma was a bit concerned about my countless hours in front of the telly watching a show meant for the over-fifties, so she bought me Sherlock, telling me that he could help me "solve my own mysteries."

I carried a battered leather satchel and spent countless hours drawing pictures of "suspects" and doing fake lineups with cuddly toys. Then I would interrogate them in my grandma's study, the halogen lamp tilted down towards Kermit the Frog as I screamed, "So you claimed that you were nowhere near the school cafeteria at the time of the alleged cookie theft, yet we found traces of raw cookie dough on your hands! Somebody better start talking."

As I got older, the crimes increased in severity from shoplifting to armed robbery. One of my favorite games was "stakeout," where Sherlock Dog and I would follow a known felon around my grandma's living room, occasionally peeping through the window at her neighbors' houses and downing endless Thermoses of orange soda that I pretended was coffee. If a man was planting roses, I assumed that he was trying to bury body parts.

But my sleuthing skills got put to proper use the night my dad left. I remember him tapping gently on my door and telling me that we needed to talk. I bristled, thinking that he was going to bust me and my best friend for stealing half a beer out of the refrigerator. So when he said, "Basically, your mum and I are having some problems and we will probably end up getting a divorce," my mind refused to compute the information. Our family had been so perfect. I pulled my pink terrycloth bathrobe tighter and asked him to repeat himself.

"You know that you and your sister are the most important things in the world to me," he said, his eyes darting from side to side, "and I'll always love you. But I need to find my happiness now, and I think it's best for everyone if I go ahead and leave so that we can all make a fresh start. It's the right time." His face was set in a cold, impassive stare, but he looked as though he was about to cry.

"But, Dad," I begged, "where are you going? It's New Year's Eve."

"Memphis," he said as I followed him into his room where he had placed several dress shirts and crisply folded slacks on the bed next to his suitcase.

"But where will you stay? Hotels will have been full for months—" In that second, I understood. I was worried about him driving around alone and having to sleep in his car, racked with grief. But then I saw it—the crumpled paper from a dry cleaning hanger. I realized then that he hadn't chosen the date for some symbolic reason because we were beginning a new cycle on the calendar. He wanted to go to a fucking New Year's Eve party with someone else. It was so obvious. He must have had the whole thing planned for ages.

Watching him put his suitcase into the Cadillac as snow flurries blurred my view, I wished that I could turn the world back to before Sherlock Dog and *Murder, She Wrote* taught me the art of perception.

A week later, my mum came into my room at 10:30, whispering something about "a stakeout." "I don't want to leave you by yourself here," she said—my sister was at my grandparents' house—"I know it's probably crazy to take you with me, but I just didn't want you to wake up at home alone. So put on some pants, we're going to figure out where your father has been spending his nights!"

"You can't do that," I said, rubbing my eyes and sliding out of bed. "He knows your car. He'll spot you in a second."

"No, that's why we're going with Jake and Mary. They're parked outside."

My mum co-owned an antique store, and Jake was one of her most loyal customers. He was what a kind person would term a "hoarder," while a more blunt individual would label him barking mad, since every crevice of his two-story house was packed with questionable antiques. Winding my way to the bathroom in his house involved walking a tiny pathway through stacks of old newspapers, random oak chairs, stuffed squirrels, and dirty dishes precariously piled on top of yellowing carpet and overflowing ashtrays.

His personal appearance was as haphazard as his front room: He had a Grizzly Adams–style full beard and bushy eyebrows that merged into one flowing arc. He was secretly in love with my mum, which is why his wife insisted on accompanying him every time he came to her aid.

"We're going in the serial killer van? I hate that thing!"

She paused in the hallway. Her eyes were puffy, and I could tell that she'd been crying. "On second thought, honey, why don't you stay here? It's not really appropriate for you to come along, and it will only take about an hour."

But I was filled with righteous indignation and rage. "No," I said, opening the front door. "I want to bust that son of a bitch." I put my hand on her shoulder. "But we should really be wearing all black, like the Ninja stuff in movies."

So I went up to my closet and got a black ski-mask to match my tracksuit. We headed out to the van, where Jake was waiting with a Thermos of coffee.

"This is just like one of those cop shows," he said.

"How do you know where he's going to be?" I asked him, my adrenaline pumping.

"He's still at work, so we're going to park there and wait until he comes out. I think he's with D—[a petite yet rather dumpy nurse who worked the night shift at the hospital]."

I remember the van pulling into some trees outside the hospital, and waiting until we saw my dad coming out to his car. I felt a surge of love then, and it dawned on me how much I'd missed him. But I quickly pushed my love to the back of my mind, because I was being a traitor. When you are thirteen, still at the phase of completely idolizing your parents before realizing that they are human and rebelling, everything is black and white. My mum was a Jedi knight, my dad was the Evil empire (part of my nerdiness was being a huge sci-fi geek).

We tailed Dad for twenty minutes, through loads of traffic, keeping two cars between us and his black Cadillac. "Don't get too close," my mum kept saying. "He'll see us!"

Finally the car turned down a quiet, tree-lined side street, and we waited at the traffic lights for about thirty seconds before shadowing him. "Turn the car headlights off." I hissed at Jake after we saw him pull into a driveway.

"We need to stay across the street," he said. "Now, we wait."

"Great," I said, climbing into the very back and muttering under my breath, "I've got a better idea." I looked out the grimy backseat window at the grand home he had walked into, with its manicured garden and white lights lining the bushes. I wondered if she was married, or had ever given any thought to the home she destroyed.

Jake whipped round. "What's that noise back there?" he demanded. He was strangely precious about his collection of miscellaneous tat.

"Nothing. Just looking around." I sifted through a glass coffee table, reams of tissue paper, and bubble wrap and found a pair of bolt-cutters.

"Screw waiting," I said, unlatching the back door.

"Catherine! What are you doing? Get back in here!"

"She fucked up my holiday season," I said. "It's payback time, bitch!" So, running through the snow, I took the bolt-cutters and snipped through the green wire, neatly severing it—and suddenly, the entire house went dark. At the same time, I heard a cacophony of canine commotion as two huge Rottweilers lunged against the chain-link fence separating the front from the backyard.

I ran like hell, my Keds losing traction, and as I skidded I dropped the bolt-cutters.

"Run!" I heard Jake's wife yell. "The house lights are coming on."

I doubled back to grab the bolt-cutters, and racing by Dad's car, I saw something that made my heart stop: a Texas license plate. But we were in Arkansas. Which meant that this wasn't Dad's car at all, and we must have been following the wrong guy since the traffic lights.

Cursing Jake for being stupid, I leaped into the back of the van.

"Catherine, I can't believe you did that," Mum said, looking flushed. "But I have to admit that it was hilarious!"

I didn't have the heart to tell her that we'd targeted the wrong guy until about a month later. So much for being a super sleuth.

In hindsight, of course, I realized that my "perfect family" hadn't been so perfect for a while. Dad had stopped showing up for dinner and started working later hours, and when he was home he retreated into his study. By emotionally withdrawing from all of us, he was present physically but not mentally.

Which is why I find the moment when a relationship morphs from the utter mutual admiration of the first few heady weeks to a more normal and balanced existence so difficult: I always want to leave them before they start withdrawing and leave me. Like the Stone Roses said, I want to be adored.

# TWENTY-SIX

So what's the deal with women constantly putting fingers up my bum?" I was standing at a cocktail party with Michael, who had been trying to talk me out of my crazy marriage plan.

But after about four beers, our conversation moved swiftly into the gutter. "I've been dating for almost twenty-five years, and suddenly in the last five every woman I date tries it. I mean, I like it on occasion— but part of me wonders when putting a finger up a man's backside became part of the cultural Zeitgeist."

"The mid-nineties, I think," I said, taking a swig of Corona. "I put it down to the trickle-down porn effect. It's the same reason why Brazilian waxes have become ubiquitous." I slid my lime wedge into the drink, causing foam to shoot out over the bottle. "At least with the finger-up-the-bum trend, men have a physical payoff because of the prostate stimulation. Women just end up looking more and more like plastic dolls and conforming to men's views of sexuality."

"So what's your preferred waxing style?" Somehow, his easygoing manner makes seemingly offensive questions seem perfectly pleasant. I can see how he catches politicians off guard.

"Personally, I don't like landing strips," I said. "So I go completely bare."

"If waxing offends your feminist sensibilities, why aren't you rocking a retro 1970s bush?" he asked playfully.

"Because I grew up with a male view of sexuality. I think that's why there are so many bisexual women; it's like we're eroticized from a young age to find that view of the world attractive. Besides, I love the way that sex feels with a Hollywood wax."

"So what's the latest sex trend then?"

"Nowadays it's all about the A-spot. The G-spot is on the front, where the female paranurethral glands meet the vaginal wall; the A-spot is further up. Last year it was all about anal sex, ten years ago no one was talking about doggy style. It's constantly evolving."

"So which do you think was the best?"

"To be honest, I don't think having a great knowledge of anatomy is the key thing. The key is to know what's sexy for you. When I was in love with my boyfriend, we could spend hours in the missionary position, but the sensations were incredible."

"I think that if you grow up watching porn movies, it's only natural to try and re-create scenes from them. But the key, eventually, is to figure out what you truly find sexy, rather than copying everyone else. You have to make your own porno."

I had to admit that his logic made sense. "What a great way of thinking about things," I said.

He grabbed me another beer. "So, I saw that Mark put you guys on the bridal registry. Do I seriously have to buy you two a gift?"


It wasn't even midday, and Mark and I were already at each other's throats, fighting in a taxi.

"Why aren't you talking to me?" he demanded, then, "You're mad. I can tell."

I took a deep breath. "I am not mad. I'm just trying to understand why you would put us on a fucking bridal registry when we're sworn to secrecy about this whole thing."

"Come on, sweetheart. It's a chance to get loads of gifts! I really need a web cam for my computer, and the new breakfast sandwich maker is so cool!"

"You are so goddamned immature! You make a fortune, and you're selling me out for a waffle iron?" I gritted my teeth and continued, since I was on a roll. "Meanwhile, you haven't done a thing to help with the wedding. I've had to book the florist and pick flowers for the pictures, and I've handled the tux rental, and also booked a restaurant for afterwards for fifteen people, no easy feat in Notting Hill on a Saturday afternoon—are you even listening to me?"

The cab driver pulled over on Kensington High Street and let me out. "You two getting married?" he asked.

Momentarily stunned, I sputtered, "Well, yes. Yes, we are." I hadn't quite realized how loud and heated our debate had become.

My cheeks flushed, and I considered chasing after him and telling him that this wasn't a real wedding and I'm not Bridezilla, but he was already disappearing into the traffic.

Mark stuck his tongue out and pulled a horrible face at me through the back window. I gave him the finger. So much for married life.

My hands were still shaking when I got home, so I brewed some tea, lit a cigarette, and turned on my laptop. Sometimes, despite reading about the series of disasters that plagued my love life, readers emailed me with questions on how to improve their own.

Helping others also took my mind off the fact that I was starting to freak out seriously about my upcoming fake nuptials. Even though I knew why we were taking the plunge, I would find myself checking *Modern Bride* magazine in the supermarket.

Of course, there were always the garden-variety nutters who emailed me photos of their erect members inviting me to "jump on it," usually phrased in misspelled text-speak, though there was a rather erudite Anglican priest who wanted to re-create a scene from *Last Tango in Paris*—the morbidly obese Marlon Brandon mounting the French chick with butter one, presumably—with me in a Cambridge hotel one afternoon. The whole sordid scene was almost enough to make me upchuck my eggs Benedict.

Interestingly, the vast majority of men were seeking advice on how to convince their girlfriends to have a threesome, or a practical guide to seducing them into anal sex. Women, on the other hand, wanted some insight into the inner working of men's minds. But there was one issue on which the two sexes agreed: Both wanted to know a reliable indicator of whether a potential sex partner would be good in bed. Take this, for example:

> *Dear Catherine,*
>
> *I'm a bisexual woman in my late twenties. My question is: How can I tell if a potential sex partner will be good in bed? I've heard the rumors about checking hand size, etc., and found them to be bollocks—so is there a reliable indicator of skills in the sack?*

After some careful thought, I started my reply:

> *Dear_____,*
>
> *Take a man out to dinner. I've always maintained that everything you need to know about a man's sexual prowess can be learned at the dinner table.*
>
> *Is he the adventurous type, suggesting that you go ahead*

and try that blowfish—or a meat and potatoes guy who refuses to try anything adventurous?

Sense of humor is also key here: The guy who can put you at ease when you spill a glass of wine is the one you want next to you when you accidentally break wind through your vagina.

Is he generous or stingy when leaving a tip? Rude to waiters? He'll be the guy getting huffed when you try to suggest adding a new technique or sex toy, because he has serious self-esteem problems.

Watch the way he dresses. While it's fine to go casual for a grocery store run, beware the man with long, unkempt hair who spends entire days in stained shirts. Chances are he'll be as lackadaisical in the sack as he is in life.

And for the men out there: You want a woman who is well-groomed, with attention to detail, but not so immaculately coiffed that she doesn't have a hair out of place. The girl who cries on the street when it rains because she doesn't have an umbrella to hand will be the same one afraid to give you a blow job lest she smear her lipstick.

Long, talon-like nails are another warning sign. If I were a man, I'd be searching for the girl with neatly manicured, but short nails. There are some places that long nails just can't go.

Since by nature sex is messy and involves the exchange of body fluids, you don't want someone too fastidious when it comes to fucking.

With males and females, confidence is key. You want someone who can hold your eye in conversation, and who has manners, holds the door open for you, and remembers the little touches. They will be considerate in bed.

*After all, the bedroom is really an extension of how things*
*are going in every other room.*

I spent the afternoon on the King's Road, shopping for a wedding
dress with Victoria. "Can't I just wear a little black dress?" I mumbled
as we browsed the racks of 1980s-era Dynasty dresses from Steinberg
& Tolkien.

"Honey, even if it's not totally legit, this is still a wedding," she said.
"Besides, we're going to take loads of photos and need to make it look
convincing for immigration."

She pulled out a 1950s pillbox hat. "What do you think?"

"I told you, I don't do hats. I'm too tall for them. Anyway, I want to
look chic and cool, not like a circus clown."

I tried on a gorgeous 1950s Chanel number that was the right size,
but made for someone about a foot shorter. Then I saw something
amazing. Strapless, iridescent, and white, it looked like my Crystal
Barbie doll from the 1980s. "This one," I said. "It's kitsch, it's eighties,
and it's perfect."

"Are you sure?" she said, wrinkling her nose. "It looks like some sort
of costume. Mind you, it is very you."

"It helps if I think of this whole thing as a movie role. I'm playing
the character of the bride. That's the way I'm going to get through
this." My eyes started tearing up as I struggled with the zipper.

She gave me a hug. "Well, you are marrying a terrific guy. I know that
it's not exactly happening the way you hoped, but people get married
for all kinds of crazy reasons. At least you guys are great friends."

"Thanks, honey," I said, tightening my grip on her hand and looking
at my reflection. I whirled around. "Considering that I've slept with
most of the guys coming, let's hope that there isn't audible laughter in
the room when I wear white."

My mum took the news of my impending nuptials surprisingly well. At first, she was a bit shocked. But after I explained my precarious position, she relented. "Well, honey, when I was in college my best friend, and your godmother, married a gay male flight attendant just so she could get the free frequent flier miles. So I guess I can't blame you for doing what you have to do."

I fought back tears. "So you're not disappointed in me?"

"Nothing you do could ever disappoint me," she said gently. "I'm so proud of you, and everything you do, and if your life is unconventional that means that my girlfriends and I can live vicariously through you. You're so talented, honey," she said, her voice breaking, "and I know that your dad feels the same way, even if he doesn't always say it."

I giggled, relieved, as I wiped away my tears. Mum had always liked Mark, whom she'd met during her frequent visits to New York. I didn't see her nearly as often now that I was on the other side of the pond. "So do you think I should invite Dad?" I said, trying to lighten the mood.

"Hell, no! Let's not push it," she said. "This will be our little family secret." She paused. "And be sure to tell my future son-in-law that I said hello."

# TWENTY-SEVEN

I never discount the role that alcohol plays in modern courtship, especially in England where drinking is a national pastime—which is why my signature dirty martini so often lived up to its name. There are the men who I instantly know I'll never have a long-term future with, but alcohol dulls the inhibitions and smooths out the rough edges of the evening, so that the awkward first kiss seamlessly leads on to a night back at his place. It's like an old friend who never lets you down.

That evening started out as a semi-hen night for me while Victoria, Amy, and I downed cocktails at Soho House. I was already very merry when Michael called me in a panic, asking if I could meet him at Number 11 Downing Street for a reception with Gordon Brown.

"I'm not sure I should," I whispered. "I'm already pretty hammered."

"They're politicians, do you think anyone will know the difference?" he asked. "Come on, I'd like the company."

So I climbed into a cab, hiccuping, and headed home to squeeze myself into a black vintage cocktail dress then turned back towards

Westminster. I could see Michael standing outside, and I approached the iron gates nervously as they ticked our names on the list.

"Are you okay?" he asked, as we headed past the intense-looking doormen.

"Actually, I'm pretty sober now," I told him as we climbed the stairs. "This is where Gordon lives? It looks so… ordinary." At the top of the stairs was a large-ish room with a hardwood floor, a makeshift bar at one end, and several large, brightly colored and rather garish paintings lining the walls. The food wasn't even on trays, but on a table in one corner of the room. Which of course created a problem for women: Every female in the room would rather starve to death than be the first person to load up with a plate of Indian. Because chances were, Gordon would want to speak to me at the exact moment I was stuffing my face with cheese and crackers. So I walked to the window overlooking the back garden, which was littered with children's toys.

I was nervous enough as it was because I was pretty sure that Michael had told Gordon's spin doctor about my piece on erotic dreams. Which would make any conversation seriously awkward.

But after half an hour I was getting bored and fidgety. The room looked like a high school dance, men from different news organizations all surrounding Gordon Brown in concentric outward-spreading circles, waiting for their turn. "I'm going to the bar," I told Michael. "Do you need anything?"

On my way back, with two full glasses of red wine, the unthinkable happened. My stiletto caught on something soft. I turned to find that my leg was entwined with Gordon Brown's. Of all the people in the room, why him? I wanted to sink into the floor. But first, I needed my foot back. "I'm sorry, I am just so sorry," I sputtered, trying to disentangle my limb while Brown pulled at his trousers. After about three minutes, which seemed like an eternity as his crowd laughed, I broke free. With another terse apology I went over to join Michael.

His head was in his hands. "Why is it that of all the people in the room, trouble seems to find you?" he asked, laughing.

"Well, I did apologize," I said miserably. "I'm so sorry. I should probably get out of here, huh?" I noticed that Sarah Brown and her cronies were eyeing me suspiciously.

"Don't worry, you were fantastic!" he said. "It was by far the most entertaining thing that happened all night. Do you want me to help you get a taxi?"

"No, don't worry, I can handle it. I'm going back to meet Victoria and Amy. Good luck with your interviews." I kissed him on the cheek and ran outside, where it immediately started to pour with rain after I cleared the iron gates. I tried in vain to squeeze beneath a buttress because tonight, of all nights, I'd forgotten my goddamned umbrella.

I was running down Whitehall, trying to escape the rain, when a taxi pulled up next to me. I was about to lean in because I thought it must be someone I knew when a very attractive man rolled down the window.

"Miss?" he said. "I can't help noticing that you seem to be having a bit of difficulty. Can I offer you a lift somewhere?"

I did the mental calculations. He was in a black cab and smartly dressed, so was probably on his way out somewhere rather than home to dismember me in his basement. I hopped in and tried to slough the water off my forearms in order to shake his hand. "Thanks so much for rescuing me," I said. "I'm Cat."

"Paul," he said, unwrapping his red scarf. "Do you need something to dry off with?"

"Cheers." I smiled, dabbing at my cleavage. "I'm soaking wet, and not in a good way." I blushed, realizing how tacky that must have sounded. But I couldn't help flirting, albeit crudely, because this guy was hot and, judging by his long legs, very tall. "I'm on my way back to Soho House to meet some friends, but you can just drop me at any Tube station and I'll be fine—"

"Wouldn't hear of it," he said. "I'll take you to the door."

"That's really sweet of you," I said.

"No problem," he said, smiling.

He had a lovely smile, and his apparent sincerity put me at ease. But I reminded myself that I was tipsy, and had to keep my guard up.

We chatted for the next few minutes about our jobs (he ran an Internet company) and he displayed no horror when I told him about my career path. Normally my job is like Marmite to men: Either they can handle it or they can't, which is why I tend to mention it early on in conversation. "I'm not shocked at all," he said, taking off his jacket to hand to me. "In fact, I find it very intriguing."

"So, are you married?" I couldn't believe I had blurted that out, but he seemed to take it in his stride.

"No," he said. "I'm single."

"Separated?"

"No, not separated either. I've never been married. Yet." I couldn't tell if it was the booze or his aftershave, which smelled faintly of cinnamon, but I was starting to get seriously turned on.

"And how old are you?"

"Thirty-nine."

"So," I said, smirking playfully, "what's wrong with you?"

He laughed. "Well, I've been told that I'm argumentative."

"Really? Well, I just got into a fight with Gordon Brown."

For the next ten minutes, I told him about the embarrassing episode, and delighted in making him laugh. He was so charming and easy to talk to. There had to be a catch to this guy.

We pulled up outside Soho House, and I offered him money.

"Well, I'm sorry to hear that your crashing his party may have started an international political incident. But I'm glad that I met you." He looked me directly in the eye. "Would you like to have dinner with me some time?"

Drunk on cheap red wine and pheromones, I lunged across the cab and we started kissing. His lips felt hot, and I remembered something I'd once read about using the middle part of your tongue because most of the nerve endings were there. Whatever this guy was doing, I was feeling it coursing through my entire body. I wanted him naked, in bed, with every fiber of my being.

The driver cleared his throat, and we broke the kiss, panting on opposite sides of the cab. I gave him my number and went upstairs to find Victoria and Amy, my heart pounding. In the loo, I discovered that my eyeliner had run halfway down my face, so I looked like Bette Davis in *Whatever Happened to Baby Jane?* If he thought I looked hot in this state, I knew that Paul and I were off to a very good start.

# TWENTY-EIGHT

A few days later, I found myself aimlessly wandering the aisles at Sainsbury's, thinking about marriage.

I've always hated grocery stores because my cluelessness about how to cook—until Victoria rebelled I used our oven for shoe and jewelry storage—means that I tend to leave the store with three magazines and a can of curry sauce, with no milk or bread in sight. Trapped in a seemingly endless queue, I flipped through *Psychologies* magazine.

It had a fascinating article that debated whether being single or married is best for long-term happiness. It seems that these days, much like selecting the right pasta sauce, the abundance of choice makes things more confusing than ever.

On the one hand there is the idealized life of the independent woman, yet on the other we still grow up conditioned by fairy tales, rippling covers of romance novels, and magazines featuring celebrity weddings, to believe in happily ever after with one person.

According to the article, one study found that women who remain single throughout most of their lives display good mental health compared to married women, while the happiness gap between single and married men is much more pronounced in favor of the latter, so it's men who benefit more from marriage.

However, women were more adversely affected by moving in and out of several relationships, leading some researchers to speculate that women are happiest if they stay single, rather than if they have many short-term relationships.

*Great*, I thought, looking up. *I'm definitely screwed.*

Then I read on. It seems that, statistically, a happy partnership is best, but happy singledom can be equally fulfilling. Next comes miserable singledom. But the worst condition, it seems, is an unhappy relationship.

Which was a refreshing take on things, since I'd been wondering lately if the whole feminist movement was some kind of cruel hoax. I had got depressed having read elsewhere that British men apparently want to marry their mums. Researchers here recently concluded that smart men with demanding jobs would rather have old-fashioned wives, like their mums, than equals, and that a high IQ hampers a woman's chance of marriage.

Personally, I was sick of the assumption that a girl who was passionate about her job was condemning herself to a future of watching *Trisha* in a tracksuit while dozens of mewling cats weaved their way through her front room.

Working women took yet another hit when American editor Michael Noer wrote in *Forbes* magazine that men were fundamentally unhappier in marriages to career women who earn more than they do. His biggest "revelation" was that men are afraid that high-flying women will cheat on them.

This is the same problem that women married to successful men have had for decades, but we are admonished in countless women's magazine articles to go to Pilates or spice up our sex lives to keep men from straying.

So maybe instead of moaning about their partners' success, men should raise their own game. After all, Victoria's boyfriend Mike is always telling me how proud he is of her high-flying career.

Besides, I've always believed that being creative and satisfied in the boardroom translates into the bedroom, and as my job success has grown my sex life had never been hotter.

When I got home from the supermarket, I said to Victoria, "I can't believe that I'm pushing twenty-nine. It's funny because I was one of those women who said, circa ten years ago, 'All of the most interesting women I know are over thirty,' with absolute sincerity."

Suddenly, I felt as I did in my senior year of high school, when college applications came due and every decision I made felt heavy and weighted with permanence, and every subject that interested me seemed laden with significance. I even took one of those career assessment tests and freaked out when my "perfect career" was listed as bartender!

Later, of course, I realized that people change careers throughout their life, and I was putting myself through an insane amount of pressure for nothing. But at the time I couldn't see past the Ivy League envelopes. If I made the right decision, I could be sipping Krug with movie producers. The wrong call would have me eating Cheese Curls, welded to a couch in the back of a trailer.

Fast-forward ten years and I felt exactly the same about relationships. Did I want the preppy, clean-cut City business executive? Choosing the wavy-haired *Guardian* reader with a split-level townhouse in Battersea and a large dog meant that I was ruling out ever marrying the lead singer of a rock band.

Victoria laughed. "You're a baby. Then again, I do have five years on you. But thirty is the time when you traditionally take stock of your life."

"But thirty is such an arbitrary age to decide to make changes," I told Victoria. "Why can't we move in seven-year cycles, like the body does? That would mean that I went through my big transition when I moved to London, and it buys me five more years, until I'm thirty-five."

"Speaking of which…" she said, hesitating. "I have some news, Cat. Mike and I are engaged."

I screamed and enveloped her in a huge hug. "Oh, my God! Congratulations! So, wait," I said, as I noticed her face scrunching up, "why do you look sad? Are you okay?"

"It's these girls at work. One of them actually said, 'Great. Now you're not going to get left on the shelf,' and I said, 'I quite like my shelf. I built it myself!' I'm in love with Mike, and I think he's The One, but part of me is terrified of losing my independence."

"There's nothing wrong with depending on people," I told her. "You'll always be independent, and you're with Mike because you want to be, not because you need to be," I reminded her.

"I'm just so afraid, look at today's divorce rates. It's really scary to rely on someone else. Even if he has agreed to my terms and conditions," she said.

I hugged her. "It's like my mum says: Life is short, and you have no idea what kind of shit is going to get thrown at you," I said. "But you guys have an amazing relationship. And if you are constantly afraid to risk getting hurt, you stay paralyzed in life—which is just another kind of pain."

I poured her a glass of wine, pondering what I had just said. "I'm going to plan you an insane hen night, and I'm so excited about having a wedding to plan!"

She shot me a look.

"Well, other than mine of course," I said hastily.

Later, in bed, I thought about the life I'd built in London, and how far I was willing to go to fight for it. I knew this marriage scheme was a risk, but, somehow, I had to take the chance.

Sitting in Mark's darkened front room watching the scene in *The Omen* when Liev Schreiber prepares to plunge the knife into his son—the perfect boy who turned out to be the Antichrist—my mind naturally turned to my ex-boyfriends.

The film was basically a scene-for-scene copy of the original, yet I was glued to the screen—desperately hoping for a different ending. Pulling the duvet higher, I wondered if relationship "remakes" work the same way.

When Mark invited me over to his place, I thought it would be a good chance to set a few ground rules before the wedding. Despite our intense sexual connection, our personalities are so similar that we end up clashing in huge fights that could rival anything from the book of Revelations.

"I know that you are going to be my husband, but you realize that we have to keep it strictly platonic," I told him. "I'm serious, Mark," I said, noticing his raised eyebrow. I knew that look. The tingling between my legs reminded me that, given my recent dating disasters, it'd been ages since I'd had a good shag.

And if my upcoming date with Paul went well, this could be the end of an on-off era. It felt a bit surreal.

"We can't hook up any more after the ceremony. Ever. It would just complicate things too much."

And yet, half a bottle of Ketel One later, he had me pinned against the corridor wall, his hands sliding up my dress as I wrapped my legs around him.

"So, sweetheart," he said, moving his hand between my legs and touching the outside of my already wet knickers, "since I'm not getting a stripper or anything for my stag night, don't you think we're both entitled to one last fling?"

"Okay," I said, feeling his massive erection pressing against my thigh. "But if I'm going to fuck you, I'm going to make it count. And tonight, you are going to play by my rules."

"Whatever you say," he said, backing away and holding his hands up in submission. "I knew you didn't wear those fishnets for nothing. You can't fool me. We're too much alike."

"Not yet," I told him as he unbuttoned his shirt. "First, I want you to strip, take a shower, and make sure to get squeaky clean everywhere. Then meet me in the bedroom." I pulled my dress up so that he could see the tops of my stockings.

When I heard the water running, I went into the bedroom and unearthed the box of toys that I'd left a few months ago. I also pulled out his box of porn and put on a tape where two enthusiastic nurses were kissing, using vibrators and something that looked like a kind of hot pink tricked-out rectal thermometer on each other. By that point, I was fingering myself lightly through my knickers, not paying too much attention to the plot.

Mark joined me before long, a white towel loosely wrapped around his waist. The sight of his muscular, hairy torso always got me going.

"Wow," he said when he saw the spread. "What's going to happen to me?"

"Shut up and come over here," I demanded. I'm not naturally dominant, but since I knew this was going to be our last night I was determined to revel in my role. I was so horny for him that I was practically salivating.

He sat on the edge of the bed, and I slid behind him on my knees. "So what surprises are in store for me tonight?" he asked.

"Shhh," I whispered. "You can't speak until I tell you to. I'm in charge tonight."

He moaned in anticipation as I wrapped a silk scarf around his head, covering his eyes, and shook his head when I asked him if it was too tight. I made him lie on the bed, face down, and tethered his wrists to the headboard posts with Japanese silk rope ties. Then I kissed down his neck and back, slowly winding my tongue down the curve of his back as I slipped my hands between his legs and cupped his balls lightly.

"Oh, God," he said, writhing on the bed.

"Shhh," I said, giggling. "Tonight you're my bitch and I'm going to have my way with you. You've been a naughty boy, haven't you?" I licked my fingers then slipped my index finger inside his arse and gently fingered his prostate, reaching underneath him with my other hand and feeling his cock get rock hard from my attentions.

"Do you like that? Does that feel good?" I always like to check on people when I'm in the dominant role, even though at this point I was fairly certain that the question was rhetorical.

"Your finger feels fantastic," he mumbled, his voice muffled by his giant feather pillow. "I'm loving it."

"I'm going to do better than that," I said, opening a bottle of massage oil/lube that I had placed next to a box of tissues on the bedside table. I slipped my knickers off as I slid down his body, still moving my finger in and out of him, then replaced it with my tongue, flicking in and out. He loved it, and pulled against the restraints.

"I'm glad you like that," I murmured, "because I'm going to fuck you in the arse, the way you fucked me. Would you like that?"

I often had boxes of sex toys that I had to test delivered to Mark's house, because he had one mailbox as opposed to five, and I therefore avoided the awkwardness of explaining to my neighbors that a box of anal beads they had received were meant for me. But unbeknown to him, I'd added a little something special to my last sex toy order: The Bend Over Boyfriend, a curved vibrator meant for male penetration.

The reviews on the site said it was supposed to be amazing, but I knew that Mark would never ask me directly to use it on him: He had to be "forced" into doing something naughty. I could feel my clit pulsing as I squirted the lube onto the tip and wrapped the belt around my waist, situating the vibe so that it pressed against my clit. The sight of him below me, rock hard and utterly at my mercy, was intoxicating. I bit my lip and rested the tip of my "cock" against him. "Tell me when you're ready," I said softly. "We're going to do this really slowly." He pushed back against me, while the vibrator rested against his bum.

I started playing with him from behind.

"Do you want me to fuck you?" I whispered, feeling my forehead slick with sweat.

"Yes," he moaned.

I started to grind in circular motions, pushing harder and deeper while fingering myself. Finally, I couldn't hold back any longer—my contractions were pulsing so hard that I could feel the blood roaring through my brain. For a split second I thought I might pass out. He started shaking, and when he started to come it seemed like the convulsions would never end. At last I collapsed on top of him.

"Wow, that was so fucking incredible," he said, kissing my forehead and ruffling my hair. "We have the filthiest sex." He smiled as we dumped the toys on the floor and I pulled the duvet up to my chest with trembling hands. "You know, Cat, the man who marries you for real is going to be one lucky son of a bitch."

Later, looking over at him blissfully slumbering next to me, I imagined for a minute what life would be like if I was really married to Mark: We were so similar, would it actually be that bad?

But it wasn't long before old patterns emerged: After the post-orgasm glow subsided, we got into a childish argument over who could have the last chicken wing that ended with him throwing it out the kitchen window. "We really should have seen this coming." He laughed, shaking his head. "We drive each other crazy, in a good way and a bad way."

Life would be so much easier if we had a rating system for men, like the one for movies, that would warn us that they were unsuitable for some viewers. In my case, though the men I dated seemed completely different on the surface, the ones I really fell for shared similar personality traits. They were all outgoing, intense alpha males who seemed to be the life of the party—but their outer confidence often hid a darker, insecure side.

By going for the same "type" in different bodies, I felt that I was hurtling towards the same inevitable conclusion each time—and the ending was not going to be pretty. So was I destined to keep dating the same guy over and over?

This time, rather than try to make the intensity of our sexual affair translate into a relationship, Mark and I had decided to keep it real.

But the fact that Mark wasn't the love of my life didn't make our relationship any less significant. As Victoria always says, "You guys obviously have a bond, it's just not meant to be permanent. At least, not in that sense."

The chicken wing fight proved that we're not going to disappear into the sunset hand in hand together. Yet our friends-with-benefits arrangement had taught me more about my own desires than any one-night stand, and shown me that I could never settle for a sexually tepid relationship.

# TWENTY-NINE

I had just been to my very first "official" sex party (I've been to informal, laissez-faire get-togethers that turned into shag-fests before, but never to a party where it has been the raison d'être) to celebrate my own, personal, self-styled "hen night." Though incredibly horny at the time, I have to say that on the whole I was a bit underwhelmed.

My preparation began weeks in advance, when I was asked to email a photo of myself so that I could be evaluated by the party's panel of experts. I passed, and when they emailed me the directions on the day I couldn't help feeling mildly terrified.

In theory, I've always been a huge fan of sex parties. I think it's much better for a woman to act out a fantasy of being with multiple partners in a safe environment with condoms and a security team, where guests are vetted beforehand, than picking up two random men in a bar or car park.

But in practice, my evening out was like combining the anxiety of going to a party where I didn't know anyone with the first time I slept with a new partner: It's as much "Will the guests laugh at my jokes?" as "Will they like the look of my labia?"

I chose a silk, knee-skimming white dress with a plunging neckline that allowed me to wear my white demi-cup bra, knickers, and matching suspenders with fishnet stockings underneath.

My stilettos raised my height to about six foot two, almost into drag queen territory, but my legs aren't good enough to be mistaken for a she-male.

My heart was in my throat as I knocked on the huge black door, my clammy hands clutching a bottle of champagne. I was greeted by an efficient-looking blonde with impeccable makeup and hair in an artfully disheveled up-do-with-tendrils style that looked like it took five minutes to arrange, but had probably been fixed in a salon.

The first hour was pretty uneventful, though I could definitely distinguish between the obvious "regulars" who moved through the party chatting up everyone in sight and nervous-looking couples who seemed to be rooted to the floor. I had the feeling of flying solo at a junior high dance, where the cool kids were all talking in a group with their backs to me, and started to wonder if coming along had been a mistake.

"Hi there," said a tall, thin brunette in a backless gown. There was no bra in sight but her breasts didn't move. I wondered if they were real. "People are always asking if I've had my breasts done," she confessed, as if reading my mind. "I'm Taryn, and this is my boyfriend, Dan," she said, pointing to a tall, lanky, and cute type who looked like he spent his weekends climbing mountains for fun. "We come to these things a lot."

I blushed. "I'm sorry for staring," I blurted out.

"That's okay," she said, "I don't mind if you look. In fact, I think you are gorgeous and my boyfriend and I were just wondering if you were interested in joining us in the playroom."

"I would love to," I said, taking her hand. "But this is my first time, so I'm not sure how far I'm going to go... I'm kind of playing it by ear."

"Don't worry, there's absolutely no pressure. If you're someone, there are ways of politely declining—you'll catch on pretty quickly to the signals."

As they led me into the playroom, I was surprised to find that, far from being a bacchanal free-for-all, there were actually a number of tacit rules. I noticed a very buxom brunette, an elegant slim blonde, and an Indian man climb onto a bed. Several other couples were writhing and moaning, their limbs tangled in a pornographic tableau that could have been an outtake from *Caligula*.

"Do you want to join us?" the brunette said, turning towards me as she unbuttoned her shirt and stripped to the waist, revealing brown nipples spilling out over a quarter-cup black lace bra. She had beautiful long legs and a gorgeous face, which was tempting. But I didn't fancy her man, and I figured that this group was like a prepackaged sandwich—I couldn't pick and choose my ingredients. It was all or nothing. So I stuck with Dan and Taryn.

Condoms were provided in big bowls in the playrooms, and the "rules" say that it's a man's responsibility to show any woman who is not his regular partner that he's wearing one.

Taryn straddled Dan on the bed, and immediately pulled her red and black knickers to one side and sat on top of him. The sight of her moaning and writhing while caressing her nipples and staring at me made me incredibly wet, so I moved in and started kissing her. I could feel her boyfriend's hand down my knickers as she continued to ride him, while sucking on my nipples. The combination of sensations was incredible.

I also liked the look of Dan's cock, despite the fact that it was uncircumcised. I'd only ever seen about three uncircumcised penises in my life, and the first one really freaked me out. It looked like a Shar-Pei dog. But his was lovely—I'd estimate it was at least nine inches, with a curve that bent in the direction of her G-spot. Lucky girl.

"You know, I love watching Dan getting off on other women." She smiled wickedly, slowly grinding against him.

I found this an incredibly horny sight, so I slipped off my knickers and straddled Dan's mouth, facing her. Normally I'm incredibly self-conscious when a man is performing oral sex, but this time I focused on his hungry tongue, buried deep in my pussy, while fingering my clit and watching him fucking his girlfriend. It felt like I was watching a live porno movie, and I came almost instantly.

"Do you want to switch?" she asked a few minutes later.

I hesitated. "No thanks," I told her, "I don't think I'm up to having penetrative sex this time. Maybe next time."

"No worries, sweetheart," she said, and turned around to kiss the brunette.

For a moment I felt stung—had I been dissed? But I knew that the golden rule of this party was not to take anything personally; some people were here to satisfy certain kinks, and I might not fit in to their criteria. If I wanted intimacy, I would stay home with one partner.

I picked up my knickers and moved to a nearby sofa, where I chatted to a first-time couple who were content to lounge and watch the action.

Later, I found Taryn and Dan again, and we all headed out to a champagne breakfast. I wanted to chat with them about their hobby.

"I'm actually really interested in you guys' attitude towards sex," I said. "I'm finding it difficult to meet a man because I'm a bit of a paradox: I want someone who wants an equal partner and doesn't mind my experience, yet wants to take care of me. Don't you two ever get jealous?"

"Even if you're a swinger, relationships are all about compromise," Taryn explained. "I would be devastated if I found out that Dan had been having an affair behind my back. Physical flings are one thing, emotional infidelity quite another."

I respected Taryn and Dan for being open enough to talk about setting ground rules for the girls they brought home (for him, no anal with another woman; she gets final approval on girl selection, etc.) but I think that unbridled hedonism starts to lose some of its appeal when you put constraints on what a person can and can't do.

I still thought that, for me, intimacy with a serious partner would be too fragile to risk. Relationships are delicate ecosystems, especially in the first few months. One jealous moment or "wrong look" in bed with a third person could ruin things. And that's not a risk I was prepared to take.

We took a cab together and Taryn and Dan dropped me a few yards from my flat, and gave me their number in case I wanted to "play" again. Hearing the staccato click of my stilettos and spotting a flash of my all-white gear, an unshaven homeless guy shrugged out from under his duvet and declared, "My God, I've seen an angel!"

I beamed and fished out £2. Why ruin the illusion?

The next day, I discussed my upcoming wedding with Amy over coffee. Since the whirlwind of planning the party started, we hadn't really had a moment alone.

"So, do you think this is completely crazy, or what?" I asked her.

"Not at all," she said, stirring her iced latte. "I think that we learn something from every relationship we have. Even if he isn't the love of your life," she added hastily.

"Well, I didn't learn much from Grant," I told her. "I'm sorry to say that I didn't get much comfort from the self-help book you gave me. The only thing that made any sense was when I watched a rerun of that show *Dog Whisperer*, hosted by the guy who rehabilitates problem dogs, and saw the expert talking about how to dominate this aggressive poodle by acting like the pack leader. Maybe I should have bought Grant a choke chain."

"That's not a bad idea," she said. "Though I'm not sure that basing an entire relationship on a problem poodle is the way forward."

I laughed. "Seriously, though, the dog trainer had some great insights. When the poodle would growl and bite, the trainer always said don't reward negative behavior. Maybe the same approach would work for men."

She rubbed my shoulder. "I know that laughter is your way of dealing with things, but I totally understand why you would be feeling down right now. You've had a rough year with men."

I cracked a smile. "You know what the most fucked-up thing is? My bogus marriage may be the only honest relationship with a man I've ever had in my life. So maybe it is for the best."

"And if Mark pisses you off? From what I hear, he would really be into the choke chain," she said.

We paid the bill and left.

# THIRTY

I was on a fantastic first date with Paul when his phone beeped during dinner, and I saw him become instantly tense. Then it happened again. By the end of dessert he had shown me twelve vulgar and somewhat alarming messages— all from his ex-girlfriend.

"We had a fling for a couple of weeks, and since I ended things she's been, well, stalking me a bit," he admitted. Then he gave me the details: He'd been dating a nineteen-year-old wannabe glamour model, and loaned her money after she got stuck in Eastern Europe.

I was sympathetic, but also rather suspicious. I'll never forget my encounter with a serial cheater who told me that his ex-girlfriend was "a total bunny-boiler." One night we were naked on the couch at his flat, and the intercom kept buzzing. Finally, I answered—only to discover that she lived there with him! He had double-locked the front door, turned out the lights, and was pretending not to be home. Besides, I'm immediately suspicious of any man who describes all his exes as "psychos"; chances are the exes are not the ones with the problem.

But let's face it: On the road to The One, we've all stopped off at a few dodgy exits. If all my ex-boyfriends came back and started following me around at once, I would have a *Night of the Living Dead* situation on my hands.

Still, when dealing with the end of the affair, there's a fine line between seducer and stalker. I have never understood the logic of someone who thinks, *She didn't pick up the first seventeen times I called, but the eighteenth will convince her to come back!* In the age of caller ID, it's excruciating to watch.

At the end of the evening it seemed quite natural to go back to Paul's flat. Most men find it a bit weird that "Your place or mine?" is a rhetorical question for me, because I never take men back to my flat.

Beside my need for an exit strategy this was partly because I lived with a flatmate in cramped quarters, and the thought of Victoria having to deal with a strange semi-nude man on our toilet seemed a bit unfair. But I'd also discovered that a man's flat was often a useful metaphor for his mental state.

A few scattered garments are okay, but a floor ankle-deep in old newspapers and ashtrays layered like the bottom of a gerbil's cage is a really bad sign. So is a suspiciously sparse flat, as it could indicate that he's married with a family home somewhere else.

Most men don't realize that, for women, a quick nip to the loo is often a fact-finding mission. We are playing mini Miss Marple to check for clues to personality types, whether the shelves are stocked with tampons and unopened pink toothbrushes (the player); loads of exfoliating scrubs, hair gel, and waxing strips (the metrosexual); or drawers filled with expired condoms (the fantasist).

A quick peek inside Paul's medicine cabinet revealed a few Kiehl's male grooming products, which seemed to indicate that he was into his appearance but not overly obsessed.

I'll never forget my ill-fated encounter with Chris, a very hot tattoo artist/bartender who took me back to his east London flat after a night at the movies. When I went to the fridge to get a beer, I found a kitchen counter that had its own ecosystem, littered with opened vats of Chinese takeaway sludge that had expired two months previously. A severed head would have been only slightly more alarming.

But the final straw came when I went to the loo, and noticed the pentagram hanging above the toilet, right next to a bunch of books on Satanism. "If you're looking for a virgin to sacrifice, you're barking up the wrong tree," I cracked, then got the hell out of there.

It's possible to take foraging too far. A girlfriend of mine once stayed behind while her man played cricket, and turned over his entire flat—then freaked out when she found pictures of his ex-girlfriend in a box under the bed. She confronted him, and he binned her for invading his privacy. I don't blame him.

My rule is that I stick to items that are visible to the naked eye. When Paul went to the kitchen to fetch some drinks, I scanned the room and noticed that the bookshelves contained actual literature (not just self-help books!) and family photos—no *Loaded* posters or beanbags in sight.

"Do you like what you see?" he asked, as he led me back to his bedroom, which was lined with mirrors. I tore his clothes off, and we watched ourselves from every vertical, horizontal, and diagonal vantage point. He had an amazing body, which I had a great view of when he was behind me.

"Do you think we're ready to take the next step in our relationship?" I deadpanned afterwards as I fished my blouse off the floor and looked at my makeup-smudged face. "Leaving some cleanser, I mean."

He looked across at me, using his hands to draw lazy circles on my shoulder. "You can leave whatever you want," he murmured. "I want to give you every incentive to stay over as often as possible. I adore you."

My heart skipped a beat, because I had never had anyone say something that bluntly before and somehow felt sure that they meant it. Well, not unless it was followed by "but I have a raging cocaine habit," or "and I would love to borrow your clothes," or "but I have to go home to my wife."

This was just so, well, normal.

"So can I come back to your place next time?" he asked as I walked out the door.

I'd have to think of an excuse: He might find the juxtaposition of lavender sheets and fur handcuffs unsettling. And if he unearthed my secret super-kinky sex toy box, he really would think I was crazy.

# THIRTY-ONE

I had just attended the wedding from hell. On the positive side, at least it wasn't my own.

I knew that my girlfriend's wedding would be tough. Sarah lived the fairy-tale romance that so many of us dreamed of: Three months after meeting her husband, a six-foot-five banker, he went down on one knee during a romantic trip to the Virgin Islands and proposed. Weeks later, she was decorating his New York condominium and planning her wedding near her family's cottage in Devon that was the site of so many happy childhood memories. Victoria and I drove down together. Mike had to work that morning so would be joining us later.

"You do know that there's a huge storm forecast this weekend," Victoria said as rain slammed into our windscreen.

I laughed. "Great. And I'm sure I'm the only single girl—a perfect target for the serial killer who will be watching our cabins hidden deep in the woods."

"If it makes you feel any better, I reckon that Mike and I will be the first to die. The loved-up couple having sex are always the first target. Just don't get into the shower!"

She was referring to eighties teen movies, whose bloody moral code meant that anyone in close proximity to a nude body was about to get axed.

"Well, at least the nerdy virgin lives longest!"

"Honey, you are far from a virgin." She laughed, pushed in the cigarette lighter, and cracked open the window, only to have rain pour in from the side. "Shit. It's really coming down out there."

She shifted gears as we climbed the winding, slick road. "Anyway, remember Alan, the usher, the groom's hot college roommate? He's going to be around, and he's single, too."

"I think I should focus on getting out alive. I don't want to get eaten, at least not in a bad way." I smiled slyly. "Anyway, it's going really well with Paul. So I don't want to jinx things."

Later, after changing into my killer ballgown, I found myself at the freak show singles' table. I was next to a random work friend who played the bagpipes, some guy with a lazy eye, and Uncle Roger, who turned out to be fifty-something, fat, balding, and fancied himself a bit of a Casanova.

Don't get me wrong, I'm thrilled for my girlfriends who are celebrating their blissfully happy unions—but I've found that navigating the minefields of wedding parties can be a terrifying prospect.

When I've brought dates in the past, watching public declarations of love makes us question the status of our own relationship, and there are always the nosy relatives who keep asking me when he's going to "pop the question."

If I'm flying solo, everyone wants to know when I'm going to settle down, or they want to fix me up with any guy who has a pulse. Some psychologists in the U.S. have actually theorized that married people are uncomfortable around singles, and want them to cop off with someone because they pose a sexual threat.

Ironically, my male friends think of wedding season as hunting season. "Emotions are running high, free booze is flowing, and picking up women is like shooting fish in a barrel," Michael told me earlier. "I learned to ballroom dance for that sole reason."

I've also done my share of picking up hot members of the wedding party. But I learned that hooking up at weddings had its downside at my girlfriend's "destination wedding" at a couples-only resort in Jamaica.

I had to share a room with a platonic male friend—and after one too many pina coladas, we ended up in bed. The next day, I returned with a horrible hangover to find that he had strewn rose petals all over the room and written a poem to declare his love, while all I felt like doing was putting my head in the toilet.

I spent the next two days hiding out at the pool bar, and was even reduced to holding my breath underwater when he walked past.

I didn't want to suffer the same fate at Sarah's wedding, especially after the DJ grabbed the microphone and asked all the single women to come forward for the bouquet toss—which was between me and three eleven-year-old girls.

I let one of the kids win, prompting a visibly sweat-stained Uncle Roger to grab my waist and say, "Don't worry, baby, you're not going to get left on the shelf!" Before lowering his tone to add, "I've got some Viagra back in my room!"

After getting rid of him, I headed to the dance floor and boogied all night to nineties dance tunes with three very cute single men—all under age twelve. We had a blast.

Later, I smoked a joint in the woods with Alan the hot usher, trying to gain insight into the male psyche. "I want what Tad has," he said, loosening his tie as he exhaled. "I mean, I've got to the point in my life where I'm ready to settle down and have a family."

"That doesn't sound very romantic," I said, coughing frantically. "Whatever happened to waiting until the right person comes along? I've always thought that I would wait until I'm forty if that's when it's meant to happen."

"See, that's the thing though," he said, taking a swig of bourbon and passing it over to me. "So much of life is down to timing. I'm sure I've dated several women who were great 'wife material' [he indicated quotes by slicing through the air, spilling a bit of bourbon down my cleavage] but I was still sowing my wild oats. I'm not saying that I won't love the woman I marry."

"Right," I said, dabbing at the booze. "But what you are saying is that you reach a certain age in your life and think, 'Right, the next woman who fits the bill is the one by default.' It's a very logical position, and I'm not saying that it's wrong. But what I'm saying is that, even though I may intrinsically feel that I'm in the right frame of mind for a relationship, I'm going to wait for the right person to come along." I realized that I was repeating myself, and he wasn't really listening. I must have been very stoned.

He looked at me for several seconds. "What's the difference? Women do the same thing. You guys are all so picky about money. Would you marry an unemployed guy? Or a drug addict?"

I thought about it, and took another shot. "I'd like to think that if he was the love of my life, I would."

"Women always think they can magically change the guy. Don't you girls ever watch talk shows?"

"That's just the thing—I wouldn't want to change him. It can work. Look at Ozzy and Sharon." I paused. "Though, to be fair, he did try to kill her a couple of times."

He snorted in a slightly patronizing manner, which reminded me how much I hated men who immediately wrote me off as the crazy girl. I could feel his eyes metaphorically rolling, and I felt the need to defend myself. My control was slipping, even though logically I knew that this guy had no power over me. It didn't make any sense: I had no emotional investment in him, so why was I so sensitive?

"So, if you felt like you were in love with me, and I had loads of baggage, you would rule me out. Whereas if I was in love with you, I'd like to think that I would fight for you."

He stubbed out the remainder of the pot and propped his hands behind his head. "Why purposely try to take the path of greatest resistance?"

"Haven't you ever heard of the road less traveled?"

"Whatever, Robert Frost. Man, this is some seriously strong weed. I feel like I can't move right now."

"I concur," I said. Stoned out of my mind, I wanted to tell him that the wedding isn't the goal. Marriage, spending the rest of your life with one person, is the goal.

But I already knew that I would be wasting my breath. Because, out here under the stars, everything became clear. Some men obviously don't want long-winded, pot-fueled debates with their wife. They want to come home to hot food and a warm body, someone who is the human equivalent of the *Heat* crossword so that they feel smart when they crack it. Everyone gets to feel rewarded.

Exhausted and hung over, Amy and I hit the road early the next morning.

"You're not having bridesmaids at your wedding, are you?" Amy asked. "Because those outfits were so naff."

"Totally. They looked like someone vomited a load of pink Pepto-Bismol on their heads. Don't worry," I said, "you can be assured that my fake wedding will be a class act all the way."

"I've noticed that you're not talking much about Paul," she

said, giving me a sideways glance. "Are you going to tell him about the wedding?"

Amy knows me well enough to understand that when I'm not full of funny anecdotes about disastrous sexual encounters, things must be going really well.

"I can't," I said. "At least, not yet. Can't I maintain the illusion for just a bit longer?" I knew that I couldn't keep my secret forever. In fact, I wanted to tell him with every fiber of my being. But I didn't want him to talk me out of it, since this was my ticket to a permanent visa and staying in London had become so important to me.

I would tell him. Right after the wedding.

# THIRTY-TWO

For an instant, waking up next to Paul, I forgot and lost myself in his arms, grinding involuntarily against his hard-on and snuggling under the duvet. It was bliss—until I remembered that I was getting married today. I bolted up and jumped into the shower, yelping as I stepped under the trickling water because I forgot that you have to wait about ten minutes before the goddamned thing actually gets warm. I usually have coffee and read the papers in the interim. With other men I had been out of their flat before the sun rises. But I felt strangely comfortable at his place.

"Hey, beautiful."

I saw him snaking around the bathroom door and stripping off his dressing gown.

"God, I love waking up and seeing you in my shower." He opened the door. "Mind if I come in?"

I kissed him, and he placed a hand between my legs. I'm not usually a fan of getting it on in bathtubs, because the water washes away my natural lubrication. But he slid his fingers inside me, while I braced myself against him.

"If you keep going like this, I may drop the soap," I whispered, spreading my legs wider. Then the thought of my upcoming nuptials flooded back into my head. "Actually, honey, I have to run. I'm, um, having brunch with some friends, and it's been arranged for ages. I can't be late!"

Since we were having lunch after the ceremony, this was technically true. But as I toweled off, I still felt like shit for not leveling with him. I was worried that he would try to talk me out of it, or offer to marry me himself. In a weird way, I was protecting him by not telling him. At least, that's what I told myself.

"Darling, do you want me to make you some coffee?" he asked, putting his dressing gown over my shoulders.

I shook my head. "No," I said, "I really have to run. How long do you think it will take to get a cab?"

"Hang on, let me call them." Fortunately, Paul was used to my intensity when it came to work deadlines, so the urgent nature of my request didn't seem to strike him as unusual. As I pulled my sweater over my head, Paul came back into the bedroom. "It's going to take half an hour."

"Half an hour? Shit! I'm going to be really late!" Panicking, I tried to steady myself. I noticed that my phone was off, which must be why I hadn't heard the alarm. I turned it on, and there were already several messages from Victoria asking me where I was.

"Don't worry, I'll take you," he said easily.

"Are you sure it's not too much trouble?" I asked in a small voice.

"Of course not. I told you," he said, cupping my chin and looking down into my eyes, "I want to make sure that you're well looked after."

"Thanks so much. I would invite you along but (*I'm getting fucking married today!*) it's kind of a girl thing. This way, we can, you know, talk about you when you're not around."

"Hopefully good things," he said, with an interrogative smile.

"Where are you?" the 9:02 text from Victoria read. "We have to leave in forty-five minutes!"

I called her. "Hey, it's me," I said weakly.

"Cat, where are you?" she said. "The limo is coming at nine thirty!"

"You booked a limo?" I said, not thinking.

Paul looked at me quizzically. How the hell was I going to explain this one?

I began to sweat. Not the healthy workout perspiration, but the beads of sweat that ooze out from my adrenal glands when stress starts pumping. It wasn't a pretty smell. I could feel my heart pounding, and got the horrible feeling that I used to have in high school, coming home late when I had booze on my breath and the smell of sex on me. I was, to put it bluntly, about to get busted.

"Her cousin's wedding," I said, by way of explanation. God, that sounded lame. But luckily he seemed too engrossed in staring at me lovingly to notice. He just smiled politely. In this case, I decided that ignorance definitely was bliss.

"Well, don't worry about me being late for brunch," I said cheerfully. "I've already had a shower, so I just need to do a quick change."

"You had better be fucking Superman-in-a-phone-booth fast because we *have* to be there by ten, otherwise we'll miss our slot."

God. You would think that she was the one having the fake wedding. "Calm down, honey," I said. "I promise, we will make it. I'll be there in ten."

"Wow," Paul said, careering around the Old Street roundabout towards our little side street. "She must be really hungry."

"Yeah, you know women. In the morning. Before their coffee." Suddenly at a loss for words, I ran my palm over his knees and felt him draw in a breath.

"God, sweetheart, you are so sexy," he said. "Are you sure I can't convince you to skip this whole brunch nonsense so that I can spend the day licking you?"

"Sorry," I said as we pulled up outside my flat, and I noticed to my horror that Mark was walking up from Starbucks with a tuxedo on. "Okay, well, see you later, honey."

I raced to the door, waving jauntily, and keyed in the entry code. "Cat!" I could hear Mark yelling from across the street but I let myself in, slammed the door behind me, and looked out the glass lobby window just in time to see Mark walking out in front of Paul, who had slowed down to let him pass. Thank God they'd never met, I thought, as Mark signaled his thanks and Paul pulled away.

He knocked on the door, and I opened it. "Come on upstairs," I said. "Let's do this thing."

Twenty minutes later, the limo came for Mark, Amy, Victoria, and me.

"Wow," Mark said, holding the car door open for me, "I have to say, Cat, you look absolutely stunning."

"Thanks," I said, smiling. This was one instance when I could honestly say that I did look beautiful. Victoria had worked magic with my hair, which she admitted "smelled like an ashtray," by twisting it into an up-do (she's inherited her French mum's effortless grace with scarves and chic hairstyles), and the dress looked gorgeous with my Gina rhinestone stiletto sandals.

"Those shoes are amazing," Mark said.

"I'm glad you like them," Victoria said, "because they're your wedding gift to her. I used your credit card to buy them."

"What the hell?" he said, loosening his bow tie. "That's totally ridiculous!"

"Look, you didn't help out with the wedding, so rather than have a huge blowout fight with you, since you can't have make-up sex, Cat decided to be passive aggressive and spend loads of money instead without telling you. Now it's all better."

He laughed. "Well, at least now I feel like a real married couple."

I was staring out the window.

"Cat? Are you okay?"

Actually, I was freaking out. Everything seemed to be happening in slow motion, and suddenly I couldn't breathe.

Amy held my hand and asked me if I was okay, and kept telling me to take deep breaths. "Just close your eyes and go to the happy place," she said.

"I just came from the happy place, a.k.a. my boyfriend's bedroom," I murmured, pulling my bodice top up since my left nipple was threatening rebellion. "But I don't know how long it's going to stay happy once he realizes what's going on."

The car crawled past South Kensington Tube, and we drove down Sydney Street then pulled up in front of the registrar's office. Victoria adjusted my dress as David Parkside embraced me outside.

"Darling," he said, opening a bottle of champagne, "you look stunning."

I had invited him because Mark had invited some of his friends, in hopes of getting gifts and free drinks, and I wanted some grounded support. His advanced age had actually been an advantage: After all, he'd been married twice in this very registrar's office, so he'd assured me that "all the fabulous couples come here. Even celebrities." All of which was cold comfort in my current situation, but still.

Standing on the steps in front of the King's Road, I thought about perception and reality. Anyone looking at Mark and me from the outside would assume that we were blissfully in love and about to start our lives together.

Victoria took photos with her digital camera while Mark and I linked arms and tried to look relaxed.

"How are you feeling?" I whispered out of the corner of my mouth, still keeping the smile fixed on my face.

"To be honest," he said, "I'm shit scared." He put his hands on my shoulders. "But we can't have a great writer like you getting kicked out of the country." He smiled down at me. "So take a deep breath, and get ready."

We entered the room first, which was decorated in a soothing pale yellow and was lined with plants, and were given a list of songs to choose from, including the office's top ten most requested. Among the classical wedding marches were several inexplicable choices. "'True'? What do you think?" I asked him, giggling nervously.

"There is no way in hell that I'm walking down the aisle to Spandau Ballet, so you can forget that," he snapped. I noticed that he was sweating, like me.

"What's this? 'Everybody Hurts' by REM? 'I'm Not In Love'? Who the hell would pick that? Talk about a bad omen!"

"We'll just take 'Pachelbel's Canon,' please," Mark said, handing the flyer back to the registrar.

Gripping the floral arrangement tightly, I stepped out into the hallway to wait for my cue.

Victoria stuck her head round the door. "Cat," she said, "are you okay with this? Because if you want, we can call the whole thing off right now."

I thought about London, and about my destiny. I also thought about my friends, and the fact that my bonds with them have outlasted most of my relationships. So maybe forging a permanent bond with someone I consider a best friend isn't the worst thing in the world.

In the past few months I've found someone to give me emotional support, multiple orgasms, a shoulder to cry on, and physical bliss. So what if they weren't all with the same guy?

My mobile vibrated from the table behind me, and I glanced surreptitiously at the screen: "You are so beautiful. Can I convince you to come over after brunch? Let me know if there is anything that I can do to help with your stressful work situation. I am crazy about you. xx Paul"

I wondered if I could sneak off and satisfy my fantasy of getting fucked in my wedding dress, but I didn't have long to ponder.

Peeking into the room, the surreal nature of my situation struck me. I could see David Parkside serving champagne into flutes and clinking glasses with Michael, another of my ex-lovers. Victoria and Mike were holding hands, doubtless thinking about their own big day. Amy looked like she was about to vomit into her handbag from her hangover.

But they were my friends, and they were all there because they loved me. At that point, I had several unconventional soulmates, so meeting the right guy will just be the icing on the cake. I looked back towards the open window in the hallway and could see the white net curtains fluttering in the light breeze, and thought for a fleeting second about making an escape.

But when I heard the faint strains of music I opened the door, took a deep breath, and went in. My heart was fluttering and my adrenaline racing, but at least I was living an adventure. I don't need the cookie-cutter fairy-tale happy ending after all. It's much more fun to write my own.

# ACKNOWLEDGMENTS

There are a few people I would like to thank, without whom this book would not have been possible:

Thank you to Rowan Yapp, Nikki Barrow, and everyone else at John Murray for their passion for the book.

Thank you to my amazing agent, Clare Conville, who believed in my idea.

Thanks to my mum, who always encouraged me to follow my dreams.

Thank you to my dad, who always supported me, even after he realized that I was tackling rather risqué subject matter.

Thank you to my amazing friends, who have never made me feel short of soulmates.

Thank you to Vincent Moss, for his constant advice, support, and endless cups of tea.

Thank you to my friend Amina Akhtar, who has regaled me for years with tales of her love life, and given me some great advice.

Thank you to my grandma, who taught me how to read. Though I hope she doesn't read this book.

Finally, I would like to say thank you to all the men I've dated, the good ones for enriching my life, and the bad ones for making me fight harder.

# ABOUT THE AUTHOR

Catherine Townsend writes the weekly sex and dating column "Sleeping Around" in the *Independent*.

Born in Arkansas, USA, Catherine was a gossip columnist for *New York Magazine* before moving to the UK. She writes regularly for *Glamour*, *Cosmopolitan*, and *Marie Claire*, has contributed to various newspapers, and has commented on radio and TV. She has a BA and MA in journalism.